Real-Resumes for Social Work & Counseling Jobs...
including real resumes used to change careers and transfer skills to other industries

Anne McKinney, Editor

PREP PUBLISHING

FAYETTEVILLE, NC

PREP Publishing

1110½ Hay Street

Fayetteville, NC 28305

(910) 483-6611

Library of Congress Cataloging-in-Publication Data

Real-resumes for social work & counseling jobs : including real resumes used to change careers and transfer skills to other industries / Anne McKinney, editor.
      p. cm. -- (Real-resumes series)
      ISBN 978-1475093919; 1475093918 (trade pbk.)
    1. Résumés (Employment) 2. Social service. 3. Counseling.
I. McKinney, Anne, 1948- II. Series.

  HF5383 .R3962 2002
  650.14'2--dc21   2002020590
                                                                          CIP

Printed in the United States of America

By PREP Publishing

Table of Contents

A WORD FROM THE EDITOR:
ABOUT THE REAL-RESUMES SERIES

Welcome to the Real-Resumes Series. The Real-Resumes Series is a series of books which have been developed based on the experiences of real job hunters and which target specialized fields or types of resumes. As the editor of the series, I have carefully selected resumes and cover letters (with names and other key data disguised, of course) which have been used successfully in real job hunts. That's what we mean by "Real-Resumes." What you see in this book are *real* resumes and cover letters which helped real people get ahead in their careers.

The Real-Resumes Series is based on the work of the country's oldest resume-preparation company known as PREP Resumes. If you would like a free information packet describing the company's resume preparation services, call 910-483-6611 or write to PREP at 1110½ Hay Street, Fayetteville, NC 28305. If you have a job hunting experience you would like to share with our staff at the Real-Resumes Series, please contact us at preppub@aol.com or visit our website at http://www.prep-pub.com.

The resumes and cover letters in this book are designed to be of most value to people already in a job hunt or contemplating a career change. If we could give you one word of advice about your career, here's what we would say: Manage your career and don't stumble from job to job in an incoherent pattern. Try to find work that interests you, and then identify prosperous industries which need work performed of the type you want to do. Learn early in your working life that a great resume and cover letter can blow doors open for you and help you maximize your salary.

This book is dedicated to those seeking jobs in the social work and counseling field. We hope the superior samples will help you manage your current job campaign and your career so that you will find work aligned to your career interests.

Real-Resumes for Social Work & Counseling Jobs...
including real resumes used to change careers
and transfer skills to other industries

Anne McKinney, Editor

Introduction:
The Art of
Changing
Jobs...
and Finding
New Careers

As the editor of this book, I would like to give you some tips on how to make the best use of the information you will find here. Because you are considering a career change, you already understand the concept of managing your career for maximum enjoyment and self-fulfillment. The purpose of this book is to provide expert tools and advice so that you *can* manage your career. Inside these pages you will find resumes and cover letters that will help you find not just a job but the type of work you want to do.

Overview of the Book

Every resume and cover letter in this book actually worked. And most of the resumes and cover letters have common features: most are one-page, most are in the chronological format, and most resumes are accompanied by a companion cover letter. In this section you will find helpful advice about job hunting. Step One begins with a discussion of why employers prefer the one-page, chronological resume. In Step Two you are introduced to the direct approach and to the proper format for a cover letter. In Step Three you learn the 14 main reasons why job hunters are not offered the jobs they want, and you learn the six key areas employers focus on when they interview you. Step Four gives nuts-and-bolts advice on how to handle the interview, send a follow-up letter after an interview, and negotiate your salary.

The cover letter plays such a critical role in a career change. You will learn from the experts how to format your cover letters and you will see suggested language to use in particular career-change situations. It has been said that "A picture is worth a thousand words" and, for that reason, you will see numerous examples of effective cover letters used by real individuals to change fields, functions, and industries.

The most important part of the book is the Real-Resumes section. Some of the individuals whose resumes and cover letters you see spent a lengthy career in an industry they loved. Then there are resumes and cover letters of people who wanted a change but who probably wanted to remain in their industry. Many of you will be especially interested by the resumes and cover letters of individuals who knew they definitely wanted a career change but had no idea what they wanted to do next. Other resumes and cover letters show individuals who knew they wanted to change fields and had a pretty good idea of what they wanted to do next.

Whatever your field, and whatever your circumstances, you'll find resumes and cover letters that will "show you the ropes" in terms of successfully changing jobs and switching careers.

Before you proceed further, think about why you picked up this book.
- Are you dissatisfied with the type of work you are now doing?
- Would you like to change careers, change companies, or change industries?
- Are you satisfied with your industry but not with your niche or function within it?
- Do you want to transfer your skills to a new product or service?
- Even if you have excelled in your field, have you "had enough"? Would you like the stimulation of a new challenge?
- Are you aware of the importance of a great cover letter but unsure of how to write one?
- Are you preparing to launch a second career after retirement?
- Have you been downsized, or do you anticipate becoming a victim of downsizing?
- Do you need expert advice on how to plan and implement a job campaign that will open the maximum number of doors?
- Do you want to make sure you handle an interview to your maximum advantage?

- Would you like to master the techniques of negotiating salary and benefits?
- Do you want to learn the secrets and shortcuts of professional resume writers?

Using the Direct Approach

As you consider the possibility of a job hunt or career change, you need to be aware that most people end up having at least three distinctly different careers in their working lifetimes, and often those careers are different from each other. Yet people usually stumble through each job campaign, unsure of what they should be doing. Whether you find yourself voluntarily or unexpectedly in a job hunt, the direct approach is the job hunting strategy most likely to yield a full-time permanent job. The direct approach is an active, take-the-initiative style of job hunting in which you choose your next employer rather than relying on responding to ads, using employment agencies, or depending on other methods of finding jobs. You will learn how to use the direct approach in this book, and you will see that an effective cover letter is a critical ingredient in using the direct approach.

The "direct approach" is the style of job hunting most likely to yield the maximum number of job interviews.

Lack of Industry Experience Not a Major Barrier to Entering New Field

"Lack of experience" is often the last reason people are not offered jobs, according to the companies who do the hiring. If you are changing careers, you will be glad to learn that experienced professionals often are selling "potential" rather than experience in a job hunt. Companies look for personal qualities that they know tend to be present in their most effective professionals, such as communication skills, initiative, persistence, organizational and time management skills, and creativity. Frequently companies are trying to discover "personality type," "talent," "ability," "aptitude," and "potential" rather than seeking actual hands-on experience, so your resume should be designed to aggressively present your accomplishments. Attitude, enthusiasm, personality, and a track record of achievements in any type of work are the primary "indicators of success" which employers are seeking, and you will see numerous examples in this book of resumes written in an all-purpose fashion so that the professional can approach various industries and companies.

The Art of Using References in a Job Hunt

You probably already know that you need to provide references during a job hunt, but you may not be sure of how and when to use references for maximum advantage. You can use references very creatively during a job hunt to call attention to your strengths and make yourself "stand out." Your references will rarely get you a job, no matter how impressive the names, but the way you use references can boost the employer's confidence in you and lead to a job offer in the least time.

Using references in a skillful fashion in your job hunt will inspire confidence in prospective employers and help you "close the sale" after interviews.

You should ask from three to five people, including people who have supervised you, if you can use them as a reference during your job hunt. You may not be able to ask your current boss since your job hunt is probably confidential.

A common question in resume preparation is: "Do I need to put my references on my resume?" No, you don't. Even if you create a references page at the same time you prepare your resume, you don't need to mail, e-mail, or fax your references page with the resume and cover letter. Usually the potential employer is not interested in references until he meets you, so the earliest you need to have references ready is at the first interview. Obviously there are exceptions to this standard rule of thumb; sometimes an ad will ask you to send references with your first response. Wait until the employer requests references before providing them.

An excellent attention-getting technique is to take to the first interview not just a page of references (giving names, addresses, and telephone numbers) but an actual letter of reference written by someone who knows you well and who preferably has supervised or employed you. A professional way to close the first interview is to thank the interviewer, shake his or her hand, and then say you'd like to give him or her a copy of a letter of reference from a previous employer. Hopefully you already made a good impression during the interview, but you'll "close the sale" in a dynamic fashion if you leave a letter praising you and your accomplishments. For that reason, it's a good idea to ask supervisors during your final weeks in a job if they will provide you with a written letter of recommendation which you can use in future job hunts. Most employers will oblige, and you will have a letter that has a useful "shelf life" of many years. Such a letter often gives the prospective employer enough confidence in his opinion of you that he may forego checking out other references and decide to offer you the job on the spot or in the next few days.

With regard to references, it's best to provide the names and addresses of people who have supervised you or observed you in a work situation.

Whom should you ask to serve as references? References should be people who have known or supervised you in a professional, academic, or work situation. References with big titles, like school superintendent or congressman, are fine, but remind busy people when you get to the interview stage that they may be contacted soon. Make sure the busy official recognizes your name and has instant positive recall of you! If you're asked to provide references on a formal company application, you can simply transcribe names from your references list. In summary, follow this rule in using references: If you've got them, flaunt them! If you've obtained well-written letters of reference, make sure you find a polite way to push those references under the nose of the interviewer so he or she can hear someone other than you describing your strengths. Your references probably won't ever get you a job, but glowing letters of reference can give you credibility and visibility that can make you stand out among candidates with similar credentials and potential!

The approach taken by this book is to (1) help you master the proven best techniques of conducting a job hunt and (2) show you how to stand out in a job hunt through your resume, cover letter, interviewing skills, as well as the way in which you present your references and follow up on interviews. Now, the best way to "get in the mood" for writing your own resume and cover letter is to select samples from the Table of Contents that interest you and then read them. A great resume is a "photograph," usually on one page, of an individual. If you wish to seek professional advice in preparing your resume, you may contact one of the professional writers at Professional Resume & Employment Publishing (PREP) for a brief free consultation by calling 1-910-483-6611.

Part One: Some Advice About Your Job Hunt

What if you don't know what you want to do?

Your job hunt will be more comfortable if you can figure out what type of work you want to do. But you are not alone if you have no idea what you want to do next! You may have knowledge and skills in certain areas but want to get into another type of work. What *The Wall Street Journal* has discovered in its research on careers is that most of us end up having at least three distinctly different careers in our working lives; it seems that, even if we really like a particular kind of activity, twenty years of doing it is enough for most of us and we want to move on to something else!

That's why we strongly believe that you need to spend some time figuring out ***what interests you*** rather than taking an inventory of the skills you have. You may have skills that you simply don't want to use, but if you can build your career on the things that interest you, you will be more likely to be happy and satisfied in your job. Realize, too, that interests can change over time; the activities that interest you now may not be the ones that interested you years ago. For example, some professionals may decide that they've had enough of retail sales and want a job selling another product or service, even though they have earned a reputation for being an excellent retail manager. We strongly believe that interests rather than skills should be the determining factor in deciding what types of jobs you want to apply for and what directions you explore in your job hunt. Obviously one cannot be a lawyer without a law degree or a secretary without secretarial skills; but a professional can embark on a next career as a financial consultant, property manager, plant manager, production supervisor, retail manager, or other occupation if he/she has a strong interest in that type of work and can provide a resume that clearly demonstrates past excellent performance in *any* field and *potential* to excel in another field. As you will see later in this book, "lack of exact experience" is the last reason why people are turned down for the jobs they apply for.

> Figure out what interests you and you will hold the key to a successful job hunt and working career. (And be prepared for your interests to change over time!)

> "Lack of exact experience" is the last reason people are turned down for the jobs for which they apply.

How can you have a resume prepared if you don't know what you want to do?

You may be wondering how you can have a resume prepared if you don't know what you want to do next. The approach to resume writing which PREP, the country's oldest resume-preparation company, has used successfully for many years is to develop an "all-purpose" resume that translates your skills, experience, and accomplishments into language employers can understand. What most people need in a job hunt is a versatile resume that will allow them to apply for numerous types of jobs. For example, you may want to apply for a job in pharmaceutical sales but you may also want to have a resume that will be versatile enough for you to apply for jobs in the construction, financial services, or automotive industries.

Based on more than **20** years of serving job hunters, we at PREP have found that your best approach to job hunting is **an all-purpose resume** and **specific cover letters tailored to specific fields** rather than using the approach of trying to create different resumes for every job. If you are remaining in your field, you may not even need more than one "all-purpose" cover letter, although the cover letter rather than the resume is the place to communicate your interest in a narrow or specific field. An all-purpose resume and cover letter that translate your experience and accomplishments into plain English are the tools that will maximize the number of doors which open for you while permitting you to "fish" in the widest range of job areas.

Your resume will provide the script for your job interview.
When you get down to it, your resume has a simple job to do: Its purpose is to blow as many doors open as possible and to make as many people as possible want to meet you. So a well-written resume that really "sells" you is a key that will create opportunities for you in a job hunt.

This statistic explains why: The typical newspaper advertisement for a job opening receives more than 245 replies. And normally only 10 or 12 will be invited to an interview.

But here's another purpose of the resume: it provides the "script" the employer uses when he interviews you. If your resume has been written in such a way that your strengths and achievements are revealed, that's what you'll end up talking about at the job interview. Since the resume will govern what you get asked about at your interviews, you can't overestimate the importance of making sure your resume makes you look and sound as good as you are.

Your resume is the "script" for your job interviews. Make sure you put on your resume what you want to talk about or be asked about at the job interview.

So what is a "good" resume?
Very literally, your resume should motivate the person reading it to dial the phone number or e-mail the screen name you have put on the resume. When you are relocating, you should put a local phone number on your resume if your physical address is several states away; employers are more likely to dial a local telephone number than a long-distance number when they're looking for potential employees.

If you have a resume already, look at it objectively. Is it a limp, colorless "laundry list" of your job titles and duties? Or does it "paint a picture" of your skills, abilities, and accomplishments in a way that would make someone want to meet you? Can people understand what you're saying? If you are attempting to change fields or industries, can potential employers see that your skills and knowledge are transferable to other environments? For example, have you described accomplishments which reveal your problem-solving abilities or communication skills?

The one-page resume in chronological format is the format preferred by most employers.

How long should your resume be?
One page, maybe two. Usually only people in the academic community have a resume (which they usually call a *curriculum vitae*) longer than one or two pages. Remember that your resume is almost always accompanied by a cover letter, and a potential employer does not want to read more than two or three pages about a total stranger in order to decide if he wants to meet that person! Besides, don't forget that the more you tell someone about yourself, the more opportunity you are providing for the employer to screen you out at the "first-cut" stage. A resume should be concise and exciting and designed to make the reader want to meet you in person!

Should resumes be functional or chronological?
Employers almost always prefer a chronological resume; in other words, an employer will find a resume easier to read if it is immediately apparent what your current or most recent job is, what you did before that, and so forth, in reverse chronological order. A resume that goes back in detail for the last ten years of employment will generally satisfy the employer's curiosity about your background. Employment more than ten years old can be shown even more briefly in an "Other Experience" section at the end of your "Experience" section. Remember that your intention is not to tell everything you've done but to "hit the high points" and especially impress the employer with what you learned, contributed, or accomplished in each job you describe.

Once you get your resume, what do you do with it?
You will be using your resume to answer ads, as a tool to use in talking with friends and relatives about your job search, and, most importantly, in using the "direct approach" described in this book.

When you mail your resume, always send a "cover letter."
A "cover letter," sometimes called a "resume letter" or "letter of interest," is a letter that accompanies and introduces your resume. Your cover letter is a way of personalizing the resume by sending it to the specific person you think you might want to work for at each company. Your cover letter should contain a few highlights from your resume—just enough to make someone want to meet you. Cover letters should always be typed or word processed on a computer—never handwritten.

Never mail or fax your resume without a cover letter.

1. Learn the art of answering ads.
There is an "art," part of which can be learned, in using your "bestselling" resume to reply to advertisements.

Sometimes an exciting job lurks behind a boring ad that someone dictated in a hurry, so reply to any ad that interests you. Don't worry that you aren't "25 years old with an MBA" like the ad asks for. Employers will always make compromises in their requirements if they think you're the "best fit" overall.

What about ads that ask for "salary requirements?"
What if the ad you're answering asks for "salary requirements?" The first rule is to avoid committing yourself in writing at that point to a specific salary. You don't want to "lock yourself in."

There are two ways to handle the ad that asks for "salary requirements."
First, you can ignore that part of the ad and accompany your resume with a cover letter that focuses on "selling" you, your abilities, and even some of your philosophy about work or your field. You may include a sentence in your cover letter like this: "I can provide excellent personal and professional references at your request, and I would be delighted to share the private details of my salary history with you in person."

What if the ad asks for your "salary requirements?"

Second, if you feel you must give some kind of number, just state a range in your cover letter that includes your medical, dental, other benefits, and expected bonuses. You might state, for example, "My current compensation, including benefits and bonuses, is in the range of $30,000-$40,000."

Analyze the ad and "tailor" yourself to it.
When you're replying to ads, a finely tailored cover letter is an important tool in getting your resume noticed and read. On the next page is a cover letter which has been "tailored to fit" a specific ad. Notice the "art" used by PREP writers of analyzing the ad's main requirements and then writing the letter so that the person's background, work habits, and interests seem "tailor-made" to the company's needs. Use this cover letter as a model when you prepare your own reply to ads.

Date

Exact Name of Person
Title or Position
Name of Company
Address (no., street)
Address (city, state, zip)

Dear Exact Name of Person (or Dear Sir or Madam if answering a blind ad):

I would appreciate an opportunity to talk with you soon about how I could benefit your organization through my background in education as well as my experience in counseling and social services. I am particularly interested in the position of Director of the Job Training Partnership Program which was recently advertised.

As you will see from my resume, I have had a number of years experience working with children in the educational field. I began my career as a Teacher and excelled in the teaching profession. Slowly, however, I began to realize that my true calling was in the social work and social services area as I realized that the social services field could meet needs of children which were even more basic than textbook learning.

In my first position in the social work field, I counseled both young and older adults with the Joint Partnership Training Act, the federal program devoted to helping disadvantaged people develop job skills and find employment. In my work with the JTPA, I have demonstrated strong skills in marketing and advertising as well as in community liaison. In formal performance evaluations I have been described as a resourceful individual who excels in working with others at all levels.

You would find me to be a well-rounded professional with exceptional organizational skills and highly developed communication abilities.

I hope you will call or write me soon to suggest a time convenient for us to meet and discuss your current and future needs and how I might serve them. Thank you in advance for your time.

Sincerely,

Bettina L. Dolly

Alternate last paragraph:
I hope you will welcome my call soon to arrange a brief meeting at your convenience to discuss your current and future needs and how I might serve them. Thank you in advance for your time.

Employers are trying to identify the individual who wants the job they are filling. Don't be afraid to express your enthusiasm in the cover letter!

2. Talk to friends and relatives.

Don't be shy about telling your friends and relatives the kind of job you're looking for. Looking for the job you want involves using your network of contacts, so tell people what you're looking for. They may be able to make introductions and help set up interviews.

About 25% of all interviews are set up through "who you know," so don't ignore this approach.

3. Finally, and most importantly, use the "direct approach."

The "direct approach" is a strategy in which you choose your next employer.

More than 50% of all job interviews are set up by the "direct approach." That means you actually mail, e-mail, or fax a resume and a cover letter to a company you think might be interesting to work for.

To whom do you write?

In general, you should write directly to the *exact name* of the person who would be hiring you: say, the vice-president of marketing or data processing. If you're in doubt about to whom to address the letter, address it to the president by name and he or she will make sure it gets forwarded to the right person within the company who has hiring authority in your area.

How do you find the names of potential employers?

You're not alone if you feel that the biggest problem in your job search is finding the right names at the companies you want to contact. But you can usually figure out the names of companies you want to approach by deciding first if your job hunt is primarily geography-driven or industry-driven.

In a **geography-driven job hunt,** you could select a list of, say, 50 companies you want to contact **by location** from the lists that the U.S. Chambers of Commerce publish yearly of their "major area employers." There are hundreds of local Chambers of Commerce across America, and most of them will have an 800 number which you can find through 1-800-555-1212. If you and your family think Atlanta, Dallas, Ft. Lauderdale, and Virginia Beach might be nice places to live, for example, you could contact the Chamber of Commerce in those cities and ask how you can obtain a copy of their list of major employers. Your nearest library will have the book which lists the addresses of all chambers.

In an **industry-driven job hunt,** and if you are willing to relocate, you will be identifying the companies which you find most attractive in the industry in which you want to work. When you select a list of companies to contact **by industry,** you can find the right person to write and the address of firms by industrial category in *Standard and Poor's, Moody's,* and other excellent books in public libraries. Many Web sites also provide contact information.

Many people feel it's a good investment to actually call the company to either find out or double-check the name of the person to whom they want to send a resume and cover letter. It's important to do as much as you feasibly can to assure that the letter gets to the right person in the company.

On-line research will be the best way for many people to locate organizations to which they wish to send their resume. It is outside the scope of this book to teach Internet research skills, but librarians are often useful in this area.

What's the correct way to follow up on a resume you send?

There is a polite way to be aggressively interested in a company during your job hunt. It is ideal to end the cover letter accompanying your resume by saying, "I hope you'll welcome my call next week when I try to arrange a brief meeting at your convenience to discuss your current and future needs and how I might serve them." Keep it low key, and just ask for a "brief meeting," not an interview. Employers want people who show a determined interest in working with them, so don't be shy about following up on the resume and cover letter you've mailed.

STEP THREE: Preparing for Interviews

It pays to be aware of the 14 most common pitfalls for job hunters.

But a resume and cover letter by themselves can't get you the job you want. You need to "prep" yourself before the interview. Step Three in your job campaign is "Preparing for Interviews." First, let's look at interviewing from the hiring organization's point of view.

What are the biggest "turnoffs" for potential employers?

One of the ways to help yourself perform well at an interview is to look at the main reasons why organizations *don't* hire the people they interview, according to those who do the interviewing.

Notice that "lack of appropriate background" (or lack of experience) is the *last* reason for not being offered the job.

The 14 Most Common Reasons Job Hunters Are Not Offered Jobs (according to the companies who do the interviewing and hiring):

1. Low level of accomplishment
2. Poor attitude, lack of self-confidence
3. Lack of goals/objectives
4. Lack of enthusiasm
5. Lack of interest in the company's business
6. Inability to sell or express yourself
7. Unrealistic salary demands
8. Poor appearance
9. Lack of maturity, no leadership potential
10. Lack of extracurricular activities
11. Lack of preparation for the interview, no knowledge about company
12. Objecting to travel
13. Excessive interest in security and benefits
14. Inappropriate background

Department of Labor studies have proven that smart, "prepared" job hunters can increase their beginning salary while getting a job in *half* the time it normally takes. (4½ months is the average national length of a job search.) Here, from PREP, are some questions that can prepare you to find a job faster.

Are you in the "right" frame of mind?

It seems unfair that we have to look for a job just when we're lowest in morale. Don't worry *too* much if you're nervous before interviews. You're supposed to be a little nervous, especially if the job means a lot to you. But the best way to kill unnecessary fears about job hunting is through 1) making sure you have a great resume and 2) preparing yourself for the interview. Here are three main areas you need to think about before each interview.

Do you know what the company does?

Don't walk into an interview giving the impression that, "If this is Tuesday, this must be General Motors."

Find out before the interview what the company's main product or service is. Where is the company heading? Is it in a "growth" or declining industry? (Answers to these questions may influence whether or not you want to work there!)

Information about what the company does is in annual reports, in newspaper and magazine articles, and on the Internet. If you're not yet skilled at Internet research, just visit your nearest library and ask the reference librarian to guide you to printed materials on the company.

Do you know what you want to do for the company?

Before the interview, try to decide how you see yourself fitting into the company. Remember, "lack of exact background" the company wants is usually the last reason people are not offered jobs.

Understand before you go to each interview that the burden will be on you to "sell" the interviewer on why you're the best person for the job and the company.

How will you answer the critical interview questions?

Put yourself in the interviewer's position and think about the questions you're most likely to be asked. Here are some of the most commonly asked interview questions:

Q: "What are your greatest strengths?"

A: Don't say you've never thought about it! Go into an interview knowing the three main impressions you want to leave about yourself, such as "I'm hard-working, loyal, and an imaginative cost-cutter."

Q: "What are your greatest weaknesses?"

A: Don't confess that you're lazy or have trouble meeting deadlines! Confessing that you tend to be a "workaholic" or "tend to be a perfectionist and sometimes get frustrated when others don't share my high standards" will make your prospective employer see a "weakness" that he likes. Name a weakness that your interviewer will perceive as a strength.

Q: "What are your long-range goals?"

A: If you're interviewing with Microsoft, don't say you want to work for IBM in five years! Say your long-range goal is to be *with* the company, contributing to its goals and success.

Q: "What motivates you to do your best work?"

A: Don't get dollar signs in your eyes here! "A challenge" is not a bad answer, but it's a little cliched. Saying something like "troubleshooting" or "solving a tough problem" is more interesting and specific. Give an example if you can.

Research the company before you go to interviews.

Anticipate the questions you will be asked at the interview, and prepare your responses in advance.

Q: "What do you know about this organization?"

A: Don't say you never heard of it until they asked you to the interview! Name an interesting, positive thing you learned about the company recently from your research. Remember, company executives can sometimes feel rather "maternal" about the company they serve. Don't get onto a negative area of the company if you can think of positive facts you can bring up. Of course, if you learned in your research that the company's sales seem to be taking a nose-dive, or that the company president is being prosecuted for taking bribes, you might politely ask your interviewer to tell you something that could help you better understand what you've been reading. Those are the kinds of company facts that can help you determine whether or not you want to work there.

Q: "Why should I hire you?"

A: "I'm unemployed and available" is the wrong answer here! Get back to your strengths and say that you believe the organization could benefit by a loyal, hard-working cost-cutter like yourself.

In conclusion, you should decide in advance, before you go to the interview, how you will answer each of these commonly asked questions. Have some practice interviews with a friend to role-play and build your confidence.

Go to an interview prepared to tell the company why it should hire you.

STEP FOUR: Handling the Interview and Negotiating Salary

Now you're ready for Step Four: actually handling the interview successfully and effectively. Remember, the purpose of an interview is to get a job offer.

A smile at an interview makes the employer perceive of you as intelligent!

Eight "do's" for the interview

According to leading U.S. companies, there are eight key areas in interviewing success. You can fail at an interview if you mishandle just one area.

1. **Do wear appropriate clothes.**

You can never go wrong by wearing a suit to an interview.

2. **Do be well groomed.**

Don't overlook the obvious things like having clean hair, clothes, and fingernails for the interview.

3. **Do give a firm handshake.**

You'll have to shake hands twice in most interviews: first, before you sit down, and second, when you leave the interview. Limp handshakes turn most people off.

4. **Do smile and show a sense of humor.**

Interviewers are looking for people who would be nice to work with, so don't be so somber that you don't smile. In fact, research shows that people who smile at interviews are perceived as more intelligent. So, smile!

5. **Do be enthusiastic.**

Employers say they are "turned off" by lifeless, unenthusiastic job hunters who show no special interest in that company. The best way to show some enthusiasm for the employer's operation is to find out about the business beforehand.

6. Do show you are flexible and adaptable.

An employer is looking for someone who can contribute to his organization in a flexible, adaptable way. No matter what skills and training you have, employers know every new employee must go through initiation and training on the company's turf. Certainly show pride in your past accomplishments in a specific, factual way ("I saved my last employer $50.00 a week by a new cost-cutting measure I developed"). But don't come across as though there's nothing about the job you couldn't easily handle.

7. Do ask intelligent questions about the employer's business.

An employer is hiring someone because of certain business needs. Show interest in those needs. Asking questions to get a better idea of the employer's needs will help you "stand out" from other candidates interviewing for the job.

8. Do "take charge" when the interviewer "falls down" on the job.

Go into every interview knowing the three or four points about yourself you want the interviewer to remember. And be prepared to take an active part in leading the discussion if the interviewer's "canned approach" does not permit you to display your "strong suit." You can't always depend on the interviewer's asking you the "right" questions so you can stress your strengths and accomplishments.

Employers are seeking people with good attitudes whom they can train and coach to do things their way.

An important "don't": Don't ask questions about salary or benefits at the first interview.
Employers don't take warmly to people who look at their organization as just a place to satisfy salary and benefit needs. Don't risk making a negative impression by appearing greedy or self-serving. The place to discuss salary and benefits is normally at the second interview, and the employer will bring it up. Then you can ask questions without appearing excessively interested in what the organization can do for you.

Now...negotiating your salary
Even if an ad requests that you communicate your "salary requirement" or "salary history," you should avoid providing those numbers in your initial cover letter. You can usually say something like this: "I would be delighted to discuss the private details of my salary history with you in person."

Once you're at the interview, you must avoid even appearing *interested* in salary before you are offered the job. Make sure you've "sold" yourself before talking salary. First show you're the "best fit" for the employer and then you'll be in a stronger position from which to negotiate salary. **Never** bring up the subject of salary yourself. Employers say there's no way you can avoid looking greedy if you bring up the issue of salary and benefits before the company has identified you as its "best fit."

Don't appear excessively interested in salary and benefits at the interview.

Interviewers sometimes throw out a salary figure at the first interview to see if you'll accept it. You may not want to commit yourself if you think you will be able to negotiate a better deal later on. Get back to finding out more about the job. This lets the interviewer know you're interested primarily in the job and not the salary.

When the organization brings up salary, it may say something like this: "Well, Mary, we think you'd make a good candidate for this job. What kind of salary are we talking about?" You may not want to name a number here, either. Give the ball back to the interviewer. Act as though you hadn't given the subject of salary much thought and respond something like this: "Ah, Mr. Jones, I wonder if you'd be kind enough to tell me what salary you had in mind when you advertised the job?" Or ... "What is the range you have in mind?"

Don't worry, if the interviewer names a figure that you think is too low, you can say so without turning down the job or locking yourself into a rigid position. The point here is to negotiate for yourself as well as you can. You might reply to a number named by the interviewer that you think is low by saying something like this: "Well, Mr. Lee, the job interests me very much, and I think I'd certainly enjoy working with you. But, frankly, I was thinking of something a little higher than that." That leaves the ball in your interviewer's court again, and you haven't turned down the job either, in case it turns out that the interviewer can't increase the offer and you still want the job.

Salary negotiation can be tricky.

Last, send a follow-up letter.

Mail, e-mail, or fax a letter right after the interview telling your interviewer you enjoyed the meeting and are certain (if you are) that you are the "best fit" for the job. The people interviewing you will probably have an attitude described as either "professionally loyal" to their companies, or "maternal and proprietary" if the interviewer also owns the company. In either case, they are looking for people who want to work for *that* company in particular. The follow-up letter you send might be just the deciding factor in your favor if the employer is trying to choose between you and someone else. You will see an example of a follow-up letter on page 16.

A follow-up letter can help the employer choose between you and another qualified candidate.

A cover letter is an essential part of a job hunt or career change.

Many people are aware of the importance of having a great resume, but most people in a job hunt don't realize just how important a cover letter can be. The purpose of the cover letter, sometimes called a **"letter of interest,"** is to introduce your resume to prospective employers. The cover letter is often the critical ingredient in a job hunt because the cover letter allows you to say a lot of things that just don't "fit" on the resume. For example, you can emphasize your commitment to a new field and stress your related talents. The cover letter also gives you a chance to stress outstanding character and personal values. On the next two pages you will see examples of very effective cover letters.

A cover letter is an essential part of a career change.

Please do not attempt to implement a career change without a cover letter such as the ones you see in Part Two of this book. A cover letter is the first impression of you, and you can influence the way an employer views you by the language and style of your letter.

Special help for those in career change

We want to emphasize again that, especially in a career change, the cover letter is very important and can help you "build a bridge" to a new career. A creative and appealing cover letter can begin the process of encouraging the potential employer to imagine you in an industry other than the one in which you have worked.

As a special help to those in career change, there are resumes and cover letters included in this book which show valuable techniques and tips you should use when changing fields or industries. The resumes and cover letters of career changers are identified in the table of contents as "Career Change" and you will see the "Career Change" label on cover letters in Part Two where the individuals are changing careers.

**Addressing the Cover
Letter:** Get the exact
name of the person to
whom you are writing. This
makes your approach
personal.

First Paragraph: This
explains why you are
writing.

Second Paragraph: You
have a chance to talk
about whatever you feel is
your most distinguishing
feature.

Third Paragraph: You
bring up your next most
distinguishing qualities and
try to
sell yourself.

Fourth Paragraph: Here
you have another
opportunity to reveal
qualities or achievements
which will impress your
future employer.

Final Paragraph: She
asks the employer to
contact her. Make sure
your reader knows what
the "next step" is.

**Alternate Final
Paragraph:** It's more
aggressive (but not too
aggressive) to let the
employer know that you
will be calling him or her.
Don't be afraid to be
persistent. Employers are
looking for people who
know what they want to
do.

Date

Exact Name of Person
Exact Title
Exact Name of Company
Address
City, State, Zip

Dear Exact Name of Person (or Dear Sir or Madam if answering a blind ad):

With the enclosed resume, I would like to make you aware of my desire to explore employment opportunities with your organization. I am especially interested in the position of Rape Center Director which you recently advertised.

I actually stumbled into my social work career after I applied for a position as an Eligibility Specialist. I then made a successful transition from the private sector where I had been selling insurance, and I quickly realized that I wanted to make my professional home in the social work field. Once I had experienced the profound sense of satisfaction that comes from helping others in need, I was committed to a social services career.

In subsequent positions, I have worked for two departments of social services in California. In my current position as a Case Worker II in San Diego, I interview and hire potential clients to determine their eligibility for assistance, and I perform liaison with a vast network of helping organizations as I seek to locate assistance for individuals in need of emergency shelter, medical care, counseling, and other services.

I believe my education in banking and finance as well as my strong computer skills would be valuable assets in the role of Rape Center Director. I can provide outstanding references, and I hope very much that we will have an opportunity to discuss in person the position you are seeking to fill. I can assure you in advance that I am a highly motivated individual who would committed to serving the needs of your community's rape victims.

Sincerely,

Stacey Wilson

Date

Exact Name of Person
Title or Position
Name of Company
Address (no., street)
Address (city, state, zip)

Dear Exact Name of Person (or Dear Sir or Madam if answering a blind ad):

I would appreciate an opportunity to talk with you soon about how I could contribute to your organization through my experience in the social services field.

Specially recruited for my current position as a Job Coach, I currently supervise eight job coaches while managing 10 developmentally challenged clients. In the absence of the day program director, I oversee a population of 125 clients.

When I joined the WAVE Program in my current job, it was in an embryonic state of development. With a reputation as a social and outgoing person, I aggressively called on business and community leaders in order to establish new employment opportunities for developmentally challenged adults. Through persistence and relentless follow-through, I have transformed this small local program into a "model" operation which is frequently studied by other state departments.

Although I am highly regarded in my current position and can provide outstanding references at the appropriate time, I am selectively exploring opportunities in other social services environments. To a large degree, I feel that the challenging goal I undertook when I assumed my current position has been achieved, and I am restless for new and more complex challenges. I thrive on the challenge of solving problems so that the less fortunate can have a better quality of life.

I hope you will write or call me soon to suggest a time when we might meet to discuss your goals and needs and how I might serve them. I feel certain that I could become a valuable and productive member of your team.

Sincerely yours,

Steven Alexander

Date

Exact Name of Person
Title or Position
Name of Company
Address (number and street)
Address (city, state, and zip)

Dear Exact Name:

I am writing to express my appreciation for the time you spent with me on 9 December, and I want to let you know that I am sincerely interested in the position of Controller for your private practice which you described.

I feel confident that I could skillfully interact with your staff of counselors and psychologists in order to provide the most effective services, and I am adept at billing through Medicaid and Medicare as well as through private insurers. I want you to know, too, that I would not consider relocating to Salt Lake City to be a hardship! It is certainly one of the most beautiful areas I have ever seen.

As you described to me what you are looking for in a controller, I had a sense of "déjà vu" because my current boss was in a similar position when I went to work for him. He needed someone to come in and be his "right arm" and take on an increasing amount of his management responsibilities so that he could be freed up to do other things. I have played a key role in the growth and profitability of his private practice, and he has come to depend on my sound financial and business advice as much as my day-to-day management skills.

It would be a pleasure to work for a successful individual such as yourself, and I feel I could contribute significantly to your business not only through my accounting and business background but also through my strong qualities of loyalty, reliability, and trustworthiness. I send best wishes for the holidays, and I look forward to hearing from you at your convenience.

Yours sincerely,

Jacob Evangelisto

In this section, you will find resumes and cover letters of social work and counseling professionals—and of people who want to work in the field of social work and counseling. How do social work professionals differ from other job hunters? Why should there be a book dedicated to people seeking jobs in the social work field? Based on more than 20 years of experience in working with job hunters, this editor is convinced that resumes and cover letters which "speak the lingo" of the field you wish to enter will communicate more effectively than language which is not industry-specific. This book is designed to help people (1) who are seeking to prepare their own resumes and (2) who wish to use as models "real" resumes of individuals who have successfully launched careers in the social work field or advanced in the field. You will see a wide range of experience levels reflected in the resumes in this book. Some of the resumes and cover letters were used by individuals seeking to enter the field; others were used successfully by senior professionals to advance in the field.

Newcomers to an industry sometimes have advantages over more experienced professionals. In a job hunt, junior professionals can have an advantage over their more experienced counterparts. Prospective employers often view the less experienced workers as "more trainable" and "more coachable" than their seniors. This means that the mature professional who has already excelled in a first career can, with credibility, "change careers" and transfer skills to other industries.

Newcomers to the field may have disadvantages compared to their seniors. Almost by definition, the inexperienced social work professional—the young person who has recently earned a college degree, or the individual who has recently received certifications respected by the industry—is less tested and less experienced than senior managers, so the resume and cover letter of the inexperienced professional may often have to "sell" his or her potential to do something he or she has never done before. Lack of experience in the field she wants to enter can be a stumbling block to the junior manager, but remember that many employers believe that someone who has excelled in anything—academics, for example—can excel in many other fields.

Some advice to inexperienced professionals...
If senior professionals could give junior professionals a piece of advice about careers, here's what they would say: Manage your career and don't stumble from job to job in an incoherent pattern. Try to find work that interests you, and then identify prosperous industries which need work performed of the type you want to do. Learn early in your working life that a great resume and cover letter can blow doors open for you and help you maximize your salary.

Special help for career changers...
For those changing careers, you will find useful the resumes and cover letters marked "Career Change" on the following pages. Consult the Table of Contents for page numbers showing career changers.

An experienced social worker reported that one of her clients expressed surprise that she got paid for what she did -- "all you do is talk," the client said. "Yes," she responded, "but it took me a long time to learn how to talk like this."

Date

Exact Name of Person
Exact Title
Exact Name of Company
Address
City, State, Zip

Dear Exact Name of Person (or Dear Sir or Madam if answering a blind ad):

With the enclosed resume, I would like to make you aware of my background as an articulate human services professional with exceptional planning and motivational skills who offers experience providing guidance and supervision to a variety of child and adolescent populations.

As you will see from my resume, I have a Bachelor of Arts in Psychology from the University of Colorado, and am pursuing my Master's degree in Counseling Psychology in my spare time. I am a licensed Client Behavior Intervention Technician, and have additional certifications in First Aid, CPR, and Non-Violent Crisis Intervention.

At Colorado Behavioral Services, I worked as a Client Behavior Intervention Technician, serving a client population with conduct disorders, oppositional defiant disorder, and other behavioral problems. I directly supervised and assisted two clients, a six-year-old and a thirteen-year-old, and assumed temporary responsibility for two other middle school clients while filling in for other technicians.

If you can use a dedicated human services professional who is known for the ability to build a strong rapport with clients, I hope you will welcome my call soon when I try to arrange a brief meeting to discuss your goals and how my background might serve your needs. I can provide outstanding references at the appropriate time.

Sincerely,

Isabel Raines

Alternate Last Paragraph:
If you can use a dedicated human services professional who is known for the ability to build a strong rapport with clients, I hope you will write or call me soon to suggest a time when we might meet to discuss your needs and goals and how my background might serve them. I can provide outstanding references at the appropriate time.

ISABEL RAINES

1110½ Hay Street, Fayetteville, NC 28305 • preppub@aol.com • (910) 483-6611

OBJECTIVE   To benefit an organization that can use a dedicated human services professional with exceptional communication and organizational skills who offers education and experience in working with a diverse population of children and adolescents.

EDUCATION   Pursuing a **Master's** degree in **Counseling Psychology** at Akron State University, Akron, CO in my spare time.
Earned a **Bachelor of Arts** in **Psychology**, University of Colorado, Boulder, CO, 2001.
• Awarded the Allen Normal Alumni Association academic scholarship .
Completed additional training which included Client Behavior Intervention, Non-Violent Crisis Intervention, Adult & Child CPR.

CERTIFICATIONS   Licensed Client Behavior Intervention Technician.
Certified in Adult & Child CPR by the American Red Cross.

EXPERIENCE   **CLIENT BEHAVIOR INTERVENTION TECHNICIAN.** Colorado Behavioral Services, Akron, CO (2002-present). Provided supervision and care to children and adolescents suffering from behavioral disorders who were referred by the Departments of Mental Health and Social Services; was personally responsible for two clients and assisted with two others occasionally, accompanying them to school and to various after-school activities.
• Discussed treatment plans, appropriate behaviors while in school, and rewards for good behavior with clients; created goals for each client according to their treatment plan.
• Planned and developed after-school activities, transporting clients to and from these scheduled outings.
• Ensured that clients adhered to their medication schedules.
• Performed liaison with officials from the client's school, Colorado Behavioral Services, the Department of Social Services, and the client's mental health professional.
• Encouraged positive interaction between clients and their peers, providing appropriate rewards for good behavior.
• Through my efforts, one client achieved dramatic improvement academically; placed on the A/B Honor Roll, she was almost completely removed from BEH/LD classes.

DAYCARE PROVIDER. Shelley's Daycare, Carrboro, CO (1999-2001). Started with this company as a "floater," and quickly advanced to head teacher; provided direct care and supervision to children ages six weeks to five years.
• Developed and implemented lesson plans and daily activities; monitored children's behavior in the classroom and during outside play periods.

RESIDENT ASSISTANT. Hopkins House, Akron, CO (1999). While completing my Psychology degree at Colorado, worked in this emergency group home for adolescents who had been removed from their homes due to abusive or neglectful situations, behavioral disorders, etc.
• Monitored resident behavior both in the home and on organized field trips and outings, assisting them in determining and maintaining conduct appropriate to their situation.
• Served as a mentor while providing the residents with a structured atmosphere; assisted them with their homework, and interacted with them in home environments.

PERSONAL   Excellent personal and professional references are available upon request.

Date

Exact Name of Person
Title or Position
Name of Company
Address (number and street)
Address (city, state, and zip)

Dear Exact Name of Person (or Sir or Madam if answering a blind ad):

I would appreciate an opportunity to talk with you soon about how I could contribute to your organization through my education and experience as well as through my personal strengths as an articulate, compassionate, and dedicated young professional.

With a degree in Psychology from Palomar College at San Marcos, I have applied my time management and organizational skills to maintain a high GPA while also gaining work experience in health care settings ranging from a medical office to a facility for mentally and developmentally disabled adults. In addition to course work in my major area of concentration, I excelled in courses in the science field including microbiology, biology, chemistry, and physiology. I recently completed an internship through which I gained hands-on experience with the Community Alternative Program for Disabled Adults.

A well-rounded and adaptable individual with good listening skills, I offer the ability to quickly learn and apply new ideas and methods, and outstanding organizational and detail skills.

I would like to point out that the address on my resume is my permanent address, but that I am planning to move to the San Francisco area. I graduated from Palomar on December 15 and am presently looking for career opportunities in the San Francisco area.

I hope you will welcome my call soon to arrange a brief meeting to discuss your current and future needs and how I might serve them. Thank you in advance for your time.

Sincerely,

Mercedes S. Benz

Alternate last paragraph:
I hope you will call or write me soon to suggest a time convenient for us to meet and discuss your current and future needs and how I might serve them. Thank you in advance for your time.

MERCEDES S. BENZ

1110½ Hay Street, Fayetteville, NC 28305 • preppub@aol.com • (910) 483-6611

OBJECTIVE   I am eager to contribute to an organization that can use an enthusiastic self-starter who offers an excellent education in social work along with hands-on experience in dealing with people of all age groups, ethnic, cultural, and socioeconomic backgrounds.

EDUCATION   **Bachelor of Science degree in Social Work (B.S.W.)**, Palomar College, San Marcos, CA, 2002.
- Was inducted into the **Social Work Honor Society, Chi Zeta Phi**, because of excellent grades and demonstrated potential for leadership in this field.
- Was selected to the **Golden Key National Honor Society** honoring the top 15% of juniors and seniors among North Carolina universities.
- Was accepted for membership into the **National Association of Social Workers (NASW)** based on being enrolled in an accredited and respected school of social work.
- Achieved a GPA of 3.82 overall and 3.9 in my major.
- Received the Honor Society Award for the highest scholastic achievement in my class while attending high school at St. Marcos Junior College, St. Marcos, CA.

EXPERIENCE   **CAP/DA CASE MANAGER (Social Work Student Intern). Hartt County Memorial Hospital Department of Social Services.** Davis, CA (2002). Worked with the Community Alternative Program for Disabled Adults (CAP/DA), and was evaluated as one of the brightest interns participating in this program; excelled in assessing and coordinating all care for nine patients including home health, mental health, housing, economic, and social needs.
- On my own initiative, established new community resources including "HEAR NOW" which provides hearing aids to people who cannot afford them; developed a new information resource for the elderly, handicapped, and disabled seeking housing.
- Refined my counseling skills while gaining indepth knowledge of the health field.
- Planned goals and objectives with CAP patients; ordered medical supplies/equipment.
- Assisted Adult Services Unit in conducting adult protective services investigations of abuse and neglect.
- Became skilled in preparing a wide variety of paperwork used in social work.
- Prepared written correspondence/business letters to clients and outside contacts.
- Attended CAP Advisory Board meetings and CAP staff meetings.
- Was recognized as an advocate and for outstanding "networking" ability; networked successfully with other community resource professionals and gained an excellent understanding of how the community social services organizations interrelate.

ASSISTANT, COMMUNITY RELATIONS DEPARTMENT. Hartt County Memorial Hospital. (1997-02). While working in the hospital's Community Relations Department and Employee Wellness Center, assisted in planning and coordinating events while also being responsible for making reservations for hospital functions.
- Gathered data from hospital employees through conducting interviews to compile data related to the hospital's Employee Fitness Program; attended hospital board meetings.

TELEMARKETER. Plantation Village Retirement Community. Wilmington, NC (1995-96). As the sole telemarketer, initiated all telephone contact with senior citizens/prospective clients and explained to them the concept and benefits of a retirement community.

PERSONAL   Am a creative and dynamic "opportunity finder" who excels in discovering new resources. Enjoy a challenge and am able to adapt to changing environments.

Date

Exact Name of Person
Exact Title
Exact Name of Company
Address
City, State, Zip

CASE MANAGER   Dear Exact Name of Person (or Dear Sir or Madam if answering a blind ad):

With the enclosed resume, I would like to make you aware of my desire to explore employment opportunities with your organization. I have recently completed my B.S.W. degree in Social Work and offer strong communication and counseling skills.

As you will see from my resume, I have excelled in counseling positions in a camp environment, in a home for displaced children, and at the YMCA. While working as a Resident Counselor at the Methodist Home for Children, I became known for my creativity and program development skills. On my own initiative, I organized a store at the home so that youth aged 9-19 could learn money-handling and budgeting skills. I was commended for my efforts which resulted in building self-esteem and a feeling of self-worth.

In a job as a Case Manager at the YMCA, I worked as an intern with the Big Brothers/Big Sisters of Bunce County. In that capacity, I organized an after-school program at Palm Middle School designed to build self-esteem in children. Known as "High School Bigs," the program I developed began with 10 children and grew to serve 40 children, and after my internship the program received formal funding so that it can continue. For my efforts and initiative, I received a certificate of appreciation from Guidance by Partners in Education.

As a teenager, I discovered my orientation toward the social work field while working as a Camp Counselor at Moore Summer Fun Camp with children aged 6-13. I also volunteered as Office Manager and Receptionist at the Coalition for the Homeless, where I developed a book of poems written by the homeless clients of this nonprofit organization.

If you can use a caring and enthusiastic young professional with a true desire to make a difference in the lives of others, I hope you will contact me to suggest a time when we might meet to discuss your needs. I can provide excellent references.

Sincerely,

Rachel H. Hunter

RACHEL H. HUNTER

1110½ Hay Street, Fayetteville, NC 28305   •   preppub@aol.com   •   (910) 483-6611

OBJECTIVE   I want to contribute to an organization that can use an outgoing young professional who offers considerable sales skills and proven management potential along with a desire to serve the public and work with others in achieving top-quality results.

EDUCATION   **Bachelor of Social Work (B.S.W.) degree,** Meredith College, Bunce, OK, 2002.
Activities included Resident Advisor, Resident Hall Association, Weaver Hall Council **President,** Sigma Omega Chi **President,** Psychology Club, Social Work Club, Alpha Psi Omega Historian, Monarch Playmakers, Puppetry and ARC Association.
Training: Professional training included Teaching Parent Model and PC Essentials.

COMPUTERS   Windows operating systems and Microsoft Word, Works, Excel, WordPerfect, SPSS, Internet

EXPERIENCE   **RESIDENT COUNSELOR.** Methodist Home for Children, Bunce, OK (2002-present). At this home for displaced children, provide training related to life skills for youth aged 9-19 while also implementing parent training; developed programs for each child which resulted in building self-esteem and a feeling of self-worth.
- **Program Development:** On my own initiative, organized a store at the home so that children could earn money and learn skills in handling money and budgeting for their expenses; designed and managed the store's policies and procedures.

CASE MANAGER. YMCA, Bunce, OK (Spring 2001). As an Intern with the Big Brothers/ Big Sisters of Bunce County, interviewed and placed prospective mentors and worked as the trusted "right arm" to the program manager.
- **Program Development:** Organized an after-school program designed to build self-esteem in children and worked closely with children making failing grades; the "High School Bigs" program at Palm Middle School was widely praised and considered a success. Began with 10 students and grew the program to 40 students. The program received funding after its pilot year and is being continued.
- **Award:** Received Certificate of Appreciation from Guidance by Partners in Education.

HISTORIAN. Saint Ann Catholic Church, Bunce, OK (1999-2000). Developed a scrapbook which provided the school's first permanent record of its after-school program; planned photographic events and arranged photo opportunities with children, tutors, and staff.

OFFICE MANAGER & RECEPTIONIST. Coalition for the Homeless, Bunce, OK (1999). While working as a volunteer, applied my creativity in developing a book of poems by the homeless clients of this nonprofit organization serving the less fortunate.
- **Social worker responsibilities:** Processed intakes, made referrals to other agencies, supplied clients with clothing and hygiene kits, and followed up.

CAMP COUNSELOR. Moore Summer Fun Camp, Moore County, OK (Summer, 1998). Found many opportunities to express my creativity and resourcefulness while scheduling events, planning educational programs, and working with children aged 6-13.
- **Programming:** Planned a talent show for the children and nurtured their creativity.

SALES REPRESENTATIVE. Cole's Department Store, Robbins, OK (1994-98). Began working as a youth and worked for four years part-time.

PERSONAL   Am a caring, nurturing professional who wants to make a difference in the social work field.

Date

Exact Name of Person
Exact Title
Exact Name of Company
Address
City, State, Zip

Dear Exact Name of Person (or Dear Sir or Madam if answering a blind ad):

With the enclosed resume, I would like to make you aware of my desire to explore employment opportunities with your organization. I am especially interested in the position of Rape Center Director which you recently advertised.

I actually stumbled into my social work career after I applied for a position as an Eligibility Specialist. I made a successful transition from the private sector where I had been selling insurance, and I quickly realized that I wanted to make a career in the social work field. Once I had experienced the profound sense of satisfaction that comes from helping others in need, I was committed to a social services career.

In subsequent positions, I have worked for two departments of social services in California. In my current position as a Case Worker II in San Diego, I interview and hire potential clients to determine their eligibility for assistance, and I perform liaison with a vast network of helping organizations as I seek to locate assistance for individuals in need of emergency shelter, medical care, counseling, and other services.

I believe my education in banking and finance as well as my strong computer skills would be valuable assets in the role of Rape Center Director. I can provide outstanding references, and I hope very much that we will have an opportunity to discuss in person the position you are seeking to fill. I can assure you in advance that I am a highly motivated individual who would be committed to serving the needs of your community's rape victims.

Sincerely,

Stacey Wilson

STACEY WILSON

1110½ Hay Street, Fayetteville, NC 28305 • preppub@aol.com • (910) 483-6611

OBJECTIVE

To benefit an organization through my excellent communication skills as well as experience in office administration and automation, including all secretarial and clerical skills.

EDUCATION

Earned a certificate in *Banking and Finance*, American Institute of Banking, New York, NY.
Have successfully completed 73 credits towards a *Business Education* degree, Sacramento State University, Sacramento, CA.

COMPUTERS

Familiar with many of the most popular computer operating systems and software, including Windows, Microsoft Word and Excel, Corel WordPerfect, Lotus 1-2-3, and others.

EXPERIENCE

CASE WORKER II. San Diego County Department of Social Services, San Diego, CA (2002-present). Interviewed and evaluated potential clients to determine their eligibility for assistance as well as to pre-screen and assess their needs for emergency intervention such as food stamps, housing, medical care, or shelter from abusive situations.
*   Provided clients with referrals to other service providers and charitable organizations within the community that would offer them assistance.

CASE WORKER. Department of Social Services, Sacramento, CA (1995-01). I interviewed clients for AFDC, food stamps, and Medicaid codes according to and complying with agency and state guidelines; responsible for accuracy and completeness of paperwork; typed 50/60 wpm transcription.
*   Performed periodic interviews and accounting; terminated or reopened cases according to need; performed analysis of claims and daily expenses.
*   Made decisions about emergency intervention and provided good community relations.
*   Acquired experience with data entry, word processing, and spreadsheets.
*   Working knowledge of automated accounting and finance environment.

ELIGIBILITY SPECIALIST III. Employment Eligibility Center, Department of Social Services, New York City Human Resources Administration, Brooklyn, NY (1993-94). Conducted interviews to evaluate the client's eligibility for public assistance and coding for Medicaid and food stamps while handling a caseload of 760 families.
*   Wrote summary case reports and applied my knowledge of accounting and medical claim codes; made referrals to detoxification, rehabilitation, ESC, and SSA offices
*   Performed periodic accounting, re-budgeting, and data entry as needed.
*   Completed financial reports that included monthly financial schedules and revenue analyses, claims, enrollment, and operating expenses.

INSURANCE SALES AGENT. Telespectrum Worldwide, Sacramento, CA (1990-92). Started with this large national company as a Telemarketing Sales Representative, and quickly advanced to a position as an Agent when the company started calling on insurance campaigns.
*   Completed the presentation of insurance packages pre-sold by the Telemarketing Sales Representatives, answering customer questions and concerns, then closing the sale.
*   Called on all active campaigns presenting the products of Telespectrum's clients, including credit card protection programs, long distance services, insurance, and travel packages.
*   Interacted with a large number of customers daily at this large outbound call center.

PERSONAL

Excellent personal and professional references are available upon request.

CAREER CHANGE

Exact Name of Person
Exact Title
Exact Name of Company
Address
City, State, Zip

CASE WORKER   Dear Exact Name of Person (or Dear Sir or Madam if answering a blind ad):

With the enclosed resume, I would like to make you aware of my interest in exploring positions within student affairs, academic affairs, and student life at your institution.

From my enclosed resume you will see that I have earned three degrees: a B.A. in Sociology from Tulane University; an M.A. in Sociology from Tulane University; and a Master of Divinity in Theology from Tulane University. Although I have succeeded professionally as a chaplain through Tulane Divinity School and as a case worker with the Department of Social Services, I have decided that I would like to make a career change and specialize in student services.

You will notice on my resume that, while earning my M.A. in Sociology, I performed extensive analysis and interviewing of administrators and freshmen in order to learn about students' experiences in adjusting to the large university setting. My findings and analysis served in part as the inspiration for a course at UNC-G that is helping students adapt to life at the school. I co-authored "First Experiences of the Bureaucratic Kind: Freshman Experience with Campus Bureaucracy," published in *The Journal of Higher Education.*

While involved in field experiences through Tulane Divinity School, I had many opportunities to refine my counseling skills. I was evaluated as "a caring individual who people learn to trust," and I was commended for my ability to "initiate new ideas and carry through with those ideas." I am known as a compassionate individual who genuinely cares about people, and I am also respected as an excellent organizer.

Although I am held in the highest regard in my current position as a Case Worker II, I have decided that I want to use my social service skills to aid students. I am positive that my strong counseling, teaching, and motivational skills could be valuable assets within the academic community.

If you can use a compassionate and intelligent individual who excels in building effective relations and helping others reach personal and professional goals, I hope you will call or write me soon to suggest a time when we might have a brief discussion of how I could contribute to your institution. I am confident that I could become a valuable member of your organization.

Sincerely,

Benny Paris

BENNY PARIS

1110½ Hay Street, Fayetteville, NC 28305   •   preppub@aol.com   •   (910) 483-6611

OBJECTIVE

To offer my reputation as a creative, compassionate individual with excellent counseling and listening skills, strong analytical abilities, and a talent for motivating people of all ages.

PUBLICATIONS

Co-authored "First Encounters of the Bureaucratic Kind: Freshman Experience with Campus Bureaucracy," published in *The Journal of Higher Education,* 2000.

EDUCATION

Master of Divinity in Theology, Tulane University, Dunham, LA, 2002.
M.A., Sociology, University of North Carolina at Greensboro, 1997.
- Achieved a 3.8 GPA while simultaneously working as a Graduate Research Assistant.
- Interviewed administrators and freshmen about students' experiences in adjusting to the large university setting; my findings and analysis served in part as the inspiration for a course at Tulane that is helping students adapt to life at school.

B.A., Sociology, Wake Forest University, Winston, LA, 1992.
Completed special training which included Red Cross Shelter Operations and Disaster Relief Caseworker course (2003) and Clinical Pastoral Education (2001).

EXPERIENCE

Am held in high regard; have been hired and rehired on three separate occasions by the Camber County Department of Social Services, Hastings, LA, in the process of earning three degrees:
COUNSELOR & CASE WORKER II. (2002-present). Have become highly skilled in handling multiple tasks and dealing with individuals of all socioeconomic levels while counseling people and coordinating public assistance case loads of up to 400 cases.
- Am adept at "tracking down" the right department or person within bureaucracies who can solve the client's needs; highly proficient in performing computer research, locating and "tracking down" a highly mobile clientele while performing liaison with employers, government agencies, and other organizations to obtain data and records.
- Observe strict attention to detail because federal audits require that paperwork be perfect; am skilled in interpreting and applying state and federal guidelines which must be stringently adhered to in matters of budgeting; process financial information while budgeting monthly income and calculating benefit amounts and Medicaid deductibles.
- Recognized for **outstanding service** in 2003 and 2002.

Gained experience in counseling and research while financing my education:
STUDENT CHAPLAIN and **ASSISTANT MINISTER.** Tulane University Divinity School Field Education, Durham, LA (2001-02). Held two separate positions:
- Carried out activities which included preaching, developing a Bible study class for older adults, leading a youth group during a retreat, and visiting hospital patients and shut-ins.
- Developed/participated in religious programs for developmentally disabled residents.

GRADUATE RESEARCH ASSISTANT. Tulane University, Dunham, LA (1998-00). As the principal research assistant for a project sponsored by the American Association of Retired Persons, examined friendship patterns, habits, and lifestyle changes of older adults (55 to 85) through random telephone calls.
- Validated and compiled research data; performed library research on related literature.
- Assisted in teaching a 300-student Introductory Sociology course.

PERSONAL

Offer excellent counseling, communication, and analytical skills. Am proficient with computers and knowledgeable of Microsoft Word and Windows 98. Excellent references.

Date

Exact Name of Person
Exact Title
Exact Name of Company
Address
City, State, Zip

CASE WORKER   Dear Exact Name of Person (or Dear Sir or Madam if answering a blind ad):

With the enclosed resume, I would like to make you aware of my background as an experienced caseworker, personnel assistant, and finance clerk with excellent communication, organizational, and computer skills, as well as prior experience in JTPA administration and compliance and a proven track record of handling heavy caseloads in social services environments.

In my current position as a Caseworker I for Chester County DSS, I manage a caseload of 250 clients, interviewing them to determine eligibility for various programs as well as providing counseling and information on community resources and employment opportunities. As a Personnel Assistant, I assisted in all phases of the hiring process, managed and monitored the employee evaluation system for a staff of 700, and processed Workers' Compensation claims, injury leave requests, payroll, and termination paperwork. I processed time sheets for JTPA participants and employees, computed hours, and balanced weekly payroll as Finance Clerk for Chester Consolidated Government.

As you will see from the enclosed resume, I hold a Bachelor's degree in Business Administration and am highly computer literate. I am proficient with commercial software and systems such as Windows, the Microsoft Office suite, WordPerfect, and Excel, and am able to quickly master proprietary systems, such as the ACCENT program used by the Department of Social Services. I feel that my strong combination of education, experience, and computer skills make me a strong asset to your organization.

While I am highly regarded by my present employer, and can provide outstanding personal and professional references at the appropriate time, I feel that my education, skills, and experience would be more fully utilized in a finance, or personnel environment.

If you can use a motivated and articulate social services professional, with previous JTPA experience and a background in case management, personnel, payroll, and finance, then I look forward to hearing from you soon, to arrange a time when we might meet to discuss your needs. I assure you in advance that I have an excellent reputation within the community and would quickly become a valuable addition to your organization.

Sincerely,

Natalie Riggins

NATALIE RIGGINS

1110½ Hay Street, Fayetteville, NC 28305   •   preppub@aol.com   •   (910) 483-6611

OBJECTIVE	To benefit an organization that can use a motivated caseworker, coordinator, personnel assistant, or finance clerk with exceptional communication and organizational skills who offers a background in managing heavy caseloads in social services environments and is familiar with the policies and requirements of JTPA, AFDC, and other federal programs.
EDUCATION	Bachelor's degree in Business Administration, Harrington College, Columbus, OH, 1997. Previously completed course work in Political Science at Simmons College, Boston, MA.
COMPUTERS	Proficient in the use of the following computer software and systems: Windows 98, Microsoft Word, Microsoft Excel, Microsoft Access, Microsoft PowerPoint, Microsoft Outlook, WordPerfect, and Lotus 1-2-3, as well as quickly mastering proprietary systems.

EXPERIENCE

CASEWORKER I. Chester County Department of Social Services, Chester, ME (2001-present). Perform a variety of tasks in this busy social services environment.
- Manage and maintain case files for an ongoing caseload of 250 clients.
- Interview clients to determine ongoing eligibility for Aid For Dependents and Children (AFDC), Medicaid, and/or food stamps.
- Counsel clients to assist them in achieving self-sufficiency by making them aware of community resources and employment opportunities.
- Review case files to ensure that clients are not fraudulently receiving assistance.
- Enter client data into the computer system, utilizing a combination of commercial and proprietary software.

PERSONNEL ASSISTANT IV. ME Department of Corrections/Central Prison, Chester, ME (2000-2001). Assisted in all phases of the operation of the personnel office, including various clerical/secretarial, hiring, employee evaluation, and benefits management tasks.
- Managed and monitored the employee evaluation system for 700 employees; entered employee performance ratings into the SIPS computer system.
- Prepared and maintained the OSHA 200 log and submitted monthly safety reports.
- Processed workers' compensation claims and secured injury leave.
- Received and verified the accuracy of time reports; prepared employee separation forms.

FINANCE CLERK. Chester Consolidated Government, Chester, ME (1999). Tasked with a number of administrative and bookkeeping duties in a fast-paced government office.
- Processed time sheets for Job Training Partnership Act participants and employees.
- Computed total individual and overall hours and balanced weekly payroll.
- Keyed information on past and present employees into the city's computer system.

ELIGIBILITY COUNSELOR. Texas Department of Social Services, Twining, TX (1992-98). Evaluated and documented each case to determine client's eligibility for assistance under the guidelines of various programs.
- Interviewed clients to determine their eligibility for AFDC, medical assistance, food stamps, and other social services programs.
- Managed a large caseload of more routine clients already receiving assistance through various programs.
- Performed client referrals, recommending community resources.
- Kept journals and documentation of all interviews and decisions on client eligibility.

PERSONAL	Excellent personal and professional references are available upon request.

Date

Dr. Preston Smith
Randolph Clinic
Suite 100
2 Arrow Drive
Philadelphia, PA

CHILD ABUSE
COUNSELOR

Dear Dr. Smith:

I would appreciate an opportunity to talk with you soon about how I could contribute to your organization through my education, experience in working with abused and exceptional children, as well as my concerned and caring leadership style.

As you will see from my resume, I am a graduate of Drexel University in Philadelphia, where I earned a B.A. degree in Psychology. I completed specialized courses including child development, personality, social psychology, the family and society, and exceptional children (autistic, learning disabled, and mentally retarded).

My actual experience with "special" children includes tutoring a child with reading disabilities and low self-esteem and working with another child who is autistic. Working with these children allowed me to help them through positive reinforcement and my strong wish to reach them. This experience enabled me to appreciate the advantages I grew up with and strengthened my desire to help others with special needs.

While a student at Drexel, I also participated through the Campus Y service organization as Program Coordinator and Advocate and Child Care Giver for the Child Abuse Prevention Program (CAPP). I cared for children whose parents were receiving counseling, helped set up a program in Durham, conducted regular business and training meetings, and participated in presenting educational programs to local and campus groups.

I hope you will welcome my call soon to arrange a brief meeting at your convenience to discuss your current and future needs and how I might serve them. Thank you in advance for your time.

Sincerely yours,

Zelda N. Gatsby

ZELDA N. GATSBY

1110½ Hay Street, Fayetteville, NC 28305   •   preppub@aol.com   •   (910) 483-6611

OBJECTIVE I want to apply my "newly minted" degree in psychology and my empathy and experience in relating to children and adolescents to an organization that can use a mature and dependable young professional.

EDUCATION **B.A., Psychology**, Drexel University at Philadelphia, PA, 2002.
- Learned to manage time and coordinate a busy schedule while working a minimum of 20 hours a week to help pay for my college expenses as well as participating in numerous volunteer activities.
- Completed specialized course work including family life and society, child development, social psychology, personality, and exceptional children: autistic, learning disabled, and mentally retarded.

EXPERIENCE **SPECIAL EDUCATION TUTOR**. Internship, Drexel University (2002). Worked with two students in a Culbreth Elementary School program for "exceptional children."
- Provided positive reinforcement and feedback for a child with reading disabilities and low self-esteem.
- Worked closely with a crisis intervention counselor and supervised the schoolwork for an autistic child.
- Learned the importance of providing positive reinforcement at every opportunity when working with children with handicaps.

PROGRAM COORDINATOR and **ADVOCATE AND CAREGIVER**. Child Abuse Prevention Program (CAPP), Drexel University (1999-02). Provided care for abused children while their parents attended counseling and conducted biweekly meetings to provide information to, and training for, volunteers.
- Gained a broad base of "hands-on" experience with abused children and became familiar with the types of situations they endured.
- Played a major role in setting up the program in Durham.
- Was highly effective in passing my knowledge and observations on to less experienced workers in order to educate them.

MEMBERSHIP CHAIRMAN. Campus Y, Drexel (1998-99). Refined my organizational skills through attention to the details of coordinating activities with 32 other committees and handling the collection of, and accounting for, membership dues from approximately 750 students.
- Set up an automated system to simplify record-keeping and accounting.

RETAIL SALES ASSOCIATE. Hammond's Dept. Store, Grove City, PA (1994-98). Excelled in providing outstanding customer service while handling daily functions including: customer sales, inventory control, stocking, and closing out the register.
- Consistently received "superior" performance evaluations in every area.

Highlights of other experience: Learned to be patient and tactful in dealing with customers as a waitress; applied my communication skills in a campaign to solicit funds from university alumni; and learned to manage both time and money as a sales associate/stocker while still in high school.

PERSONAL Am an enthusiastic and outgoing person. Have a desire to work with disadvantaged children and adolescents. Offer superior communication skills.

Date

Exact Name of Person
Title or Position
Name of Company
Address (number and street)
Address (city, state, and zip)

CHILD CARE SERVICES WORKER

Dear Exact Name of Person (or Sir or Madam if answering a blind ad.)

I would appreciate an opportunity to talk with you soon about how I could contribute to your organization through my experience in social services environments as well as through my outstanding written and verbal communication skills and concern for others.

With a background which includes working in child care services, adolescent parenting, and food stamp programs with the Somer County Department of Social Services (Cody, WY), I have become knowledgeable in these functional areas. Earlier experience included working in adjoining Buffalo County in the food stamp office where I maintained a 325-family caseload.

I am confident that I offer a background of adaptability and well-developed knowledge of a variety of social service functions certain to make me a valuable asset in any department needing a quick learner with excellent people skills. As you will see from my enclosed resume, I earned a degree in Sociology from Casper College in Casper, WY. I am a perceptive person with a keen eye for detail and am conscientious about the importance of maintaining confidentiality and being non-judgmental while working with people who are disadvantaged.

I hope you will call or write me soon to suggest a time convenient for us to meet and discuss your current and future needs and how I might serve them. Thank you in advance for your time. I will be relocating to Allentown and will be in your area permanently by February 28.

Sincerely,

Olivia C. Laurence

OLIVIA C. LAURENCE

1110½ Hay Street, Fayetteville, NC 28305 • preppub@aol.com • (910) 483-6611

OBJECTIVE   To offer a reputation as a compassionate and caring professional with extensive experience in social work organizations as well as outstanding written and verbal communication skills.

EXPERIENCE   *Refined my skills and contributed to the effectiveness of programs of the Somer County Department of Social Services, Cody, WY:*
SOCIAL WORKER II — CHILD CARE SERVICES. (1999-present). Worked in close co-operation with parents and numerous local related agencies to ensure that child care-related services were being provided to eligible children.
- Guided parents in decision making so problems could be resolved, qualified children evaluated, and referrals made for health, mental health, and social services needs.
- Handled a caseload of approximately 250 families, one-fourth of whom needed intervention.
- Established eligibility, provided case management, and followed up on cases.

ADOLESCENT PARENTING PROGRAM VOLUNTEER. (1998-99). Maintained close contacts with social workers while providing support for adolescent parents and helping them build confidence and self-worth as well as demonstrating good parenting skills and setting an example.

SOCIAL WORKER I. (1995-98). As a resource person and advisor for child care facilities, acted as the social worker for approximately 250 families while controlling $1 million in child care funds and monitoring, managing, and coordinating related services.
- Assisted parents to find safe, reliable child care, resolving conflicts between parents and providers, and interviewed parents in order to make eligibility determinations.
- Inspected facilities to verify compliance with state and federal guidelines.
- Was credited with implementing a program which educated child care providers and conducted regular seminars for child care professionals.
- Handled administrative details such as preparing statistics, completing end-of-the-month reports, and writing and presenting corrective action plans.

INCOME MAINTENANCE CASE WORKER I. (1994-95). Maintained a caseload of 380 food stamp recipients to include conducting interviews, processing reapplications, re-certifications, and changes for qualifying households with inadequate incomes.
- Obtained and verified information; determined eligibility; made referrals to other interested agencies; utilized an IBM computer for maintaining records.
- Computed income, calculated budgets, and verified information from other agents.
- Worked in close cooperation with other agencies while following up on suspected fraud.

INCOME MAINTENANCE CASE WORKER I. Buffalo County Department of Social Services, Lilith, WY (1993-94). Interviewed and maintained a caseload of 325 food stamp recipients with responsibilities which included setting up records, taking in applications, making changes, and completing monthly reports for eligible families.
- Made determinations on eligibility and referrals to other agencies.

EDUCATION   B.S., **Sociology, Casper** College, Casper, WY, 1993.

PERSONAL   Offer effective written and verbal communication skills. Have a talent for seeing the details needed to plan and carry out informative and interesting briefings, training, and programs.

Date

Exact Name of Person
Title or Position
Name of Company
Address (no., street)
Address (city, state, zip)

CLIENT ENABLER   Dear Exact Name of Person (or Dear Sir or Madam if answering a blind ad):

I would appreciate an opportunity to talk with you soon about how I could contribute to your organization through my experience and administrative skills related to the social services and mental health field.

As you will see from my resume, I have been involved since childhood in helping others as a role model and mentor. While earning my B.S. degree in Marketing and my A.A. in Business Administration, I worked with troubled youth and convinced many young people that hard work and a positive attitude combined with staying in school can overcome a bad start in life.

For the past two years after graduating from college, I have worked in classroom and camp environments with children who have varying disabilities including autism, mental retardation, cerebral palsy, and Down's Syndrome. As a teacher in a classroom of behaviorally disturbed children in Texas, I learned how to develop and implement effective lesson plans for disruptive students. As a teacher with the Ft. Worth School System, I taught reading to autistic and mentally handicapped children and, on my own initiative, I learned sign language in order to help a child with Down's Syndrome learn to better communicate in his world. Most recently I was recruited by a classroom teacher for autistic students as one of seven staff members responsible for starting up a new summer program for autistic children.

If we meet in person, you will see that I am an outgoing young professional with excellent communication skills and a very positive attitude. I truly believe that hard work and a positive attitude can help people overcome even the most disadvantaged childhood, and I take pride in the fact that I have helped many youth get off the wrong track and set high goals for themselves.

I also offer excellent computer operations skills including proficiency with Windows and Word, and I have a knack for rapidly mastering new software and hardware. I am certain I could easily learn to use whatever system you have.

I hope you will write or call me soon to suggest a time when we might meet to discuss your goals and needs and how I might serve them. I feel certain that I could become a valuable and productive member of your team.

Sincerely yours,

Pandora S. Boit

PANDORA S. BOIT

1110½ Hay Street, Fayetteville, NC 28305   •   preppub@aol.com   •   (910) 483-6611

OBJECTIVE   To benefit an organization that can use a dynamic young professional who sincerely enjoys helping others while utilizing strong organizational skills and a thoroughly positive attitude.

EXPERIENCE   **TRAINING COORDINATOR** and **CLIENT ENABLER.** The Autism Society of Texas, Dallas, TX (2000-present). Contributed to team efforts in a habilitation program which allows clients who are autistic or have related communication handicaps to develop self-care, communication, social, and leisure skills which will allow them to live independently.
- Worked closely with family members, other trainers, case managers, and the Director of Recreational and Community Service.
- Assisted clients in the development of skills such as pre-vocational tasks, ordering their own food in restaurants, or playing games in cooperation with another person.
- Completed written reports of skills, activities, progress, and concerns at each session along with monthly progress reports and regular data collection.
- Participated in community outings with clients in order to help increase their independence in areas such as using public transportation and managing money as well as carrying out household responsibilities such as doing laundry and setting the table.
- Assisted in efforts to educate the general public about autism.

ASSISTANT TO THE DIRECTOR and **TEACHER.** Camp Holly Autistic Camp, Fort Worth, TX (1998-00). Was specially recruited by a classroom teacher for autistic students as one of seven staff members to assist in starting up and implementing a new summer camp for autistic children funded by Chatham County Mental Health and grants.
- Planned and implemented activities for children and youth aged 4-20.
- As the youngest member of the teaching/administrative team, won the respect of my peers for my creativity, reliability, and willingness to always "go the extra mile."
- Helped children learn behavior skills while involving them in activities that promoted their academic, physical, and social development.

SUBSTITUTE TEACHER. Fort Worth Schools, Ft. Worth, TX (1995-97). Began as a substitute teacher with the Ft. Worth School System and taught reading skills to elementary children aged five to 11 years.
- On my own initiative, learned sign language in order to communicate with a monosyllabic child and help him gain communication tools which will help him throughout life.

SUBSTITUTE TEACHER. Ewin Middle School, Ewin, TX (1994-95). For children aged kindergarten-grade 12, provided instruction based on daily lesson plans; learned to prepare and implement effective lesson plans for classrooms containing children with behavioral problems.

Other experience: While in college, worked as a mentor/counselor three days a week with troubled youth; taught them that staying in school is essential to happiness and success.

EDUCATION &   **B. S.** degree in **Marketing**, University of Texas, Dallas, TX, 1994.
CERTIFICATION   **A. A.** degree in **Business Administration**, El Paso Community College, El Paso, TX, 1992.
Hold Substitute Teacher's Certificate #991110, District #56, July 94-June 99.

PERSONAL   Have strong personal qualities which include determination to excel, persistence in achieving goals, and living by high personal and professional standards.

Date

Exact Name of Person
Title or Position
Name of Company
Address (no., street)
Address (city, state, zip)

**COMMUNITY
SPECIALIST**

Dear Exact Name of Person (or Dear Sir or Madam if answering a blind ad):

I would appreciate an opportunity to talk with you soon about how I could contribute to your organization through my experience in the social services field.

Specially recruited for my current position as a Job Coach, I currently supervise eight job coaches while managing 10 developmentally challenged clients. In the absence of the day program director, I oversee a population of 75 individuals.

When I joined the WAVE Program in my current job, it was in an embryonic state of development. With a reputation as a social and outgoing person, I aggressively called on business and community leaders in order to establish new employment opportunities for developmentally challenged adults. Through persistence and relentless follow-through, I have transformed this small local program into a "model" operation which is frequently studied by other state departments.

Although I am highly regarded in my current position and can provide outstanding references at the appropriate time, I am selectively exploring opportunities in other social services environments. To a large degree, I feel that the challenging goal I undertook when I assumed my current position has been achieved, and I am restless for new and more complex challenges. I thrive on the challenge of solving problems so that the less fortunate can have a better quality of life.

I hope you will write or call me soon to suggest a time when we might meet to discuss your goals and needs and how I might serve them. I feel certain that I could become a valuable and productive member of your team.

Sincerely yours,

Steven Alexander

STEVEN ALEXANDER

1110½ Hay Street, Fayetteville, NC 28305   •   preppub@aol.com   •   (910) 483-6611

OBJECTIVE

To contribute to an organization that can use a hard-working professional with a history of dedication to personal goals, good communication skills, and experience in sales.

EDUCATION

Earned a **Bachelor of Science** (B.S.) degree with a major in **Psychology** and a minor in **Sociology**, Thomas Edison State University, Ewing, NJ, 2000.
- Excelled in course work including abnormal psychology, gerontology, physiological psychology, psychological tests and measurements, and experimental psychology.
- Completed training programs sponsored by Dover County in evaluating and processing distress calls as a "Contact" volunteer and dispute resolution for mediation.
- Excelled in Caregiver Training and in CPR/First Aid.

Professional Training: Crisis Intervention, Medication Training, PIC Training.

COMMUNITY INVOLVEMENT

After completing county training programs, volunteered in two service programs.
- Contributed to two five-hour shifts a month as a **Contact Volunteer** involved in answering calls from people with personal emergencies and in need of someone to listen to them and assist in locating sources to help them out of their crisis.
- Participated in a program which saved the court system time and money by using volunteer mediators to act as go-betweens and help settle disputes out of court.

EXPERIENCE

JOB COACH. WAVE Day Program, Newark, NJ (2001-present). Supervise eight other job coaches and manage 10 developmentally disabled adults; oversee a client population of 75 individuals in the absence of the day program director.

COMMUNITY SPECIALIST II. Parent Alternatives, Newark, NJ (2001). Worked with clients with Mentally Retarded/Developmental Disorder (MR/DD) and provided one-to-one services with a client with a diagnosis of TBI and substance abuse; earned a reputation as a sensitive and compassionate professional; also earned praise for my attention to detail.

FULL-TIME COLLEGE STUDENT. Thomas Edison State University, Ewing, NJ (1995-00). Earned a B.S. in Psychology with a minor in Sociology.

SALES REPRESENTATIVE and **STOCK PERSON.** Frank's Carpet and Interiors, Newark, NJ (1995). Refined my communication skills dealing with commercial and retail customers while working part-time and attending college.
- Learned how to measure floor coverings as well as how to design and set up displays .using carpet and tile.

SERVICE ADVISOR and **SALES ASSOCIATE.** Manson Chevrolet, Newark, NJ (1993-94). Learned to manage my time wisely while working in two separate operational areas for this dealership; made sure that requested maintenance and repairs were documented so they could be taken care of properly, while also learning sales techniques.
- Received a Letter of Commendation on the recommendation of a satisfied customer.

DEPARTMENT MANAGER and **SALES ASSOCIATE.** Victoria's, Newark, NJ (1992-93). Oversaw daily operations in the Garden Center as well as Automotive and Electronics departments, while also making sure that the stock room was kept organized..

PERSONAL

Enjoy helping people and have a reputation for being tactful, concerned, and a good listener.

Date

Darlene Smith
Human Resources Coordinator
Family Counseling Center, Inc.
888 Highway 2, P.O. Box 92
Bemidji, MN 63857

**COMMUNITY
SUPPORT WORKER**

Dear Ms. Smith:

I appreciate the opportunity to talk with you about my interest in the position as "Community Support Worker." I would like to express my strong feeling that I offer a background which would make me an asset to the Family Counseling Center in this capacity and in others within your organization.

In addition to the work history and accomplishments outlined on my resume, I would like to mention some personal history which will give you a better idea of why I feel I have a lot to contribute. I am the adult child of a recovering alcoholic and had a childhood, adolescence, and early adulthood filled with extensive counseling and support from organizations including A.A. This has given me an understanding and deep empathy for alcoholics, drug abusers, and their families.

I would like to emphasize that I am a native of the area and since I grew up in northern Minnesota, feel that I can use my status as a "home town girl" with knowledge of the area's lifestyle and culture. As a military officer's wife, I can add a unique view-point of one who has traveled overseas and used my skills to help other women and children feeling the depression, loneliness, and isolation of living in small towns in a foreign country. I have been very active in providing a listening ear and a "shoulder to cry on" to the families of my husband's soldiers who are themselves of all ages, nationalities, and socioeconomic levels.

I am an enthusiastic and energetic individual with excellent program development and organizational skills who enjoys travel and meeting people. Thank you for seeing me today and hope that we will be talking again soon. I do want to assure you I am confident that I can offer you the skills you are seeking for in someone to fill the "Community Support Worker" position.

Sincerely yours,

Angela S. Strong

ANGELA S. STRONG

1110½ Hay Street, Fayetteville, NC 28305   •   preppub@aol.com   •   (910) 483-6611

OBJECTIVE   To contribute through my education in sociology and criminal justice along with my attention to detail skills, as well as my "exceptional" ability to interact with others.

EDUCATION   **B.S., Sociology**, Morton College, Cicero, IL, 1994.
Am nine hours from completing a ***B.S. in Criminal Justice***.
- Graduated ***summa cum laude*** and have completed related course work including:

investigations	corrections	terrorism
social welfare policies	marriage and family	juvenile delinquency
research methods	psychology	social problems

- Was elected to membership in three honor societies for my placement as the top senior and sociology major.

A.A., Sociology, Morton College, Cicero, IL, 1992.
A.A., Criminal Justice, Morton College, Cicero, IL, 1994.

TRAINING   Completed 70-credit-hour Counseling Program, earning Certificate of Occupation, Northwest Technical, Bemidji, MN.
- Maintained certification in CPR/Basic Rescue and completed additional training in self-esteem/assertiveness/stress management, modeling classes to teach poise, preparation for teaching in literacy programs, and communication and leadership skills for the wives of military commanders.
- Excelled at Resolve Facilitator Training.
- Received certifications in PIC.

EXPERIENCE   **SOCIAL RESEARCH FIELD INTERVIEWER.** Social Policy Research, Chicago, IL (2000-present). For this social research firm, conduct studies and evaluations of various social issue programs.

FACILITATOR. "Solve" Program, Care Center, Cicero, IL (1998-99). Serve as a group counselor for perpetrators and/or victims of domestic violence.

SOCIAL RESEARCH FIELD INTERVIEWER. Opinion Research Center, Cicero IL (1997-98). Traveled extensively while conducting confidential one-on-one interviews with adolescents and their mothers in the home concerning health/behavior-related issues.

FAMILY SUPPORT PROGRAM COORDINATOR and **TREASURER.** U.S. Army, Ft. Dix, NJ (1994-97). Applied the full extent of my organizational and communication abilities to establish and single-handedly run a support network for approximately 150 families.
- Developed a telephone networking system which kept immediate and extended families in contact and informed during Operations Desert Shield and Desert Storm.
- Maintained close contact between personnel in Kuwait and Ft. Dix in a sensitive situation which demanded confidentiality and discretion.
- Managed all financial matters to support families in five organizations.

DENTAL ASSISTANT. U.S. Government, Ft. Dix, NJ (1990-1993). Utilized my well-developed organizational skills while assisting dentists with patient care.

PERSONAL   Excellent references on request.

CAREER CHANGE

Date

Exact Name of Person
Title or Position
Name of Company
Address (no., street)
Address (city, state, zip)

Dear Sir or Madam:

I was so happy to read your advertisement for a CASE DEVELOPER in the *Denver Post*. With the enclosed resume describing my background in the criminal justice field as well as my strong counseling and management skills, I would like to formally request that you consider me for the position.

As you will see from my resume, I hold a B.A. degree in Criminal Justice and have completed some work towards my M.A. degree in Counseling. Since earning my degree, I have excelled in some jobs related to the criminal justice and social services field. For example, I was a Criminal Justice Administrative Aide through an internship with the Tristan House in Pueblo, CO. In that halfway house for men and women let out of prison, I performed a wide variety of tasks vital to ensuring secure and efficient operations.

In all my jobs, including my experience unrelated to the criminal justice field, I have excelled through my strong counseling, management, and communication skills. I offer a proven ability to work well under pressure, and I can provide outstanding personal and professional references. Although my current job is certainly well paid and satisfying in many respects since I enjoy dealing with people, I am sincerely interested in making contributions to society through the criminal justice and social services field, for which I have been extensively educated. I can assure you that you would find me to be a congenial and reliable professional who always strives to do my best and to help others.

I hope you will write or call me soon to suggest a time when we could meet to discuss your current and future needs and how I might serve them. Thank you in advance for your time.

Sincerely yours,

Vera R. Vines

VERA R. VINES

1110½ Hay Street, Fayetteville, NC 28305 • preppub@aol.com • (910) 483-6611

OBJECTIVE

To offer my background in criminal justice and my desire to work in the human services field to an organization that can use my excellent written/oral communication skills, my knowledge of community resources, and my ability to establish outstanding working relationships.

EDUCATION

Pursuing **Master of Arts** (M.A.) degree in **Counseling**, The Colorado College, Colorado Springs, CO.
- During a course in correctional counseling and treatment, gained interviewing and investigative reporting skills.

Earned a **Bachelor of Arts** (B.A.) degree in **Criminal Justice**, The Colorado College, Colorado Springs, CO, 1996.
- Member, Criminal Justice Club.
- Excelled in course work related to these and other areas:

Strategies for Dealing with Adult Offenders	Correctional Counseling
Prison Procedures and Policies	Juvenile Justice
Criminal Procedures	Criminal Law Personnel
Fundamentals of Substance Abuse Counseling	Psychology
Computer Applications to Public Administration	Sociology

RELATED EXPERIENCE

Hands-on experience in the Criminal Justice field through an internship is as follows:

CRIMINAL JUSTICE ADMINISTRATIVE AIDE. Tristan House, Pueblo, CO (2001-2002). In this halfway house for men and women released from penal institutions on work programs, performed a variety of tasks vital to secure and efficient operations.
- Controlled access of inmates to and from the halfway house.
- Briefed inmates on rules and regulations of the halfway house.
- Developed knowledge of group counseling procedures.
- Refined my skills in listening to and communicating with people.

OTHER EXPERIENCE

Have excelled in positions which required excellent counseling, communication, people, and management skills:

COSMETOLOGIST. Spring Plaza, Pueblo, CO (1996-00). Developed a loyal clientele of customers who appreciated my interpersonal skills and tactful style of dealing with public.
- Although I enjoy this field and find it lucrative, I strongly desire to contribute to my fellow human beings through involvement in the criminal justice and social services field, for which I have educated myself extensively.

HOMEMAKER. Munich, Germany (1994-96). Enjoyed the opportunity to learn about Europe and gain experience dealing with people from various cultural backgrounds while living in Germany with my military spouse.

CLERK-TYPIST. Internal Revenue Service, Fairfield, CO (1992-93). Worked closely with eight Revenue officers in a Collection Division Group and provided a wide range of administrative support; maintained group timekeeping records, and maintained a filing system.
- Was commended for demonstrating outstanding time management skills while meeting deadlines.
- Also worked as a University Residence Assistant for Fairfield University while putting myself through college; supervised female college students and counseled students.

PERSONAL

Am a highly motivated individual who enjoys helping others. Am known for my common sense and good judgment as well as my ability to make sensible decisions under pressure.

Date

Exact Name of Person
Exact Title
Exact Name of Company
Address
City, State, Zip

Dear Exact Name of Person (or Dear Sir or Madam if answering a blind ad):

I would appreciate an opportunity to talk with you soon about how I could contribute to your organization through my experience, education, and skills which include a background in human services with an emphasis on correctional case work.

As you will see from my enclosed resume, I am a Case Manager at Evergreen Rehabilitation Center in Cincinnati, OH, a facility for chemically dependent personnel. While advancing in a track record of promotion and accomplishments in this demanding environment, I have been completing a bachelor's degree. As a Chancellor's List student and member of two scholarship and honors societies, I received my B.S. in Psychology (with a minor in Criminal Justice) from Miami University in December 2002.

Initially hired by Evergreen as a Security Guard and Corrections Officer, I quickly earned a promotion to Security Operations Supervisor and then to my present job as a Case Manager. I currently maintain a caseload of between 35 and 45 clients and have been effective in developing new programs which improve the quality of life and support for the facility's inmates. For instance, I implemented a Community Volunteer Program and now oversee the five volunteers who provide Bible study classes and take patients off the grounds for leisure and community activities.

I hold professional memberships in Addiction Professionals of Ohio and in the American Correctional Association.

If you can use an experienced human services professional with an excellent grasp of how to maximize community resources and provide quality social case work management, please call me to suggest a time when we might meet to discuss your needs. As an experienced Case Manager, I can assure you in advance that I could rapidly become an asset to your organization.

Sincerely,

John Calvin

JOHN CALVIN

1110½ Hay Street, Fayetteville, NC 28305 • preppub@aol.com • (910) 483-6611

OBJECTIVE

To offer a background in human services with an emphasis on correctional social work to an organization that can use a professional with excellent verbal and written communication skills as well as the ability to plan, prioritize, and carry out heavy workloads.

EDUCATION & TRAINING

B.S. in Psychology with a minor in **Criminal Justice** at Miami University; December 2002.
- Have been named to the **Chancellor's List** for academic achievement four semesters.
- Was selected for membership in Alpha Chi, a National College Honor Scholarship Society, and Psi Chi, The National Honor Society in Psychology.

Completed numerous training programs including HIV/AIDS Training, Ethics for Substance Abuse Professionals, Combat Lifesaving, and Professional Leadership Development.
Was certified as an Instructor for the OH Department of Corrections Think Smart Program.

EXPERIENCE

Am advancing in this track record of promotion with Evergreen Rehabilitation Center, Cincinnati, OH (2000-present):
CASE MANAGER. (2001-present). Implemented new programs and services while handling a caseload of between 35 and 45 clients and providing services designed to aid in the rehabilitation and adjustment of chemically dependent people and their family members.
- Trained employees and now manage a five-person team of volunteers who provide Bible study sessions and take patients to leisure and community activities.
- Am building strong contacts with mental health resources and halfway houses statewide in order to ensure the availability of employment and training options for the future.
- Handle a wide range of actions including conducting initial interviews, developing complete psychosocial histories, preparing status reports, and developing care plans.
- Prepare for and attend court hearings, meetings, and conferences on the client's behalf.
- Remain on call at all times to make management decisions as a senior staff member.

SECURITY OPERATIONS SUPERVISOR (SHIFT COMMANDER). (2001). Was promoted to supervise four security guards at this facility with approximately 78 inmates after demonstrating my ability to maintain control under crisis situations.
- Supervised operation of a command center and roving patrols as well as transportation of inmates on work release status or with hospital appointments or court appearances.

SECURITY GUARD and **CORRECTIONS OFFICER.** (1998-01). Was rapidly promoted to a supervisory role on the basis of my skills displayed while observing and assisting patients; worked with them in a therapeutic setting and assisted with group therapy.

Served my country in the U.S. Army:
ADMINISTRATIVE ASSISTANT/DRIVER. Ft. Gordon, GA (1997-98). Applied computer and organizational skills; operated and maintained wheeled vehicles; was liaison for a worker and employee relations task force.

SECURITY GUARD and **DRIVER.** Korea (1995-96). Selected for advanced responsibilities ahead of my peers, handled activities such as operating and maintaining a track vehicle, maintaining engineering systems/tools, and assisting in construction/demolition projects.

PERSONAL

Proficient with computers, use them on a daily basis; member of Addiction Professionals of Ohio and in the American Correctional Association. Held a Secret security clearance.

Date

Exact Name of Person
Title or Position
Name of Company
Address (number and street)
Address (city, state, and zip)

Dear Exact Name of Person (or Sir or Madam if answering a blind ad):

I would appreciate an opportunity to talk with you soon about how I could contribute to your organization through my wide variety of experience in working with diverse client populations while applying my counseling skills, enthusiasm, and ability to work effectively with people.

With a master's degree in Counseling and bachelor's degree in Psychology, I offer a strong educational background which I have utilized in positions which called for the ability to be a caring and concerned listener who could make effective professional judgments. You will see from my enclosed resume that I have completed internships in counseling which have given me exposure to children as young as three who have experienced physical and/or sexual abuse as well as adults receiving marriage counseling along with middle school students involved in violence intervention programs.

Known for my ability to provide effective leadership and keep group and individual sessions on target, I have consistently been able to provide high-quality care to populations of mentally or physically handicapped children, adults in a group home setting, and children participating in a variety of sports activities.

I am a self-confident individual with strong counseling skills as well as a firm grasp of the importance of program planning, case management, and administrative support required to keep programs operating and productive.

I hope you will welcome my call soon to arrange a brief meeting to discuss your needs and how I might serve them. Thank you in advance for your time.

Sincerely,

Lenore A. Raven

Alternate last paragraph:
I hope you will call or write me soon to suggest a time convenient for us to meet and discuss your current and future needs and how I might serve them. Thank you in advance for your time.

LENORE A. RAVEN

1110½ Hay Street, Fayetteville, NC 28305   •   preppub@aol.com   •   (910) 483-6611

OBJECTIVE

To obtain a permanent position in the mental health field that utilizes my educational background, organizational and program management skills, and planning abilities.

EDUCATION

Master of Education in Counseling, Stanford University, Stanford, CA, 1999.
- Graduated *magna cum laude*.

Bachelor of Arts in Psychology, The University of Arizona, Tucson, AZ, 1996.

EXPERIENCE

INDIVIDUAL AND FAMILY COUNSELING INTERN. Family Therapy Center, San Diego, CA (1999-present). Provided age- and situationally appropriate counseling for individuals in a variety of age groups ranging from children to adults, acted as a co-leader for therapy groups for sexually abused girls, and provided marital therapy.
- Helped develop the curriculum for two counseling groups — the four-year-olds and the nine to 12-year-old group of sexually abused females — including reorganizing guidelines in such a way that future leaders would have a foundation for additional groups.
- Provided a buffer between sexually and/or physically abused children and their parents during supervised visitations scheduled after gaining the childrens' trust.
- Led groups so that each member was given an opportunity for individual growth.

COUNSELING INTERN. San Diego School District, CA (1998). Assisted the counseling staff at Hansen Middle School in in-school counseling under the sponsored by "Second Step — Committee for Children," a violence intervention program.
- Participated in support activities including facilitation of violence intervention classes, attendance at parent conferences, and individual or group meetings with students.
- Experienced first hand the positive effects of an early intervention initiative which taught the students alternatives and solutions to potentially dangerous situations.

CAMP COUNSELOR. Sacramento Parks and Recreation, Sacramento, CA (summer 1997). For the city's special programs summer camp, provided support for physically and mentally handicapped children in overnight as well as day-camp settings.
- Supervised a wide range of areas including assistance with general hygiene, dressing, and meals as well as evening and overnight activities.
- Planned and conducted outdoor group activities for as many as 11 children.

FACILITY ASSISTANT. Triumph Limited International, Belgium (1995-96). As assistant to the facility manager, provided support to mentally disabled home residents as well as supervising five staff members in an intense work environment.
- Challenged residents to take the maximum responsibility for the daily decisions in life.
- Provided the least restrictive possible assistance to residents to allow them to integrate into mainstream society.
- Participated in and led team meetings to assess residents' progress and future goals.

Highlights of other experience:
- Coached high school long-distance runners as well as teaching a variety of sports to elementary and middle school youth for the YMCA.

TRAINING & PROFESSIONAL AFFILIATIONS

Attended training programs in subjects including marital therapy emphasizing integrative research and practice as well as a health forum which provided valuable information on intervention techniques and treatment facilities for eating disorders.

Member, American Counseling Association

Career Change

Date

Exact Name of Person
Title or Position
Name of Company
Address (no., street)
Address (city, state, zip)

COUNSELOR & JOB DEVELOPER

This individual demonstrates the art of making a career change just by reading her resume. When you yearn to make a change in career, it's usually best to find a related field or occupation. In her situation, social work and counseling were "cousins" of teaching and education.

Dear Exact Name of Person (or Dear Sir or Madam if answering a blind ad):

I would appreciate an opportunity to talk with you soon about how I could benefit your organization through my background in education as well as my experience in counseling and social services. I am particularly interested in the position of Director of the Job Training Partnership Program which was recently advertised.

As you will see from my resume, I have had a number of years experience working with children in the educational field. I began my career as a Teacher and excelled in the teaching profession. Slowly, however, I began to realize that my true calling was in the social work and social services area as I realized that the social services field could meet needs of children which were even more basic than textbook learning.

In my first position in the social work field, I counseled both young and older adults with the Joint Partnership Training Act, the federal program devoted to helping disadvantaged people develop job skills and find employment. In my work with the JTPA, I have demonstrated strong skills in marketing and advertising as well as in community liaison. In formal performance evaluations I have been described as a resourceful individual who excels in working with others at all levels.

You would find me to be a well-rounded professional with exceptional organizational skills and highly developed communication abilities.

I hope you will call or write me soon to suggest a time convenient for us to meet and discuss your current and future needs and how I might serve them. Thank you in advance for your time.

Sincerely,

Bettina L. Dolly

Alternate last paragraph:
I hope you will welcome my call soon to arrange a brief meeting at your convenience to discuss your current and future needs and how I might serve them. Thank you in advance for your time.

BETTINA L. DOLLY

1110½ Hay Street, Fayetteville, NC 28305   •   preppub@aol.com   •   (910) 483-6611

OBJECTIVE

To benefit an organization that can use a versatile professional with experience in the fields of education and counseling as well as excellent organizational skills and attention to detail.

EDUCATION

Bachelor of Arts degree in Elementary Education, with English minor, New Bern University, New Bern, NC, 1988.

Have completed graduate-level course work in Counseling, University of North Carolina at Wilmington, Wilmington, NC.

EXPERIENCE

JOB DEVELOPER. New Hanover County Community Services, Wilmington, NC (2001-present). For the JTPA, work with older adults aged 55 and up, providing limited counseling services in addition to helping these adults find employment.

- Arrange classes for older adults, assisting them in the registration process for nurses' aide training.
- Prepare newspaper, radio, and television advertisements to generate interest among older adults for the JTPA.

COUNSELOR/JOB DEVELOPER. New Hanover County Services, Wilmington, NC (1995-01). Counseled low-income youths aged 16 to 21, helping them find full- and part-time positions for the federal government's Job Training Partnership Act (JTPA).

- Coordinated with area businesses to explain the program and its benefits as well as to obtain information about available positions.
- Visited area high schools to recruit students into the program.
- Taught youth a number of pre-employment training courses including interviewing techniques, proper dress codes and mannerisms, filling out applications and tax forms, choosing references, and expectations on the job.
- Matched qualifications and skills of young people with job openings.
- Obtained knowledge of various federal guidelines, requirements, and procedures.
- Utilized a Macintosh computer network and database to communicate data to and receive data from the Raleigh, NC regional center.

FIFTH-GRADE TEACHER. New Hanover County Schools, Wilmington, NC (1990-95). Taught a fifth-grade curriculum including science, math, English, social studies/history, health/nutrition, and other subjects.

FIRST-GRADE TEACHER and **SPECIAL EDUCATION TEACHER.** New Bern City Schools, New Bern, NC (1988-90). Employed various styles of teaching while instructing students with vastly different educational needs.

- While teaching first-grade students, concentrated on making learning an exciting activity for these new students, providing curriculum and activities which were conducive to learning as well as motor development and social skills.
- Taught special education students aged 11 to 14, learning to relate to and design teaching strategies for mentally challenged and socially underdeveloped individuals.

PERSONAL

Have developed excellent oral and written communication skills. Am a hard-working professional with the commitment to see a job done to the best of my ability.

Date

Exact Name of Person
Exact Title
Exact Name of Company
Address
City, State, Zip

COUNSELOR   Dear Exact Name of Person (or Dear Sir or Madam if answering a blind ad):

I would like to take this opportunity to introduce you to a highly motivated and well-rounded professional with a reputation for effectiveness in counseling, human relations, and educational activities and strong personal ethics.

I feel that one of my greatest strengths is my people-oriented skills. Consistently recognized as a person others are comfortable approaching for advice and guidance, I excel in educating, redirecting, and reeducating people and helping them set and achieve their goals.

As you will see from my enclosed resume, I recently received my M.A. in Counseling and earned a B.A. in Psychology in 2000. One element of my graduate degree program was a 300-hour practicum in counseling with the Howard County Department of Social Services (Waukesha, WI). As a Facilitator and Counselor with DSS, I continued to work with victims of domestic violence and with their abusers and family members in group and individual settings. This work has allowed me to see the firsthand results of how listening and helping others in a fair and non-judgmental setting can bring about positive changes to the lives of these individuals.

As a military spouse and native of the Jamaica, I can offer life experiences gained while living and working in Europe and in the Caribbean. I believe that this multicultural background has given me perspective in dealing with people of varied backgrounds and also helped me become an adaptable individual who can provide initiative, a sense of adventure, and a high degree of flexibility and who can relate life experiences to the situations of others in a helpful manner.

If you can use an experienced counselor and educator with a special interest in helping others through excellent communication and motivational skills, please call or write me soon to suggest a time when we might have a brief discussion of how I could contribute to your organization. I will provide excellent professional and personal references at the appropriate time.

Sincerely,

Wendy Fleming

WENDY FLEMING

1110½ Hay Street, Fayetteville, NC 28305 • preppub@aol.com • (910) 483-6611

OBJECTIVE

I want to offer my outstanding abilities in counseling, human relations, and education to an organization that can use an articulate professional with a reputation for being approachable and constantly aware of others and of the best methods for guiding and helping them.

EDUCATION & TRAINING

M.A. in Counseling, Kansas State University, Manhattan, KS, June 2002; course work included emphasis on substance abuse, family & marriage counseling, and crisis intervention.
- Completed a 300-hour practicum with the Howard County Department of Social Services, Waukesha, WI, January through May 2002.
B.A. in Psychology, Carroll College, Waukesha, WI, 2000; minor in Criminal Justice.
- Was honored with Gold Medals and Silver Awards for maintaining a 3.75 GPA.
- Inducted into Alpha Chi National Honor Society and the local Eta Chapter in recognition of my academic achievements.

EXPERIENCE

Am building a reputation as a caring and adaptable professional who has an understanding of cultural and ethnic differences and of the importance of dealing with each client as an individual:
FACILITATOR AND COUNSELOR. Howard County Department of Social Services (DSS), Waukesha, WI (2002-present). In a part-time job, apply strong listening skills and a fair manner of dealing with difficult and sensitive issues while providing counseling and facilitation in individual and group settings for victims of domestic abuse and drug/alcohol abuse.
- Am gaining personal satisfaction seeing firsthand the results of positive counseling as people learn skills needed to refocus and redirect the course of their lives.
- Have gained a broader awareness of the types of issues and situations which can result in domestic violence while working with abusers and their victims.

COUNSELOR (GRADUATE STUDENT). Howard County DSS, Wakesha, WI (2001). Contributed skills which had a positive impact on the lives of victims of domestic violence, their family members, and abusers during a six-month practicum.
- Applied language skills including fluent Spanish and working knowledge of German and French while assisting clients from a range of socioeconomic and ethnic backgrounds.

YOUTH COUNSELOR (AFTERCARE SPECIALIST). Resource Institute, Sanders, WI (2000-01). Refined time management and organizational skills in this part-time job in a residence facility for children as young as 11 and young adults up to 18.
- Helped these young people by guiding them in reeducation and in redirecting the focus of their lives as they recovered from substance abuse.
- Served as a positive role model for these misguided youth.

INVENTORY CLERK. Clark's Uniform Service, Waukesha, WI (1997-00). Learned to work on a team while keeping within a strict budget accounting for an inventory of new and used uniforms for approximately 300 customer accounts.

Highlights of earlier experience:
As a military spouse, traveled and lived in Europe. As an Educator with Ashton High School, Brighton, England motivated, guided, instructed, and mentored high school students in order to help them earn the highest grades on their General Certificate of Education (GED).

PERSONAL

Member, American Counselor's Association (A.C.A.). Especially proud of my effectiveness in mentoring and guiding troubled youth and young adults and in setting standards to follow.

CAREER CHANGE

Date

Exact Name of Person
Exact Title
Exact Name of Company
Address
City, State, Zip

COUNSELOR

In a career change situation, the cover letter becomes very important. It helps to "build a bridge" to your new field. The cover letter often "explains" the resume. Sometimes the cover letter can say things which the resume doesn't say. For example, this individual points out that his desire to enter the social and counseling field was ignited during his years as a military professional, when he often counseled troubled youth.

Dear Exact Name of Person (or Dear Sir or Madam if answering a blind ad):

I would appreciate an opportunity to talk with you soon to discuss how I could contribute to your organization through the counseling and motivational skills I gained while serving my country in the U.S. Army.

While rising to the rank of Command Sergeant Major, I earned a reputation as an inspiring leader and highly effective manager of human resources. Throughout my career, I transformed marginal performers into motivated and productive individuals. I counseled hundreds of people on family, personal, financial, and career matters, and I helped numerous professionals of all ages learn how to better manage their time, energies, aggressions, and finances. Training and teaching others was a daily responsibility in all of my jobs, and I have developed and implemented training programs in dozens of organizations.

It was during my years in the military that I developed a desire to enter the counseling, social services, or probation services field after I retired. In one job I played a key role in hosting the Special Olympics and that gave me an opportunity to see how important the Special Olympics is to Down's Syndrome individuals. In several jobs I was involved in conducting inspections and investigations of complaints. Early in my military career, I excelled as a Drill Sergeant and enjoyed the opportunity to instill in young soldiers an attitude of discipline and skills in teamwork.

In addition to pursuing my B.A. in Social Science, I completed an Associate of Science degree in Criminal Justice. As a military professional, I completed numerous courses related to personnel management techniques, drug and alcohol counseling, and other similar areas.

The recipient of numerous awards and medals recognizing my exemplary character and professional contributions, I offer a true desire to help the troubled and less fortunate along with a proven ability to motivate others to want to transform their lives. If you can use my considerable counseling and communication skills as well as my management and supervisory experience, I hope you will contact me to suggest a time when we might meet to discuss your needs and how I might serve them. I feel confident I could become a valuable asset to your organization, and I certainly wish to thank you in advance for your time.

Sincerely,

Edward Steven Moss

EDWARD STEVEN MOSS

1110½ Hay Street, Fayetteville, NC 28305   •   preppub@aol.com   •   (910) 483-6611

OBJECTIVE   To offer my management experience, counseling skills, and motivational abilities to an organization that can use a mature professional with a strong desire to make a difference in the lives of others and help them become more productive and self-confident.

EDUCATION   <u>College:</u>
Bachelor of Arts (B.A.) degree, Social Services and Sociology, Claflin College, Orangeburg, SC; degree to be awarded in Jan 2003.
Associate of Science degree in Criminal Justice, Columbus Technical Community College (CTCC), Columbus, GA, 1994.
<u>Teacher Training:</u>
Completed a continuing education course in **Effective Teaching Training for Substitutes and Assistants,** CTCC, 1994.
<u>Human Services and Technical Training:</u>
Completed military training which included courses in personnel management techniques, drug and alcohol abuse counseling, civil affairs, the effects of drug and alcohol on the mentally and/or physically handicapped, and community service center operations.

EXPERIENCE   **SECURITY GUARD.** Burns Security, Orangeburg, SC (2000-present). Maintain security for the physical plant and personnel at the Boeing Aircraft plant. On my own initiative, took actions to prevent theft and property destruction as well as controlling entry and exit.

COLLEGE STUDENT. Orangeburg Technical Community College, Orangeburg, SC (2000-present). While working in the full-time job described above, used the GI Bill to further my education and earn a bachelor's degree in Social Services. Excelled academically; 3.7 GPA.

Highlights of military experience: Advanced to the rank of Command Sergeant Major while establishing a track record of accomplishments in building morale and producing well-trained teams of employees, U.S. Army:
TRAINING PROGRAM MANAGER and **COUNSELOR.** Ft. Benning, GA (1990-99). Known for my effectiveness in communicating with others and building relations with people from widely diverse backgrounds, developed and managed the individual training programs for approximately 35 supervisors and administrative staff members.
• Observed training programs and made recommendations to senior officials on changes which would make the 20,000 people who were processed annually better prepared both mentally and physically for more advanced training.

QUALITY ASSURANCE MANAGER. Korea (1988-90). Earned the respect of my superiors and was described as having a "unique ability" for motivating, counseling, and guiding others, which was demonstrated while responding to requests for assistance with a wide variety of professional and quality-of-life issues.
• Recognized as a subject matter expert, provided advice and guidance for inspection team members and supervised a staff of five.
• Refined communication and interpersonal skills dealing with a wide variety of people ranging from those with problems to the professionals, executives, and community leaders who worked with me closely to provide answers and solutions.

PERSONAL   Awarded 28 medals honors including several for service in Vietnam. Held Secret clearance.

Date

Mr. Jeff Smith
Staff Recruiter
Baltimore Home for Children

Dear Mr. Smith:

    I am writing regarding your agency's recent advertisement for a Family Preservation Specialist. Having the opportunity to meet with Mary Smith and read materials on your agency confirmed my desire to join the Baltimore Home for Children.

    As you will see from my resume, I have a six-year track record as a human resource professional. During this six years, I have been recognized for my positive belief in myself and in others to succeed against all odds. I know I have chosen a profession in which I can excel principally as a result of perseverance. I approach my profession with enthusiasm, dedication, and an overwhelming desire to help others.

    In my current position, I work with behaviorally impaired individuals, and I can bring to the Baltimore Home for Children great insights into BEH individuals. In a prior position with the Baltimore Regional Mental Health Center, I worked with children of all ages who were experiencing trauma and stress of varying types.

    My resume is a good summary, but I strongly feel that it is during a personal interview that my potential to be of service to your organization would be fully demonstrated. I welcome a meeting to learn more about the Baltimore Home for Children. I can provide outstanding personal and professional references.

    Thank you for your time and consideration.

Sincerely yours,

Joanna Garcia

JOANNA GARCIA

1110½ Hay Street, Fayetteville, NC 28305   •   preppub@aol.com   •   (910) 483-6611

OBJECTIVE   To offer a background of extensive experience in crisis intervention and in the education and support of at-risk children and young adults to an organization that can use a knowledgeable and effective professional known for offering concern and understanding.

EDUCATION   Completing **Master's degree in Counseling**, Loyola College, Baltimore, MD; December 2002.
B.S., Psychology, Loyola College, Loyola, IN, 1999.
- Graduated *magna cum laude*, was named to the university Dean's List, Psi Chi National Honor Society, and Who's Who Among American College Students.

TRAINING AND CERTIFICATION   Received advanced training and certification in Nonviolent Crisis Intervention and Crisis Prevention Intervention as well as in CPR and First Aid.

EXPERIENCE   **TEACHER OF BEHAVIORAL-EMOTIONALLY HANDICAPPED (BEH).** Mapleton Middle School, Rockville, MD (2001-present). Provide behavior modification and management while teaching as many as 15 children ages 11 to 15 who are in the sixth through eighth grades.
- Interact with juvenile court officials on behalf of these children, some of whom I have worked with for two years; maintain confidentiality of records.
- Work with the parents to provide consulting and advisory services.
- Am pursuing the goal of preparing these children to be mainstreamed into regular educational settings and functioning independently.
- Apply strong interpersonal skills and understanding of people and their behavior while entering homes where a child had been sexually or otherwise abused and helping the parents and caregivers to handle the children and deal with their problems.
- Prepare a wide variety of written material to include Individualized Education Programs (IEP), Functional Behavior Assessments, and Behavior Intervention Plans.

CASE WORKER. Baltimore Regional Mental Health Center, Baltimore, MD (1998-00). Handled a caseload of seven children while working in close cooperation with a male counterpart to provide support and services for children from six through 18 who had experienced depression; sexual, emotional, mental, or physical abuse; or who were exhibiting emotional defiance.
- Interacted with juvenile court officials on behalf of my clients.
- Provided individual and group counseling, behavior modification and management, and crisis intervention as well as designing and implementing treatment plans.
- Controlled and administered medication.
- Oversaw activities which included cultural enrichment, daily living skills, academic tutoring, occupational skills, personal hygiene, and social and interaction skills.
- Documented clinical notes and provided administrative support for vehicles, grounds, and food service support.

RESIDENTIAL TECHNICIAN. Personal, Inc., Baltimore, MD (1995-98). Worked with three teenagers (14 to 18 years of age) who required counseling and behavior management services after experiencing emotional, mental, and/or physical problems, focusing on the development of independent living and social skills.

PERSONAL   Am a compassionate and caring professional with experience and knowledge in crisis intervention and the development of individualized plans.

Date

Exact Name of Person
Title or Position
Name of Company
Address (no., street)
Address (city, state, zip)

CRISIS COUNSELOR   Dear Exact Name of Person (or Dear Sir or Madam if answering a blind ad):

I would appreciate an opportunity to talk with you soon about how my experience in the mental health field and my education in psychology could be beneficial to your organization.

As you will see from my resume, I gained a base of experience in working with mentally retarded and developmentally delayed adults in a sheltered workshop setting. This job required that I remain calm and controlled, handle aggressive adults, provide personal care including lifting and feeding clients, and apply behavior management techniques. I am very proud of my accomplishments in developing a strong rapport with several clients who were very unresponsive or, at the other extreme, displayed violent and aggressive behavior.

Through my practical experience and education, I have gained knowledge of areas including behavioral management, behavior modification, child and adolescent psychology, social research, stress management, counseling, and crisis intervention.

Known for my strong personal initiative and exemplary work ethic, I excelled in two different jobs while financing my college degree. As a Customer Service Representative at a local video store, I was recognized as "Employee of the Month." In a job as part of the university's security force, I played a key role in a community undertaking to finger-print children in order to assure their safety and well being.

I hope you will welcome my call soon to arrange a brief meeting at your convenience to discuss your current and future needs and how I might serve them. Thank you in advance for your time.

Sincerely yours,

Reata C. Astro

Alternate last paragraph:
I hope you will call or write soon to suggest a time convenient for us to meet and discuss your current and future needs and how I might serve them. Thank you in advance for your time.

REATA C. ASTRO

1110½ Hay Street, Fayetteville, NC 28305   •   preppub@aol.com   •   (910) 483-6611

OBJECTIVE   To apply my experience in the mental health field and education in psychology for the benefit of an organization that can use a caring young professional who remains calm and in control when faced with crisis situations and difficult or disruptive behavior.

EDUCATION   **B.A., Psychology,** The Ohio State University, Columbus, OH, 2000.
- Was accepted for membership in Psi Chi, the national honor society in psychology in recognition of my involvement in the Psychology Club.
- Placed on the Dean's "High Honor" List on the basis of my high GPA.
- Excelled in an internship as an Aide in a program designed to help oppositional adolescents who were very close to being institutionalized.

TRAINING   Attended several adult training center programs in these areas:
"Try Another Way" — a one-week workshop on teaching the mentally retarded seizure disorders — history, causes, and guidelines for therapy
"Sensory Motor Programming" — functions and dysfunctions of the sensory systems and intervention strategies
"Nonviolent Crisis Intervention" — managing disruptive, assaultive, and out-of-control behaviors

EXPERIENCE   **HABILITATION ASSISTANT II/WORKSHOP SPECIALIST II.** Chastain County Board of Mental Retardation, Dayton, OH (2000-present). Apply behavior management techniques while supervising and training moderately, severely, or profoundly mentally retarded and/ or developmentally delayed adults in basic work and habilitative activities in a structured classroom setting.
- Assist with personal care including lifting, toileting, feeding, and changing soiled clothing while providing consistent level of care for multihandicapped trainees.
- Used my education, training, and instincts to establish rapport with several aggressive adults with severe behavior disorders.
- Took charge of 13 clients during the two-week absence of my supervisor and with no major mishaps, injuries, or incidents of aggression despite changes in routine which normally would be expected to cause severe behaviors.
- Contributed to major changes in the behavior of a semi-aggressive female who within a six-month period learned to work almost entirely independently.
- Established a strong rapport with several severely disturbed and normally unresponsive clients who were often known to display disruptive behavior just to gain attention.

CUSTOMER SERVICE SPECIALIST. American Video, Columbus, OH (1999-00). Was recognized as an energetic, cheerful, and courteous sales and customer service specialist who makes important contributions to ensure customer satisfaction. Worked in this job while financing my college education.
- Earned recognition as "Employee of the Month" for my willingness to "go the extra mile."

SUPERVISORY SECURITY SPECIALIST. The Ohio State University, Columbus, OH (1997-99). Patrolled the college grounds and contributed to the safety and security of students. Worked closely with children and their parents while fingerprinting and videotaping as part of a nationwide program to assist in locating missing children.

PERSONAL   Am self taught in universal sign language. Offer experience in using microcomputers for word processing applications. Am a creative problem solver.

Date

Exact Name of Person
Title or Position
Name of Company
Address (no., street)
Address (city, state, zip)

Dear Exact Name of Person (or Dear Sir or Madam if answering a blind ad.):

I would appreciate an opportunity to talk with you soon about how I could contribute to your organization through my experience and education in the areas of social work and human services along with my reputation for maturity and dedication.

While earning my B.S. in Social Work and Psychology from Duke University in Durham, NC, I completed an internship with the Wake County Department of Social Services (DSS). This internship led to positions within the department, as you will see from my resume.

I feel that among my major personal strengths are my enthusiasm, knowledge of available resources, ability to quickly and easily establish rapport with clients, and my determination to exhaust all available resources in order to do everything possible to help my clients.

In my current position as a Qualified Mental Retardation Professional, I direct 20 staff and 16 residents in two intermediate care facilities. Through my experience in my past positions and current position I have worked with several different populations. I have gained experience in management, as well as developing, monitoring, maintaining individual program plans, measuring outcomes, and much more.

I believe that through my enthusiasm, organizational skills, motivational abilities, empathy, and compassion for others I can make valuable contributions to an organization that seeks a professional with these qualities.

I hope you will welcome my call soon to arrange a brief meeting at your convenience to discuss your current and future needs and how I might serve them. Thank you in advance for your time.

Sincerely yours,

Barbara H. Major

Alternate last paragraph:
I hope you will call or write me soon to suggest a time convenient for us to meet and discuss your current and future needs and how I might serve them. Thank you in advance for your time.

BARBARA H. MAJOR

1110½ Hay Street, Fayetteville, NC 28305 • preppub@aol.com • (910) 483-6611

OBJECTIVE

To offer my reputation as a compassionate, dedicated, and enthusiastic young professional to an organization that can use my education and experience related to social work and human services and my willingness to go the extra mile for my clients.

EDUCATION

Attended a graduate program leading to a **Master of Social Work (M.S.W.)** degree, Duke University, Durham, NC.
B.S., Social Work and Psychology, Duke University, Durham, NC, 1995.

TRAINING

Am CPR certified, trained in preventing and responding to aggression, and trained in dealing with inappropriate sexual behavior. Have completed 40 hours of supervisory training and am trained in CABS psychological testing.

EXPERIENCE

QUALIFIED MENTAL RETARDATION PROFESSIONAL. Tri-Development Center, Aiken, SC (2000-present). Direct/supervise two intermediate care facilities with 20 direct service staff including two House Managers, two LPN's, and 16 Mental Retardation Specialists.

- Develop, monitor, and maintain Individual Program Plans and Active Treatment Schedules for 16 residents who are all multi-diagnosed.
- Levels of mental retardation range from profound to moderate adaptivity with other diagnoses including seizure disorders, visually impaired, Cerebral Palsy, Down's Syndrome, as well as psychiatric diagnoses including schizophrenia, Intermittent Explosive Disorder, Bi-Polar Disorder, and Obsessive-Compulsive disorders.
- Develop programs including psychosocial assessments, formal needs assessments, behavior management programs, active treatment schedules, and formal training goals.
- Initiate/call Interdisciplinary Team Meetings, as well as participate in Quarterly Psychotropic Drug Reviews, and Annual Individual Program Plans; attend Weekly Management Team Meetings, Pre-admission Screenings, and Discharge Summaries.
- Work with House Managers to ensure direct service staffs' work is of the highest quality, and to schedule and write annual employee evaluations.

CRISIS INTERVENTION SOCIAL WORKER. Wake County Department of Social Services (DSS), Raleigh, NC (1998-00). Learned how to locate and maximize community resources in ways that would make the most of benefits for clients while making determinations on clients' eligibility for financial assistance from federal, state, and local programs.

- Became skilled in assessing needs within the family as well as external factors that could lead to a family being considered at high risk for abuse.
- Gained experience in crisis intervention and in finding ways to defuse problems.

SOCIAL WORKER. Wake County DSS, Raleigh, NC (1997). For the County JOBS (Job Opportunities and Basic Skills) program, assisted in the process of completing initial assessments of potential clients for the program which enabled participants to obtain an education and/or training for a career.

SOCIAL WORK INTERN. Durham Care Clinic, Durham, NC (1995-96). Gained the respect of my superiors for my maturity and dedication to providing clients with a high quality of concerned services.

PERSONAL

Am very persistent — will not give up until I am sure I have exhausted every possible source of assistance for my client. Have earned a reputation for my enthusiasm and energy.

Date

Mr. John Smith, ACSW, CCSW
Department Head

Dear Mr. Smith:

I am sending you the enclosed resume which you requested, and I want to tell you how enthusiastic I am about the opportunity to serve as your Chief of Human Services.

As a seasoned professional with more than 20 years of successful human resource experience, I have built a reputation as a talented manager who could provide exceptional leadership in developing and carrying out large-scale programs with the Georgia Department of Human Resources. My major strengths are in program design and evaluation, grant/contract proposal preparation, organizational development, and strategic planning as well as skills in marketing and sales. I am a results-oriented team player who communicates effectively with people at all organizational levels.

In my current position as Director of the Georgia Department of Social Services, I developed a program which saved more than $200 million over two fiscal years through a unique state, local, and federal initiative to reduce erroneous benefit payments. I am well known throughout the social services field for my high level of resourcefulness in the utilization of physical and human assets.

I can provide outstanding personal and professional references, and it would be a pleasure to meet with you in person to discuss the position further.

Yours sincerely,

Allison Stewart

ALLISON STEWART

1110½ Hay Street, Fayetteville, NC 28305   •   preppub@aol.com   •   (910) 483-6611

OBJECTIVE

To offer a track record of distinguished performance as a dedicated, innovative professional with proven analytical, motivational, and planning skills along with a reputation for excellence in program development, research, technical writing, and public speaking.

EXPERIENCE

DIRECTOR, GA DEPARTMENT OF SOCIAL SERVICES, Atlanta, GA (2000-present). Supervise the administration of 100 county social services departments through a staff of 1,150 employees and a billion-dollar-plus budget. Developed changes which allowed the 100 county departments to operate more efficiently and productively.

- Provided guidance for a wide range of programs, including child protective, adult, child support enforcement, food stamp, foster care and adoption, and employment programs.
- Guided the JOBS (Job Opportunities and Basic Skills) program to recognition as one of the country's most outstanding models under the 1992 Federal Family Support Act.
- Secured funding from the General Assembly for the child protective services program.
- Applied my diplomatic skills working with the governments of each of the 100 counties to ensure their programs met federal and state regulations while also dealing regularly with administrators of other state agencies (health, commerce, and the court system).
- Developed a program which saved more than $200 million over two fiscal years through a unique state, local, and federal initiative to reduce erroneous benefit payments.

REGIONAL DIRECTOR, GA DEPT. OF HUMAN RESOURCES, Atlanta, GA (1995-00). Was recruited and handpicked for the state director's position on the basis of my performance in this capacity. Provided a 33-person staff and a 17-county region with leadership in child welfare, public assistance, child support and other related programs.

- Won recognition for dealing with complex issues and negotiating with representatives from other governmental agencies at the state, county, and local level.
- Managed a child welfare program recognized as the best from among the four regions.
- Created an Aid to Families with Dependent Children (AFDC) program recognized for the lowest error rates and highest productivity in the state.

ASSISTANT CHIEF, PREVENTATIVE AND SUPPORT SERVICES, GA DEPT. OF HUMAN RESOURCES, Atlanta, GA (1992-95). Streamlined and simplified procedures and developed policies while supervising 12 employees.

- Created and implemented a model program to prevent repeat adolescent pregnancies.
- Oversaw the monitoring, evaluation, and certification of 400 contracts.

CONSULTANT, GA DEPARTMENT OF HUMAN RESOURCES, Atlanta, GA (1990-92). Developed a model training plan and peer supervision program as a technical advisor/consultant for a ten-county region's Aid to Dependent Children programs.

- Designed and administered successful marketing strategies that increased multidisciplinary approaches to Child Welfare Service delivery in the 17 regional counties.
- Guided 34 county Departments of Social Services in the creation and implementation of a new employment and training program for public assistance recipients.

Highlights of other experience: Peach County, GA (1980-89). As a Child Welfare Worker, earned recognition for my success in taking a backlog of 42 children who had been in foster care for five, ten or more years and placing all of them either with relatives or for adoptions.

EDUCATION

Master of Social Work (MSW) degree, The University of Georgia, Athens, GA.
B.S., Secondary Education, Monroe University, Monroe, GA.

Date

Exact Name of Person
Title or Position
Name of Company
Address (number and street)
Address (city, state, and zip)

DISASTER RELIEF PROJECT DIRECTOR

Dear Exact Name of Person (or Sir or Madam if answering a blind ad.):

I would appreciate an opportunity to talk with you soon about how I could contribute to your organization through my background in the specialized field of disaster relief where I have excelled through my excellent abilities in organizing and planning programs.

With a keen eye for detail and my outstanding managerial skills, I have directed disaster relief efforts following two of this country's largest disasters — Hurricane Fran and Hurricane Hugo. My accomplishments have included directing the construction of housing and offices for volunteer workers, establishing a ministry for children of migrant workers, and coordinating arrangements for feeding and housing thousands of volunteer workers following this catastrophic events.

I am confident that during my years of planning and carrying out these massive projects, I have earned a reputation as a thorough professional who can be counted on ensure that these projects are successful. I receive a great deal of personal satisfaction from seeing that I am making a direct impact on an improved quality of life for people who have lost so much.

I hope you will welcome my call soon to arrange a brief meeting to discuss your current and future needs and how I might serve them. Thank you in advance for your time.

Sincerely,

Henry A. Higgins

Alternate last paragraph:
I hope you will call or write me soon to suggest a time convenient for us to meet and discuss your current and future needs and how I might serve them. Thank you in advance for your time.

HENRY A. HIGGINS

1110½ Hay Street, Fayetteville, NC 28305   •   preppub@aol.com   •   (910) 483-6611

OBJECTIVE

To offer my broad base of experience in project management, problem solving, marketing, and administration to an organization that can use my compassion and true concern for others as well as my specialized education and experience in disaster relief and aid projects.

EXPERIENCE

PROJECT DIRECTOR. Project Relief, Charleston, SC (2000-present). Led and directed the efforts of a management team which planned and coordinated emergency and long-term response following one of the nation's largest natural disasters including hurricanes.
- Planned and supervised the construction of three housing and program sites in support of more than 12,500 volunteers over the course of the relief efforts.
- Oversaw activities which provided food and housing for an average of 350 volunteers and staff members on a daily basis.
- Planned for and managed construction activities including scheduling, logistics support, and purchasing for 280 to 300 building projects annually.
- Directed multimillion-dollar budgets.
- Played a key role in the development and founding of Rock Bay Schools, an alternative program for delinquent adolescents.
- Was one of the co-developers of successful operational plans in which large groups of volunteers were used to provide large-scale emergency relief efforts.

PROGRAM COORDINATOR. Good Samaritan, Savannah, GA (1995-00). Managed relief projects including acting as **PROJECT COORDINATOR** for hurricane relief efforts, and **CONSTRUCTION COORDINATOR** following Hurricane Howard in the Charleston, SC, area.
- Helped establish a "Ministry to Migrants" program at Johns Island, SC: this was a program involving more than 170 children in 18 migrant labor camps on the Sea Islands, SC, and addressed the basic issues of ensuring that these children received basic food, shelter, medical, and educational service as well as meeting the spiritual needs of children and families.

PRESIDENT and **GENERAL MANAGER.** Chestnut Hill Builders, Annapolis, MD (1991-95). Established and managed a successful general contracting business which built homes and remodeled upscale homes as well as doing light commercial work in the Baltimore-Annapolis area.

Highlights of earlier experience: Built a unique business which transported large yachts cross country after accomplishing continued growth as a partner in a general residential and light commercial construction company.
- Became the youngest assistant manager and manager for two different hospitality companies and gained experience in all aspects of the industry from custodial duties, to bartending, to kitchen cook, to catering, to accounting, to reservations.

EDUCATION

Received **certification as a trainer** following advanced training by the Department of Psychiatry's post-disaster mental health course, University of Maryland, Annapolis, 1995. Completed two years of college course work in Business and Liberal Arts at the Winthrop University, Rock Hill, SC.

PERSONAL

Offer a reputation as a very compassionate, caring person. Am very adept at large-scale planning and organizing the details so that projects are successful and productive.

Date

Dear Sir or Madam:

I would appreciate an opportunity to talk with you soon about how I could contribute to your organization through my formal education in social work as well as my versatile experience in social services, business management, office operations, and transportation management.

As you will see from my resume, I recently completed the B.A. in Social Work degree which I started several years ago and was unable to complete quickly because my husband was being relocated worldwide as a military professional. I am especially proud that, through my persistence and determination, I was able to complete my degree in late 2002 even while managing a successful and fast-growing small business which I started "from scratch" and directed until recently, when we relocated to Washington.

In a previous job in the human services/social work field prior to receiving my degree, I worked as an Eligibility Specialist for the County of San Bernardino and was involved in interviewing clients and assessing their needs. I gained a reputation as a caring counselor and respected co-worker, and I was encouraged to apply for a social work position in the county if we were ever again residing in San Bernardino. It was during that time that I decided that wanted to seek formal education in the social services area so that I could make my professional home in the social services field.

From my work experience in the Air Force and in office environments, I am accustomed to dealing graciously with the public while working under tight deadlines and solving difficult problems. I offer a naturally compassionate personality along with an ability to handle large volumes of work efficiently and accurately. I can provide outstanding personal and professional references.

I hope you will welcome my call soon to arrange a brief meeting at your convenience to discuss your current and future needs and how I might serve them. Thank you in advance for your time, and I will look forward to meeting you.

Sincerely yours,

Eloise J. Witherspoon

ELOISE J. WITHERSPOON

1110½ Hay Street, Fayetteville, NC 28305 • preppub@aol.com • (910) 483-6611

OBJECTIVE   I want to contribute to an organization that can use a cheerful hard worker who offers an education related to social work and human services along with experience.

EDUCATION   **Bachelor of Arts (B.A.) degree in Social Work**, University of Baltimore, Baltimore, MD, December 2002; worked at night to finish this degree while managing a business during the day.
Studied Social Work at University of Kansas, Lawrence, KS, 1985-87 and 1991.
Excelled in supervisory and management training sponsored by the U.S. Air Force, 1987-91.

EXPERIENCE   **GENERAL MANAGER**. Peggy's Cleaning Service, Baltimore, MD (2000-02). On my own initiative and with only a fifty-dollar initial investment, set up "from scratch" a business which provided cleaning services for residential and commercial property; hired and supervised clerical and cleaning personnel while personally establishing the company's 18 major accounts.
- Only two months after starting the business, generated monthly cash flow of $1700 and personally handled the finances including accounts receivable/payable, financial reporting, tax preparation, and collections.
- Was frequently commended for my gracious style of dealing with people by telephone and in person.

ELIGIBILITY WORKER. County of San Bernardino, San Bernardino, CA (1995-00). Performed assessments of clients to determine eligibility for medical assistance in the form of Medi-Cal, requiring preparation of large volumes of paperwork..
- Became acquainted with the vast interlocking network of social services organizations, and referred clients to those agencies and organizations as appropriate.
- Assisted clients in preparing personal budgets and strengthened their ability to manage their finances.
- Earned a reputation as a compassionate counselor and effective motivator.

OFFICE MANAGER'S ASSISTANT. X.Y.Z. Insurance Service, Fresno, CA (1993-94). Worked as the "right arm" of a busy office manager in a fast-paced insurance office, and excelled in activities ranging from word processing, to invoicing, to customer service.

DATA ENTRY OPERATOR. Candide's, Los Angeles, CA (1991-93). Operated a computer in order to input data provided by sales associates; worked with customers in establishing delivery dates, and verified financial/accounting transactions.

PASSENGER & HOUSEHOLD GOODS SPECIALIST. U.S. Air Force, McGuire AFB, NJ (1987-91). While serving my country in the Air Force, specialized in managing the transportation of people and property all over the globe.
- Expertly processed every kind of paperwork related to making reservations for domestic and international travel, issuing tickets, coordinating shipments of personal goods, and preparing monthly reports and bills of lading.
- Received two prestigious medals for exceptional performance and exemplary service.

COMPUTERS   Have used Word for word processing and can rapidly master new software.

PERSONAL   Am a patient, calm person who can handle a heavy work load and not get stressed out by tight deadlines. Have been told many times that I am a gifted counselor and communicator.

Date

Mr. Steve Smith
Executive Director
Hope Church and Community Center
550 E. 15th Street
Hope Mills, NC

Dear Steve:

With the enclosed resume, I would like to formally request that you consider me for another position with the Ft. Lauderdale Community Center. I am responding to the recent ad for a Social Worker for the senior citizen information/case assistance program.

As you are well aware, I have served the Ft. Lauderdale Community Center as its Emergency Assistance Coordinator. I truly enjoy working with the aging population, and I have developed an excellent reputation within the human services community. After reading the ad you placed, I am certain that I have all the qualifications you are seeking but, in addition, I offer the advantage of thoroughly understanding the internal operations of the center as a proud member of its team.

You may not be aware that, prior to becoming your Emergency Assistance Coordinator, I worked with the elderly as Activities Director of the Cedar Brook Retirement Home. I realized from that job that I had "found my calling" in working with senior citizens, and I truly thrived on bringing laughter and structure to their lives through the creative activities I planned and implemented.

With a reputation as a highly competent and conscientious individual, you will also see that I previously excelled in a track record of promotion with two convenience store chains, where I was promoted to District Manager over nine stores and then to Regional Sales Manager over 76 stores.

Although I have excelled as a manager in profit-making organizations, I have found that my take-charge, "make-it-happen" personality is well suited to the complex environment of nonprofit services organizations. As Emergency Assistance Coordinator, I have enjoyed the satisfaction of being able to make a difference in people's lives, and I am confident that I could continue to serve with distinction in this new position.

Please give me every consideration for this position, and also please give me the opportunity to formally interview for the position so that I demonstrate that I am the person you are seeking.

Yours sincerely,

Diana L. Shandy

DIANA L. SHANDY

1110½ Hay Street, Fayetteville, NC 28305 • preppub@aol.com • (910) 483-6611

OBJECTIVE
To benefit the Ft. Lauderdale Community Center as a Social Worker through my love and admiration for senior citizens, my outstanding reputation within the human services community, and my indepth knowledge of community resources and services.

AFFILIATION
Was named "Woman of the Year" in 2001 by the Ft. Lauderdale Business and Professional Women's Organization.
- Served as President, 2001 and 2002.
Served on the Board of Directors of Rape Crisis in Ft. Lauderdale, 2000-01.

EXPERIENCE
EMERGENCY ASSISTANCE COORDINATOR. Ft. Lauderdale Community Center, Ft. Lauderdale, FL (2000-present). Continuously interface with the aging population while handling casework for those seeking emergency assistance through the Center; work closely with the executive director and casework committee in developing guidelines for the quantity and quality of assistance provided to clients.
- Work closely with Department of Social Services social workers and maintain cooperative relationships with organizations providing essential human services; have earned respect for my professionalism and compassionate style.
- Had input into the creation of the center's database in my department, and maintain files.
- Inform people including senior citizens about programs and services which could be of assistance to them; provide referral, follow-up, and advocacy activities.
- Personally approach the service delivery system on the client's behalf, especially in the case of the frail or aging, when the inquirer is unable to investigate the resources available.
- Increase community awareness of information and case assistance services.
- Provide training for other staff who perform casework.
- Have established an extensive network of contacts involved in providing emergency assistance within the community; develop and maintain a notebook for staff on resources and key contact individuals within professional helping organizations as well as volunteer operations.

ACTIVITIES DIRECTOR. Cedar Brook Retirement Home, Ft. Lauderdale, FL (1998-99). Excelled in working with aging, and enjoyed the process of bringing laughter and structure to the lives of senior citizens.

Other experience (1990-97): Excelled in a track record of promotion with Quick Foods, Inc. and Hurry-Up Food Marts, Inc.; earned a reputation as an excellent manager.
- Began as a Cashier-Clerk with Hurry-Up, then was promoted to Assistant Manager and Store Manager, then to District Manager.
- Was recruited by Quick Foods, Inc. to be District Manager of nine stores in Georgia and then was promoted to Regional Sales Manager over 76 stores.

EDUCATION
University of Florida, Ft. Lauderdale campus: Completed courses in archaeology, Bible, business education, and computer science.
Florida State University: Earned A.S. degree in Business, 1989.

PERSONAL
Am an energetic, take-charge individual who enjoys solving problems and finding solutions to human resources dilemmas. Solid speaking, writing, and computer skills.

Date

Exact Name of Person
Title or Position
Name of Company
Address (no., street)
Address (city, state, zip)

ENRICHMENT PROGRAM MANAGER

Dear Exact Name of Person (or Dear Sir or Madam if answering a blind ad):

I would appreciate an opportunity to talk with you soon about how I could contribute to your organization through my skills as an educator and planner who possesses strong abilities in organizing programs.

An honors graduate of the University of Tampa, FL, I completed my college career with a 3.8 cumulative grade point average. Since graduating I have been working as the site director at the largest of Orange County's 33 "Prime Time" after school enrichment programs. In this program which provides care for more than 70 elementary age children, I have gained experience in planning activities, handling finances, training employees, and working with administrators to plan the best quality program possible.

I am very proud of the fact that I financed my education through jobs in the areas of customer service, inventory control, and sales. Working while maintaining a high grade point average gave me experience in handling pressure and effectively managing my time.

I hope you will welcome my call soon to arrange a brief meeting at your convenience to discuss your current and future needs and how I might serve them. Thank you in advance for your time.

Sincerely yours,

Quincy L. Finian

Alternate last paragraph:
I hope you will call or write soon to suggest a time convenient for us to meet and discuss your current and future needs and how I might serve them. Thank you in advance for your time.)

QUINCY L. FINIAN

1110½ Hay Street, Fayetteville, NC 28305 • preppub@aol.com • (910) 483-6611

OBJECTIVE   To apply my experience and education to an organization that can use a hard worker with skills as a planner and organizer as well as management, accounting and finance, and instructional abilities.

EDUCATION   **B.A., Geography and Social Studies**, The University of Tampa, Tampa, FL, 2000.
- Was named to the Chancellor's List for a perfect 4.0 GPA, spring 1999 and fall 2000.
- Made the Dean's List in recognition of "academic excellence" every other semester at University of Tampa.
- Graduated "**summa cum laude**" with a 3.8 cumulative GPA.
- Completed specialized course work including:

Computer graphics	Cartography
History	Sociology
Education	Geography

TRAINING   Was certified in First Aid and CPR, Hillsboro Community College, FL, 2000; was recertified in February 2002.

EXPERIENCE   **ENRICHMENT PROGRAM MANAGER**. Orange County Schools, Orlando, FL (2000-present). Supervise six assistants while managing the largest of the county's 33 "Prime Time" after-school enrichment programs: have more than 70 students ranging in age from five to 12.
- Planned and coordinated each week's activities.
- Gained accounting experience collecting weekly fees and keeping complete and accurate records.
- Served as the liaison between administration and the public.
- Provided excellent guidance to staff members and have had several earn promotion to manage their own sites.
- Earned a reputation for "flawless" record keeping.
- Increased my instructional and counseling skills working closely with the children.

YOUTH COUNSELOR. YMCA, Orlando, FL (1998-00). Refined my skills in teaching and counseling young people while ensuring the safety and supervising groups of more than 40 five to 12 year olds.
- Held the responsibility for planning weekly activities and sometimes transported groups of children for outside activities.
- Worked closely with parents as the contact point between them and the organization.

Other experience: Financed my education and gained additional experience in jobs including the following:
- Refined my customer service skills, polished my sales techniques, and learned inventory control in a specialized retail sales outlet.
- Worked as a Lab Assistant in a dyeing plant and learned proper laboratory procedures.
- Learned to handle a fast pace preparing food, operating the cash register, and taking orders in a fast-food restaurant.
- Gained additional experience in customer service, inventory control, and sales in earlier jobs in a retail toy store and grocery store.

PERSONAL   Offer some experience in programming Apple computers. Am a quick learner who offers outstanding management capabilities.

Date

Exact Name of Person
Title or Position
Name of Company
Address (number and street)
Address (city, state, and zip)

Dear Exact Name of Person (or Sir or Madam if answering a blind ad.):

With the enclosed resume, I would like to introduce myself and my desire to explore suitable positions within your organization which can utilize my experience in providing leadership to nonprofit organizations. I am relocating back to the St. Paul/ Minneapolis area where I own a townhouse, and I believe my extensive background in nonprofit management may be of interest to you.

As you will see from my resume, I have most recently served as Executive Director of an organization in Kentucky, where I have managed recruitment and training of a 65-person volunteer staff while also supervising three professional staff personnel. I have developed effective collaborative efforts among numerous community organizations while simultaneously identifying gaps in community services and developing programs to fill those needs.

In my previous position in Wisconsin, I was promoted from Community Services Coordinator to Director of a community shelter with a staff of 30 human services professionals and paraprofessionals. In addition to developing and maintaining the $800,000 budget, I was active in grant-writing and in numerous community activities which raised the shelter's profile.

I am the recipient of numerous awards and honors for my contributions and service, and I have enjoyed the respect of my colleagues in being elected to leadership positions in professional organizations and high-profile committees. I am widely respected for my ability to develop and maintain effective working relationships, organizational partnerships, and collaborative efforts.

If you can use my considerable leadership abilities and team-building skills, I hope you will contact me to suggest a time when we might meet to discuss your needs and goals and how I might meet them. Thank you in advance for your time.

Sincerely,

Kelly Lee Myers

KELLY LEE MYERS

1110½ Hay Street, Fayetteville, NC 28305   •   preppub@aol.com   •   (910) 483-6611

OBJECTIVE

To offer my strong management skills and proven track record in fund-raising, community relations, and program development to an organization that can use an experienced, motivated professional with a solid background in the directing of nonprofit programs, crisis intervention services, and volunteer activities.

EXPERIENCE

EXECUTIVE DIRECTOR. Rape Crisis Volunteers of Frankfort, Frankfort, KY (2000-present). When I relocated back to Frankfort, was immediately rehired by Rape Crisis Volunteers as Direct Services Coordinator.

- Gained widespread respect for my leadership and ability to build collaborative coalitions and viable partnerships, and was promoted to Executive Director in 2001.
- As Executive Director, have monitored and directed all aspects of a major crisis intervention agency: implementing policies, determining budgetary requirements, guiding various programs and functions, and managing an organizational budget of $200,000 for a program providing counseling, support groups, advocacy, and referral for victims of sexual assault 24 hours a day, 7 days a week.
- Identified gaps in services in the community, and created new programs to fill those gaps.
- Responsible for developing ongoing training programs for law enforcement officers and awareness and prevention programs while also overseeing recruitment and training of a staff of 65 volunteers.

Volunteers of America Campbell Shelter, Madison County, WI (1996-2000). *Was promoted in the following "track record" of advancement by a county-wide Community Shelter with an annual budget of $800,000.*
DIRECTOR. (1998-2000). While managing the Campbell Community Shelter, directed a staff of 30 human services professionals and paraprofessionals. Acted as liaison between the shelter and the community, establishing relationships with the voluntary Advisory Council, local organizations, and the business community. Developed and maintained an $800,000 budget. Effective fund-raising through grant writing, solicitations, and special events generated ten percent of the shelter's annual budget. Interacted with the local government, serving on several committees for Madison County and other government bodies.

COMMUNITY SERVICES COORDINATOR. (1996-98). Directed and supervised a program with more than 150 volunteers, providing preventive, restorative, and aftercare services to the homeless. Organized fund-raising and special events and served as liaison to the Public Affairs committee. Was responsible for case management, quality assurance in case records, and supervision of the food services and custodial staff.

DIRECT SERVICES COORDINATOR. Rape Crisis Volunteers of Frankfort (1992-1994). Supervised, recruited, and trained volunteers in an agency program meeting the needs of sexual assault survivors. Responsible for planning, organizing, and implementing direct services to meet the needs of primary and secondary victims of sexual assault.

EDUCATION

Enrolled in Kentucky State University's Non-Profit Management Program, Frankfort, KY.
- This is a program of executive education for leading professionals in the nonprofit organizational management field.

Earned Bachelor of Arts, Sociology, Kentucky State University, 1992.
- Program included internships in geriatric and alcohol rehabilitation centers.

Date

Exact Name of Person
Title or Position
Name of Company
Address (no., street)
Address (city, state, zip)

Dear Exact Name of Person (or Dear Sir or Madam if answering a blind ad):

I would appreciate an opportunity to talk with you soon about how I could contribute to your organization through my experience and education in the areas of social work and human services along with my reputation for maturity and dedication.

Having earned my B.S. in Social Work and Psychology, I am attending a graduate program leading to a Master of Social Work (MSW) degree with a concentration in clinical social work. While attending Iowa State University in Ames, IA, I completed an internship with the Chickasaw County Department of Social Services (DSS). This internship led to positions within the department, as you will see from my resume.

I feel that among my major personal strengths are my enthusiasm, knowledge of available resources, ability to quickly and easily establish rapport with clients, and my determination to exhaust all available resources in order to do everything possible to help my clients.

In my current position as a Social Worker in the Family and Children's Services of the Chickasaw County DSS, I am involved in crisis intervention and in resolving problems which place families at risk for abuse. Through my experience as an intern as well as in both temporary and permanent positions, I have gained experience in developing care plans with both short- and long-term goals, interviewing and assessing client needs, and locating resources from other community agencies.

I believe that through my enthusiasm, motivational abilities, empathy, and compassion for others I can make valuable contributions to an organization that seeks a professional with these qualities.

I hope you will welcome my call soon to arrange a brief meeting at your convenience to discuss your current and future needs and how I might serve them. Thank you in advance for your time.

Sincerely yours,

Teresa E. Malamut

TERESA E. MALAMUT

1110½ Hay Street, Fayetteville, NC 28305　　•　　preppub@aol.com　　•　　(910) 483-6611

OBJECTIVE

To offer my reputation as a compassionate, dedicated, and enthusiastic professional to an organization that can use my education and experience in social work and human services.

EDUCATION

Attend a graduate program leading to a Master of Social Work (M.S.W.) degree, University of Iowa, Iowa City, IA.

B.S., Social Work and Psychology, Iowa State University, Ames, IA, 1998.

- Earned a 3.2 GPA while completing specialized course work including the following:

  abnormal psychology　　social psychology　　　　　psychological statistics
  juvenile delinquency　　social policies and analysis　　working with groups

- Held offices and earned honors including: elected as president of the Social Work Club; elected vice president of Psi Chi Psychology Club; elected president of Sigma Omega Chi Honor Society; was honored with the "Outstanding Social Work Student Award."

EXPERIENCE

CRISIS INTERVENTION SOCIAL WORKER. Chickasaw County Department of Social Services (DSS), Waterloo, IA (1998-present). Learned how to locate and maximize community resources in ways that would make the most of benefits for clients while making determinations on potential clients' eligibility for financial assistance from federal, state, and local programs.

- Became skilled in assessing needs within the family as well as external factors that could lead to a family being considered at high risk for abuse.
- Gained experience in crisis intervention and in finding ways to defuse problems.
- Learned to read between the lines while interviewing and assessing client needs.

SOCIAL WORKER. Chickasaw County DSS, Waterloo, IA (1998). For the Chickasaw County JOBS (Job Opportunities and Basic Skills) program, assisted in the process of completing initial assessments of potential clients for the program which enabled participants to obtain an education and/or training for a career.

- Helped clients by developing case plans which included short-term and long-term goals.
- Ensured participants in the program received support in areas such as transportation, child care, tuition assistance, and educational tools; this support ensured clients were able to complete the program and find jobs which allowed them to be independent.
- Made home visits which gave the clients emotional and motivational assistance.

SOCIAL WORK INTERN. Iowa State University, Waterloo, IA (1997). Gained the respect of my superiors at the Chickasaw County DSS for my maturity and dedication to providing clients with a high quality of concerned services.

- Displayed organizational and written communication skills while developing and editing a 100-page resource manual for patients at a free health care clinic.
- Contributed to the community by seeing that information about this new one-of-a-kind clinic and other area resources for services were made available.
- Used my research skills to compile information from numerous sources into one manual.
- Analyzed statistical data collected from confidential questionnaires to give staff members insight into how the clients really felt about the department's programs.

PERSONAL

Am very persistent — will not give up until I am sure I have exhausted every possible source of assistance for my client. Have earned a reputation for my enthusiasm and energy.

Date

Exact Name of Person
Title or Position
Name of Company
Address (no., street)
Address (city, state, zip)

FAMILY & INDIVIDUAL COUNSELOR

Dear Exact Name of Person (or Dear Sir or Madam if answering a blind ad):

I would appreciate an opportunity to talk with you soon about how I could benefit your organization with my knowledge and experience in social work, family and individual counseling, case management, and resourcing allied health agencies.

As you will see from my resume, I offer a Master of Social Work degree and have gained excellent counseling experience during my recent fieldwork position providing individual/family counseling for dual-diagnosed children and adolescents. I am also expert at accessing school, community and allied health agency resources and programs, as well as liaising with professionals affiliated with these institutions.

My position as an editor for a medical bulletin refined my communication skills and has greatly assisted me in preparing accurate and concise treatment plans and other corresponding paperwork and documentation. While at both the University of Michigan and the Andrews Mental Health Clinic, I improved my understanding of medical administration, public relations, and successfully navigating bureaucratic red tape.

You would find me to be an honest, versatile professional dedicated to improving the quality of life of needy and troubled children and families.

I hope you will call or write me soon to suggest a time convenient for us to meet and discuss your current and future needs and how I might serve them. Thank you in advance for your time.

Sincerely,

Glory Y. Lassie

Alternate last paragraph:
I hope you will welcome my call soon to arrange a brief meeting at your convenience to discuss your current and future needs and how I might serve them. Thank you in advance for your time.

GLORY Y. LASSIE

1110½ Hay Street, Fayetteville, NC 28305   •   preppub@aol.com   •   (910) 483-6611

OBJECTIVE

To benefit an organization seeking a hard-working professional with excellent communication, planning, and organizational skills who possesses knowledge related to social work, social functioning, case management, and resourcing allied health agencies..

EDUCATION

Master of Social Work degree, University of Michigan, Ann Arbor, MI, 2001; completed coursework and fieldwork in one year.
Graduated *magna cum laude* with a **Bachelor of Social Work** degree, Kettering University, Flint, MI, 1999.

Completed a wide range of courses and workshops at the Andrews Mental Health Clinic, Flint, MI, including coursework in vocational rehabilitation, life events of adolescents, functional family therapy, children traumatized by violence, group counseling, accessing allied health services, reframing behavior to increase family functioning, posttraumatic stress syndrome in children, and the treatment, risks, and medication of clinical depression.

EXPERIENCE

THERAPIST. Andrews Mental Health Clinic, Ann Arbor, MI (2001-present). Gained valuable case management and therapy experience while performing my field work as an individual/family therapist for dual-diagnosed children and adolescents.
* Prepared treatment plans as well as other paperwork and documentation.
* Liaised with schools and community allied health agencies.
* Co-led substance abuse group.
* Member of Clinic Treatment Team.

EDITOR. Frontline Nursing Service, Vincennes, KS (2000-01). Excelled in researching, writing, editing, and designing camera-ready copy for a quarterly medical professional bulletin.
* Became proficient with Aldus, WordPerfect, Lotus 1-2-3, and other software.
* Produced a quality product within a tight deadline.

EXECUTIVE SECRETARY/PERSONNEL MANAGER. Simmons Children's Research Hospital, Flint, MI (1998-00). Provided secretarial support in addition to handling certain personnel management functions.
* Performed new employee orientation and handled all employee performance, wage, and benefit problems, in addition to maintaining employee information database.
* Compiled and wrote reports for referral to top-level management.

Held several different executive secretary and administrative support positions for various departments at the University of Michigan, Ann Arbor, MI:
ADMINISTRATIVE ASSISTANT. Child Development Center (1995-97). Handled all confidential materials pertaining to faculty and staff.
* Utilized allied health agencies resources and programs for patient referral.

PRINCIPAL SECRETARY. Deeds Hospital (1993-95). Promoted due to recognition by top-level management of my professionalism and initiative; managed the office and assisted the Executive Director of External Affairs.

PERSONAL

Am a dedicated professional aspiring to help improve both an individual's and a family's quality of life. Member of the National Association of Social Workers.

Date

Personnel Director
Reed Family Mental Health Center
180 New Road
Smithville, NM

FAMILY ADVOCACY SPECIALIST

Dear Sir or Madam:

I am responding to your advertisement in the newspaper for a Social Worker II. I am enclosing a resume along with the completed State Application for Employment PS-110.

I was quite excited when I read the ad in the newspaper because I offer all the skills and abilities you seek. Fluent in Spanish, I have counseled clients in both languages while providing case management services to individuals with a wide range of problems and impairments.

In my most recent job as a social worker, I served as the "subject matter expert" on family advocacy issues at a military community in Puerto Rico, and I implemented an innovative community education program for reporting abuse.

What my resume does not reveal is my affable nature and warm personality that is well suited to the social services field, which I truly enjoy. Although my chosen profession is one in which case workers encounter tragic and sad human realities on a daily basis, I am confident of my ability, refined through experience, to help anyone improve his or her situation.

I am an experienced social services professional who would enjoy contributing to your needs and goals, and I hope you will favorably review my application and call me to set up an interview at your convenience. Thank you in advance for your time.

Sincerely yours,

Jana G. Favors

JANA G. FAVORS

1110½ Hay Street, Fayetteville, NC 28305　　•　　preppub@aol.com　　•　　(910) 483-6611

OBJECTIVE

To contribute to an organization that can use a skilled social worker who is fluent in Spanish and who offers extensive education as well as "hands-on" experience in handling problems including child abuse, mental illness, and family violence.

EXPERIENCE

FAMILY ADVOCACY SPECIALIST. U.S. Army Family Support Division, Puerto Rico (2000-present). Played a key role in implementing and coordinating the Atlantic Family Advocacy Program at this military community in Puerto Rico; performed assessments of clients in crisis situations involving child or spouse abuse, and made appropriate referrals to military and civilian agencies.

- Both in Spanish and English, counseled clients on a short-term basis.
- Conducted surveys to identify deficiencies in services for abused spouses or children.
- Implemented an innovative community education program which included training programs for soldiers which publicized information and grounds for reporting suspected abuse.
- Trained military police, social services representatives, youth services staff, social services volunteers, as well as personnel in other organizations and agencies in the procedures for identifying and referring suspected child abuse.

EDUCATION SPECIALIST. U.S. Army, Ft. Benning, GA (1998-00). At this U.S. military base, worked as Training Coordinator in the Child Development Services Branch; advised and trained those providing day care to preschoolers on age-appropriate activities, and assured that centers/homes were arranged to enhance the physical, emotional, social, and cognitive development of children.

- Completed extensive assessments on each home or center module regularly.
- Planned training modules which were used as instructional guides for caregivers.
- Completed assessments/screenings of children identified as having problems such as development delay or behavioral difficulty.
- Gained valuable insight into the factors that cause stress in caregiving and counseled workers about how to anticipate, avoid, and cope with such problems.
- Provided both individual training as well as group sessions.

SCHOOL SOCIAL WORKER. Harper Institute of Special Habilation, Albuquerque, NM (1993-97). Worked with nearly every kind of social services problem while counseling individuals and families; dealt with problems associated with unhappy marriages, unwed parenthood, and financial difficulties as well as problems related to caring for the ill and handicapped.

- Developed programs appropriate for mentally retarded and Down's Syndrome children.
- Created educational materials and provided instruction related to first aid, sex education, nutrition, home management and home economics, and other areas.
- Became extensively involved in delinquency prevention; counseled juveniles.
- Worked closely with doctors to serve mentally and emotionally disturbed patients.

EDUCATION & TRAINING

Bachelor of Science (B.S.) degree, University of New Mexico, Albuquerque, NM, 1992. Completed extensive professional development training related to family advocacy, parent effectiveness, substance abuse, children's services, and programming services for the mentally and physically impaired.

PERSONAL

Am considered an experienced public speaker and have also completed extensive training related to preparing and delivering briefings. Truly enjoy the social services field.

May 24, 2002

Murray Center
Dept: XC
P.O. Box 33
Washington, DC

FAMILY RESOURCE
SPECIALIST

Dear Sir or Madam:

I would enjoy an opportunity to meet with you in person to discuss with you the ways in which I could become a valuable part of your team in the mental health and human services area. I am writing in response to your ad for a Habilitation Specialist II.

You will see from my resume that, since graduating with my B.S. degree from Cypress College in El Cajon, CA, I have worked in preventive medicine, coordinated treatment for the mentally retarded and physically disabled, provided crisis intervention services to children up to young adults, and developed "from scratch" a program providing services to at-risk families.

I am proud of the fact that I have made valuable contributions to every organization I have served. Even in my internship with the U.S. Army Medical Department, I became the department's first intern to receive an Army Achievement Award as a result of my efforts in research and program development. Most recently, I played a key role in developing a new program serving at-risk military families, and I taught a highly effective parenting class." In a prior job I worked in a short-term, inpatient crisis intervention hospital for children and won the highly respected "I Make A Difference" award in my first quarter of employment based on a secret election by peers and patients. A Qualified Mental Retardation Professional (QMRP), I have also coordinated programs for the mentally retarded and physically disabled.

You would find me in person to be a caring and enthusiastic young professional who genuinely thrives on the challenge of helping others. I can provide exceptionally strong personal and professional references.

I hope you will write or call me soon to suggest a time when we might meet to discuss your current and future needs and how I might serve them. Thank you in advance for your time.

Sincerely yours,

Charlene L. Eagle

CHARLENE L. EAGLE

1110½ Hay Street, Fayetteville, NC 28305 • preppub@aol.com • (910) 483-6611

OBJECTIVE

To benefit an organization that can use a human services and mental health professional who has earned a reputation as a compassionate hard worker while serving the needs of at-risk families, performing crisis intervention for children up through young adults, and coordinating programs for the physically disabled and mentally handicapped.

EDUCATION

B.S., **Community** *Health Education*, Cypress College, El Cajon, CA 1998.

EXPERIENCE

FAMILY RESOURCE SPECIALIST. Army Community Service (ACS), Italy (1998-present). In an essentially "entrepreneurial" role after being hired for one of two newly created positions, utilized my resourcefulness and enthusiasm in establishing a network throughout the community; developed a clientele of "at-risk" military families and eventually provided support services and education for over 100 families while personally handling a normal caseload of 20 families at any one time.
- Effective at earning the trust and respect of others, in numerous situations was the only professional in the community who could gain access to a home when problems arose.
- Made home visits to families at risk for spouse abuse or child neglect/abuse for the Family Advocacy Program; prepared home studies for prospective adoptive parents.
- Represented families' interests as an "expert" on the Family Advocacy Case Management Team; was a member of the Community Early Childhood Intervention Board.
- Maintained confidential case files while working closely with agencies or personnel.
- Taught a highly effective parenting class, as well as classes designed to teach household management skills, self-esteem and coping principles, and orientation classes.

MENTAL HEALTH ASSISTANT. South Park Hospital, El Cajon, CA (1997). In a short-term, inpatient crisis intervention hospital for children up through very young adults, provided one-on-one care to children and adolescents while organizing activities and schedules for nonmedical tasks and guiding informal group sessions.
- Was highly respected for my skills: in my first quarter of employment, was nominated for and won the "I Make a Difference Award" in a secret ballot by peers and patients.
- Through my ability to remain calm under pressure, was very effective at answering calls on the hospital's "hot line" and in counseling children and adolescents in crisis.

TREATMENT COORDINATOR. Lincoln Rehabilitation Center, El Cajon, CA (1995-97). For a client load of 21 mentally retarded/physically disabled adults, developed, oversaw, and evaluated personal programs which would increase their level of independence.
- Became a **Qualified Mental Retardation Professional (QMRP).**
- Was selected to serve on the Special Review Committee which made decisions on cases.
- Simultaneously volunteered as a **Children's Facilitator** with the city's Office of Mental Health: gained my first exposure to abused children and parents who were resistant to counseling while attending court-mandated programs.

PREVENTIVE MEDICINE INTERN. U.S. Army Medical Department, Ft. Dix, NJ (1989). Excelled in an internship created especially for me, and then became the department's first intern to be awarded an Army Achievement Award as a result of my initiative and accomplishments in research and program development. Interviewed 20 preventive medicine professionals and used the results to produce a comprehensive tool for the Community Health Nursing Department which is still being utilized.

PERSONAL

Am CPR and First Aid certified. Can provide strong personal and professional references.

Date

Exact Name of Person
Title or Position
Name of Company
Address (no., street)
Address (city, state, zip)

**FAMILY SERVICES
CASE WORKER**

Dear Exact Name of Person (or Dear Sir or Madam if answering a blind ad):

I would appreciate an opportunity to talk with you soon about how I could contribute to your organization through my experience in the social services field.

After earning my degree in Sociology with a concentration in Social Welfare from the University of Washington, I excelled as a Family Service Assistant with Project Headstart. I quickly earned a reputation as a self-starter with unlimited personal initiative while assisting with that highly worthwhile program which facilitates the development of eligible children.

Subsequently I have earned rapid promotion to increasing responsibilities as a Caseworker. Currently handling a heavy caseload of approximately 120 individuals, I am the "go-to" individual in charge of training junior social workers in the areas of Food Stamps and Workfirst. I am proud that I have become a "model" for others to follow in terms of my strong case management style as well as my ability to remain composed and gracious in stressful circumstances.

My husband and I are in the process of relocating to your area, and I am exploring opportunities with organizations which can use a talented problem solver and skilled manager of time and other resources. I offer a reputation as a congenial colleague who relates effectively to people at all organizational, social, and economic levels.

I hope you will write or call me soon to suggest a time when we might meet to discuss your goals and needs and how I might serve them. I feel certain that I could become a valuable and productive member of your team.

Sincerely yours,

Maria Knowles

MARIA KNOWLES

1110½ Hay Street, Fayetteville, NC 28305 • preppub@aol.com • (910) 483-6611

OBJECTIVE

To benefit an organization through my education and experience in the field of social work, including my ability to handle a heavy caseload in a well-organized manner, along with my dedication, compassion, and enthusiasm for helping others.

EDUCATION

B.A. in Sociology with a concentration in *Social Welfare*, University of Washington, Seattle, WA, 1998.
- Recognized for academic achievements while excelling in courses including Social Work Methods, Abnormal Behavior, Psychology of Personality, and Social Problems.
- Was on the Dean's List; earned academic scholarships from Delta Sigma Theta Sorority and from Holy Metropolitan AME Zion Church.
- Completed extensive training related to the Headstart Program, 2002.
- Completed training related to child abuse and other areas, 1998-present.

EXPERIENCE

Have excelled in a track record of promotion with the Tacoma Department of Social Services, Tacoma, WA:
2002-present: CASEWORKER II (T & F). Handle a heavy caseload of approximately 120 individuals while assuming the responsibility for interviewing and determining eligibility of low-income applicants for the Workfirst Program.
- Perform counseling as needed, contact collaterals and employers.
- Handle liaison with the full range of state and governmental agencies.
- Train new caseworkers and other workers.
- Take applications for Workfirst and Food Stamps.
1999-01: CASEWORKER I. Before being promoted to the job above, excelled in handling a heavy caseload of approximately 120 individuals while interviewing and determining eligibility of low-income applicants for the Workfirst Program.

FAMILY SERVICE ASSISTANT. Project Headstart, Tacoma, WA (1998-99). For a child development program for state-eligible children, assisted the component coordinator with the implementation of health, Social Services, and parent involvement goals.
- As a member of the Educational Board for Project Head Start, assisted other board members with any changes needed on the education plan for the program.

SUBSTITUTE TEACHER. Pacific Heights Forest Junior High, Pacific Heights, WA (1996-98). Taught both EMH and BEH classes in the absence of the regular teachers.
- Took over a classroom after the school lost its BEH teacher; researched appropriate methods of instruction for "special needs" students and designed the curriculum.

COUNSELOR. Coleridge Place, Seattle, WA (1995). Conducted counseling sessions and monitored residents; administered UA and BA tests.

EMERGENCY ASSISTANCE WORKER. Self-Reliance Program, Seattle, WA (1994-95). In this internship, aided in conducting counseling sessions and providing emergency assistance; coordinated the Crisis Intervention Program; handled a caseload.

ACTIVITIES

Served actively on campus organizations including holding office in an organization that performed community service work. Past member, Smart Start Board of Directors. Member of Washington Social Services Association. Member, Order of the Eastern Stars.

Date

Exact Name of Person
Exact Title
Exact Name of Company
Address
City, State, Zip

Dear Exact Name of Person (or Dear Sir or Madam if answering a blind ad):

With the enclosed resume, I would like to express my interest in exploring employment opportunities with your organization.

As you will see from my resume, I am a dedicated social worker with the proven ability to handle a heavy caseload. In my current position as a Social Worker I, I handle a caseload of 375 families as I work directly with families and children in the Department of Social Services' day care services. With an outstanding personal and professional reputation, I was rehired by the Department of Social Services in Clearwater in 1999 after returning to this area because I had previously served with distinction as a Social Worker for the department in 1994-95.

With a reputation as a versatile and adaptable professional, I relocated frequently with my husband, who was a military professional, and I can say with sincerity that I made contributions to every community in which we lived. In 2000, I received the prestigious Molly Pitcher Award and the Community Service Medal given by the commander of the military base in Bamburg, Germany, because of my leadership and community service.

You will see from my resume that I am fluent in Spanish and have a working knowledge of Italian. I have utilized my Spanish language skills in professional positions as a Teacher in high school and middle schools, and I have also worked as a College Instructor teaching Spanish.

I thoroughly enjoy the social work field, and I believe my well-organized nature and strong communication skills have been the keys to my success in a high-turnover profession. I truly thrive on the satisfaction of helping others, and I have become an outstanding investigator, problem solver, and administrator.

If you can use a congenial social worker with a proven ability to make contributions to my field, I hope you will contact me soon to suggest a time when we might meet to discuss your needs. I can provide excellent professional and personal references at the appropriate time. Thank you in advance for your time.

Sincerely,

Rae Lynn Deerfield

RAE LYNN DEERFIELD

1110½ Hay Street, Fayetteville, NC 28305   •   preppub@aol.com   •   (910) 483-6611

OBJECTIVE I want to contribute to an organization that can use a dedicated young social worker who offers experience in handling a large case load while providing quality social services and excellent administrative support to adolescents, children, and families.

EDUCATION **B.A. in Sociology with Psychology minor,** University of Richmond, VA, 1996. Received three special acknowledgments for my work in helping students in other clubs and organizations in my role as Student Government Fiscal Assistant.
A.A. degree in Psychology, Tidewater Community College, Portsmouth, VA, 1992.

HONORS Received the prestigious **Molly Pitcher Award**, 2000, and the **Community Service Medal** for my outstanding accomplishments in serving the community in Bamburg, Germany.

EXPERIENCE *Have been advancing to increased responsibilities with the Department of Social Services, Clearwater, FL; was rehired by the Department when I returned to Clearwater because I had excelled previously as a Social Worker in 1994-95:*
2000-present: SOCIAL WORKER I. Work in day care services handling a caseload of 375 families; work directly with children and families. Perform liaison with organizations including the Red Cross and United Way. Work with child protective services and foster care agencies in investigating abuse and neglect. Continue to serve as Hurricane Coordinator.

1999-2000: CASE WORKER I. Handled a caseload of 300 while determining income eligibility for Food Stamps; dealt with the frequent changes in clients' income levels and other factors influencing eligibility. Served as Hurricane Coordinator for Hurricane Floyd.

Highlights of previous experience:
1998: INSTRUCTOR, LIFE SKILLS. U.S. Government Youth Services Program, Germany. Excelled in this part-time job teaching life skills to children aged 5-18.
1996-97: TEST EXAMINER. Bamburg Education Center, Germany. Administered tests to military professionals related to job knowledge and skill levels.
1996: SUBSTITUTE TEACHER. U.S. Government Schools, Germany. Taught Spanish to middle and high schoolers; taught the elementary Smart Start curriculum.
1995: SPANISH INSTRUCTOR. Céntral Texas College, Ft. Bragg, NC. Taught entry-level Spanish to Special Forces students and helped them pass the Defense Language Proficiency Test which was a requirement for job advancement.
1994-95: SOCIAL WORKER. Department of Social Services, Clearwater, FL. Screened low-income families with dependent children in order to assess their needs for electricity, rent, and the resources to pay essential bills; counseled clients and helped them set priorities. Prepared paperwork to obtain federal funds or government money for verified needs.
1993-94: DAY CARE INTERN. Children's Hospital, Miami, FL. Worked with children who were physically battered, emotionally mistreated, mentally abused, or neglected. Learned about programs available for intervention; gained experience in placing children in foster care. Learned to deal with abusive personalities.
1992-93: SITE COORDINATOR. Relief Work, Miami, FL. Was responsible for hiring and supervising 60 people to help distribute goods and services to victims of Hurricane Andrew.

VOLUNTEER Active volunteer with the Red Cross and Habitat for Humanity, 1996-present.

PERSONAL Outgoing and caring individual who can provide excellent references. Physically fit.

Date

Larry Smith
Diamond Corporation
1222 Somerset Ave.
Charleston,SC

**FAMILY SERVICES
SOCIAL WORKER**

Mr. Smith:

I would appreciate an opportunity to talk with you soon about how I could contribute to the Department of Social Services as a field service representative for migrant workers.

As you will see from my resume, I currently work for the Department of Social Services and am involved in screening low-income families with dependent children to assess their needs for basic services and resources while counseling them and helping them set priorities. In a previous position I was involved in hiring 60 people to help distribute goods and services to victims of Hurricane Andrew, and I gained experience in working with the vast network of agencies and organizations that join hands to help people in such emergencies. I received special recognition for my leadership during that disaster from the city.

In prior experience I worked with abused and neglected children at Children's Hospital in Charleston, and I have spent much time helping people in rest homes.

Fluent in Spanish, I feel certain I could be a valuable asset to DSS as a field service representative to migrant workers. I have been told many times that I am "mature beyond my years" in terms of having common sense, and I do feel I am very effective in assuring that public funds are used for legitimate needs. I am very knowledgeable of the internal workings of the Department of Social Services.

I hope you will call or write me soon to suggest a time convenient for us to meet and discuss your current and future needs and how I might serve them. Thank you in advance for your time.

Sincerely yours,

Rita L. Chuck

RITA L. CHUCK

1110½ Hay Street, Fayetteville, NC 28305   •   preppub@aol.com   •   (910) 483-6611

OBJECTIVE   To contribute to society as a poised young social worker.

EDUCATION   **B.A. degree in Sociology with a minor in Psychology**, Jacksonville University, Jacksonville, FL, 1997.
A.A. degree in Psychology, Edison Community College, Fort Myers, FL, 1993.

LANGUAGES   Fluently speak Spanish and understand Italian.

EXPERIENCE   **SOCIAL WORKER**. Department of Social Services, Charleston, SC (2000-present). Screen low-income families with dependent children in order to assess their needs for electricity, rent, and the resources to pay other essential bills; counsel clients and help them set priorities.
- Prepare paperwork in order to obtain federal funds or government money for verified needs.
- Have learned to work tactfully and delicately with people in serious financial situations, and have also become skilled at counseling uncooperative people.
- Believe strongly in the value of working with other social workers to share ideas and to gain insight into the proper approaches to a client's problem.

DAY CARE INTERN. Children's Hospital, Charleston, SC (1999). In this hospital environment, gained insight into the many ways in which children are physically battered, emotionally mistreated, mentally abused, or neglected; also learned about the variety of programs and services which are available to provide intervention and problem solving for abusive parents and their children.
- Gained experience in placing children in foster care.
- Refined my ability to deal with abusive personalities and help some of them begin the path to recovery.

SITE COORDINATOR. Project Relief, Jacksonville, FL (1995-99). Handled the responsibility of hiring 60 people to help distribute goods and services to victims of Hurricane Andrew.
- Gained insight into how numerous relief agencies, social service agencies, and religious organizations work together in crisis; worked closely with the Salvation Army, Red Cross, and FEMA to provide medical aid, money, trailer homes, and other support.
- Used my counseling skills while helping people cope with the loss of loved ones and material assets; counseled people who were suddenly homeless as well as people who were suicidal.
- Saw first hand that finding satisfactory employment is often the key to regaining self-esteem, and was instrumental in helping many people find jobs.
- Received special recognition from the city for the leadership and organizational skills I provided during this natural disaster; also received a special award from the U.S. Army for my service and contributions.

SENIOR SECRETARY. Baroni & Associates, Tampa, FL (1991-94). Rapidly became a valuable and versatile worker in this small office; operated computers, handled filing, assisted in maintaining accounting entries, and became involved in both sales and financing.

PERSONAL   Have been told on many occasions that I am mature "beyond my years." Enjoy helping people, but hold to a basic principle that even people in need should not be allowed to take advantage of me personally or of the system which tries to serve their needs.

Date

Mr. Rick Smith
Camp Director
Youth Alternatives, Inc.
Camp Fun 'n Games
Loris, WY

Dear Rick:

With the enclosed resume, I would like to formally make you aware of my interest in the position as Social Services Coordinator with Youth Alternatives, Inc., at Camp Fun 'n Games.

As you already know, I have proudly played a key role in the successful establishment and implementation of the Loris facility as a Family Services Worker. While providing a positive role model to the youth we serve, I have always gone out of my way to encourage and assist my peers, and I have consistently and cheerfully shouldered the heaviest and most complex caseload. When I joined the Youth Alternatives organization in 2000, I excelled in handling extensive public relations responsibilities, and my efforts played a key role in generating the referrals we needed in order to make the program a success.

It is now my desire to serve the Youth Alternatives program as Social Services Coordinator, and I offer strong communication, mediation, consensus-building, and problem-solving skills which would be useful in such a supervisory role. I am respected by my peers for my ability to develop innovative and effective treatment plans, and other Family Workers routinely seek my guidance in a variety of areas. Because of my previous 10 years as an Adult Probation Officer, I am very knowledgeable of the resources available within the law enforcement and social services community, and I have established contacts within the public and private sector.

I am well known for my desire to take initiative and provide leadership when new concepts and new programs need a disciplined and resourceful professional. For example, when I was an Adult Probation Officer, I was honored by being selected as one of the state's first three House Arrest Officers, and I played a key role in pioneering the house arrest concept in Wyoming, which was adopted statewide. Similarly as a Family Services Worker, I used my initiative to start up a parents' group, and I now teach a monthly class attended by 12 or more parents. My public speaking and communication skills have been refined through my teaching responsibilities as well as through my involvement in graduation and other activities.

My commitment to the Youth Alternatives program is proven, and I am confident I could further enhance the program in Loris by assuming a supervisory role. I am confident that my strong skills in mediation, arbitration, consensus-building, and problem solving would be valuable assets in such a supervisory capacity.

Sincerely,

Nathaniel Bellweather

NATHANIEL BELLWEATHER

1110½ Hay Street, Fayetteville, NC 28305 • preppub@aol.com • (910) 483-6611

OBJECTIVE

I want to contribute to an organization that can use an experienced problem-solver and decision-maker who offers strong communication and organizational skills along with a proven ability to motivate, persuade, and inspire others.

EDUCATION

Bachelor of Arts (B.A.) degree in Human Services, Casper College, Casper, WY, 1990.
- Extensive coursework in Business Administration, Accounting, Economics, and Psychology. Extensive professional training related to arbitration, mediation, and problem solving; also completed extensive training in first aid and emergency procedures.

EXPERIENCE

FAMILY SERVICES WORKER. Youth Alternatives, Inc., Loris, WY (2000-present). Played a key role in the start-up of a new facility which provides a wilderness therapeutic environment with fully accredited school services for 60 youth aged 10-16 in grades 5-12; started over 30 years ago, and now the organization provides services in five states, mostly through state contracts.
- Performed extensive public relations in an effort to help establish this new facility; my activities helped to generate needed referrals as I "sold" the facility and the concept of the program to principals, guidance counselors, the social services community, and others. Served on the budget committee and assisted in fund-raising efforts.
- Have been a member of school accrediting committees and quality assurance committees; have conducted inspections of other camp operations.
- Work as part of a professional team comprised of three Family Workers and a supervisor; consistently manage the largest and most difficult caseload.
- Perform extensive interviewing and assessment while interviewing families and youth for potential placement in this out-of-home environment for youth at risk.
- Provide a positive role model for youth while also teaching a group class for parents attended by 12 people monthly; lead discussions on topics designed to facilitate good decision-making and refine parents' ability to communicate with their children.
- Assist youth in learning coping skills and techniques related to anger management.
- Handle a caseload of 20 youth, and prepare extensive written reports and correspondence.
- Have established a track record as an effective mediator through my ability to resourcefully build consensus and mediate/arbitrate controversial situations.

ADULT PROBATION OFFICER. Wyoming Department of Corrections, Cheyenne, WY (1990-00). Supervised a caseload of 147 probationers with 75% of them being felons.
- Communicated extensively with hundreds of social services agencies and law enforcement professionals in the course of doing my job.
- As an entry-level Probation Officer, handled a heavy volume of collections as I handled collection of restitution and court costs.
- In 1994, was honored by being selected as one the state's first three House Arrest Officers; pioneered the concept of house arrest and played a key role in its successful implementation. The program was subsequently adopted for use statewide.
- Learned how to interact effectively with judges, attorneys, and other agencies and professionally carried out the duties of an officer of the court.
- Became skilled in working with people from all backgrounds and learned how to treat others with respect, no matter what their circumstances, offenses, or character flaws.

PERSONAL

Highly motivated individual with outstanding skills in influencing and motivating others. Can provide outstanding personal and professional references.

Date

Exact Name of Person
Title or Position
Name of Company
Address (no., street)
Address (city, state, zip)

Dear Exact Name of Person (or Dear Sir or Madam if answering a blind ad):

I would appreciate an opportunity to talk with you soon about how I could benefit your organization with my knowledge and experience in social work, family and individual counseling, case management, and resourcing allied health agencies.

As you will see from my resume, I earned a Bachelor of Science degree in Social Work from East Carolina University and have subsequently gained excellent case management experience. During one fieldwork position, I provided foster home supervision and determined child removal to foster homes. I am skilled in accessing school, community and allied health agency resources and programs as well as liaising with professionals affiliated with these institutions.

My organizational and time-management abilities are excellent, as I was a full-time student while also working full-time to pay for my college expenses.

You would find me to be an honest, versatile professional dedicated to improving the quality of life of needy and troubled children and families.

I hope you will call or write me soon to suggest a time convenient for us to meet and discuss your current and future needs and how I might serve them. Thank you in advance for your time.

Sincerely,

Evangeline Pawson

Alternate last paragraph:
I hope you will welcome my call soon to arrange a brief meeting at your convenience to discuss your current and future needs and how I might serve them. Thank you in advance for your time.

EVANGELINE PAWSON

1110½ Hay Street, Fayetteville, NC 28305   •   preppub@aol.com   •   (910) 483-6611

OBJECTIVE

To benefit an organization seeking a hardworking professional with excellent communication, planning, and organizational skills, who possesses knowledge related to social work, social functioning, case management, and resourcing allied health agencies.

EDUCATION

Bachelor of Science degree in Social Work, with a concentration in Community Services, East Carolina University, NC, 1994; earned Dean's List honors.
Related courses include Process of Social Work Intervention, Interviewing Fundamentals, Social Legislation/Case Law, Social Research Methods, Human Behavior, Crisis Intervention, Introduction to the Exceptional Child, Police & the Community, and Social Environment.

EXPERIENCE

RAPE CRISIS VOLUNTEER. Dade County Rape Crisis Service, Miami, FL (2000-present). Serve as companion and victim advocate while providing emotional support, information, and encouragement to victims of sexual assault and their family members.
- Help maintain a 24-hour telephone service and meet with victims in the emergency room, law enforcement center, or the rape crisis office.
- Actively participate in fundraising events and health fairs; attend volunteer meetings.
- Maintain and respect confidentiality at all times.
- Refined essential intervention skills including active listening, communication, and the ability to interact with a broad variety of people.
- Learned both medical and legal aspects of rape including police and court procedures.

SOCIAL WORKER. Wake County Department of Social Services, Raleigh, NC (1995-2000). Gained valuable case management and social work experience while performing my field work as a foster care intern; became familiar with local, state, and federal regulations pertaining to foster homes.
- Determined relicensing of foster homes by observing child-foster parent interaction, interviewing children and foster parents, and documenting summaries of visits with the proper agencies.
- Assisted social team workers and court authorities in removal of children from parents for placement in foster homes.
- Conducted supervisory visits between children and biological parents.
- Provided a wide range of administrative functions, including reviewing professional manuals, participating in group discussions, and attending staff meetings.
- Liaised with schools and community allied health agencies; made applicable referrals.
- Assisted in deciding on-site child removal to foster homes
- Praised by evaluator for "taking advantage of every opportunity to learn about and visit community resources, and has liaised appropriately between client and referral sources."

Learned outstanding planning and time-management skills paying for my college expenses working a variety of jobs while simultaneously attending college full-time:
SUPERVISOR. Lady Sophisticates, Greenville, NC (1993-94). Refined my ability for easily establishing a rapport with people from diverse backgrounds while assisting in the daily operations of this upscale women's clothing store.

ADMINISTRATIVE ASSISTANT. East Carolina University Library Technical Services, Greenville, NC (1990-91). Provided book inventory, record keeping, shelving, customer-service, and data entry.

MEMBERSHIP

National Association of Social Work

Date

Exact Name of Person
Title or Position
Name of Company
Address (no., street)
Address (city, state, zip)

**GUIDANCE
COUNSELOR**

Dear Exact Name of Person (or Dear Sir or Madam if answering a blind ad):

I would appreciate an opportunity to talk with you soon about how I could contribute to your organization through my education in the areas of psychology, counseling, and guidance as well as through my motivational and communication skills.

As you will see from my resume, I offer strongly developed time management abilities as proven by my background which combines full-time work in a technical laboratory environment with college attendance. I am presently in graduate school where I am studying Psychology and Counseling at Illinois State University.

I feel that my practical experience, which has included rape crisis counseling and technical school-level field placement and guidance counseling, has helped prepare me to provide concerned care to clients. My background of work experience in medical settings and counseling skills make me a professional who could easily step into a medical counseling situation.

I hope you will welcome my call soon to arrange a brief meeting at your convenience to discuss your current and future needs and how I might serve them. Thank you in advance for your time.

Sincerely yours,

Leslie T. Arts

Alternate last paragraph:
I hope you will call or write soon to suggest a time convenient for us to meet and discuss your current and future needs and how I might serve them. Thank you in advance for your time.

LESLIE T. ARTS

1110½ Hay Street, Fayetteville, NC 28305   •   preppub@aol.com   •   (910) 483-6611

OBJECTIVE

To contribute to an organization that can use my well-developed interpersonal communication, counseling, and planning skills as well as my education and experience related to the areas of counseling and guidance and medical technology.

EDUCATION

Attend Illinois State University, Normal, IL, completing course work toward a **master's degree in Psychology and Counseling**.
B.A., Sociology, Illinois State University, Chicago, IL, 1992.
A.A., Human Resources, Kankakee Community College, Kankakee, IL, 1990.
Participated in a master's degree program in **Guidance Counseling**, Roosevelt University, Chicago, IL, 1990-91.

- Participated in an internship emphasizing field placement and guidance counseling in the career development office of Loyola Technical Community College, IL.
- Have completed specialized course work including the following:

child and adolescent development	theories of counseling
counseling techniques	career counseling
theories of personality	family counseling
group counseling	psychopathology
adult development and aging	tests and measurements

EXPERIENCE

MEDICAL TECHNOLOGIST. Mason Regional Hospital, Chicago, IL (2000-present). Handle a variety of functions including entering and retrieving laboratory data using specialized computer-linked systems, scheduling activities, and organizing work load.

- Provided concern and a calm, reassuring attitude while working directly with patients.
- Became known as a highly organized and skilled team member while working with medical personnel in emergency and critical care environments.
- Drew blood from patients as well as performing analytical tests on blood specimens, and other body fluids.

SUPERVISORY MEDICAL TECHNICIAN. University of Chicago Medical Center, Chicago, IL (1992-97). Advanced into leadership roles which included preparing work schedules, training other employees, evaluating job performance, and establishing lab procedures.

- Earned praise and advancement based on my organizational and motivational skills.
- Developed my written and verbal communication talents in actions including preparing standard operating procedures guidelines as well as training and counseling others.

COMPUTER KNOWLEDGE

Offer experience in using personal computers for word processing as well as in the entry of technical laboratory data.

TRAINING & CERTIFICATIONS

Was selected for a year of advanced medical lab training in military schools after excelling in the basic course and in my job performance.
Hold the following certifications:
National Certification #292344536, 1992.
American Medical Technologists #5064204, 1997.
Department of Health and Human Services certification as a Lab Technologist, 1995.

PERSONAL

With experience as a volunteer counselor at the Rape Crisis Center of Chicago, feel that I have a reputation for offering empathy and true concern for the problems of others.

Date

Shelly Smith
Director of Human Resources
Home Health and Hospice Care
P.O. Box 88
Goldsboro, NC 27533-0088

HIV CASE MANAGER

Dear Ms. Smith:

With the enclosed resume, I would like to make you aware of my interest in exploring employment opportunities with your organization. I hope you will recall that we spoke briefly at Youngstown First Presbyterian Church about two weeks ago, when we attended the wedding of a mutual friend, Cassanda Porque.

As I mentioned to you when we talked, I have been employed with Home Health and Hospice Care for about a year and a half. I want to grow with the organization and am especially interested in the position of HIV Case Worker. You will see from my resume that I am currently excelling as a Social Worker for HIV Case Management.

You will also see from my resume that I maintain a strong commitment to furthering my education in my field. I have earned both an associate's degree and a bachelor's degree, and I actively seek out opportunities to attend workshops and seminars that will enhance my knowledge and make me a better social worker.

I will call you soon to make sure that you have received the resume and to answer any questions you may have at that time. Thank you for your time. I look forward to talking with you again soon about how I can continue to contribute through my job knowledge, experience, and personal strengths and abilities.

Sincerely,

Amy Cashwell Brown

AMY CASHWELL BROWN

1110½ Hay Street, Fayetteville, NC 28305　•　preppub@aol.com　•　(910) 483-6611

OBJECTIVE

To continue working in Social Work or case management while applying my superior communication skills and my ability to handle crises; adapt easily to new situations.

EXPERIENCE

Have advanced in the following track record of responsibility within Home Health & Hospice Care, Inc., Tallahassee, FL.
2000-present: SOCIAL WORKER FOR HIV CASE MANAGEMENT. Work with the mentally ill, the elderly as well as juveniles, and criminal offenders.
- Perform comprehensive assessments of client's health care, psychosocial, environmental, and financial needs; develop and implement plans of care.
- Coordinate with multiple providers, programs, and agencies; work with CAP-DA and Personal Care.

1995-00: CERTIFIED HOME HEALTH CARE PROVIDER. Completed thorough and timely documentation of each client's care and progress.
- Continued to build a reputation for being able to adapt and fill in at various settings while working with people of widely varying personalities, economic classes, social levels, and cultures as well as all races and ages of people (with an emphasis on HIV patients).
- Worked with CAP-DA and Personal Care.

Worked with disturbed youth and adolescents and applied principles of behavior modification:
BEHAVIORALLY EMOTIONALLY HANDICAPPED (BEH) ASSISTANT. Orange County Schools, Orlando, FL (1992-95). Worked closely with teachers at Stafford Elementary School while monitoring progress in the areas of developing and improving behavior and social skills.
- Completed activities with an emphasis on crisis intervention, preparing support documentation, and the application of effective behavior modification techniques.

YOUTH PROGRAM ASSISTANT (YPA) I. Orange County Mental Health Association, Orlando, FL (1991-92). For an intensive youth services organization, worked with adolescents and children, including juvenile offenders and the mentally ill, while emphasizing effective behavior modification techniques.
- Worked with Developmentally Disabled (DD) and Mentally Retarded (MR).
- Established goals and provided crisis intervention services.
- Prepared periodic progress reports on clients; made decisions on methods of achieving proper behavior and the development of social skills.

CUSTOMER SERVICE REPRESENTATIVE. Four County Electric Membership Cooperative, Miami, FL (1989-90). Ensured a high quality of service and support for customers while assisting in office operations: data processing, typing, faxing, and processing payments.

While attending college, also gained practical work experience in jobs including: PROGRAM ASSISTANT for a Dade County Mental Health-sponsored Adult Developmental Acclimation Program and SUPERVISOR at Orange Grove Family Care Home, Miami, FL.

EDUCATION & TRAINING

B.S. in Criminal Justice with a minor in Sociology, Florida State University, FL, 1995.
Associate of Applied Science degree, Miami-Dade Community College, Miami, FL, 1993.
Certification: Certified Case Manager; completed HIV Case Management Training, AIDS Care Branch of the Division of Epidemiology.

Exact Name of Person
Title or Position
Name of Company
Address (no., street)
Address (city, state, zip)

HOUSING ADVOCATE

Dear Exact Name of Person (or Dear Sir or Madam if answering a blind ad):

I would appreciate an opportunity to talk with you soon about how I could contribute to your organization through my experience as a Housing Advocate and Community Support Specialist.

As you will see from my resume, I earned my degree in Social Work and worked at night in a full-time job in order to finance my education. Currently I am wearing two "hats" as I function in twin roles. As a Housing Advocate, I develop and maintain effective working relationships with local housing authorities in order to assure the availability of affordable housing for low-income families. Simultaneously as a Community Support Specialist, I assist case managers in a residential program for mentally ill clients.

Through these simultaneous positions, I have greatly refined my time management skills as well as my ability to establish strong bonds with community leaders and decision makers.

I am in the process of relocating to your area, and I am exploring opportunities with organizations which can use a talented problem solver and skilled manager of time and other resources. I offer a reputation as a congenial colleague who relates effectively to people at all organizational, social, and economic levels.

I hope you will write or call me soon to suggest a time when we might meet to discuss your goals and needs and how I might serve them. I feel certain that I could become a valuable and productive member of your team.

Sincerely yours,

Eloise Witherspoon

ELOISE J. WITHERSPOON

1110½ Hay Street, Fayetteville, NC 28305   •   preppub@aol.com   •   (910) 483-6611

OBJECTIVE   To contribute to an organization that can use a cheerful hard worker who offers an education and experience related to social work and human services.

EDUCATION   **Bachelor of Arts (B.A.) degree in Social Work**, California State Polytechnic University, Pomona, CA, December 1994; worked at night to finish this degree while managing a business during the day.

EXPERIENCE   *Applied my communication and people skills in these simultaneous positions, Tacoma, WA, 2000-present:*
HOUSING ADVOCATE. Pierce County AIDS Foundation (PCAF). Fill a high-visibility role as liaison and coordinator for activities of the PCAF which has the mission of improving the general public's understanding of AIDS, preventing its spread, and assisting AIDS/HIV patients.
- During this program's first year as a grant recipient, administered funds and refined my public speaking skills representing the organization at numerous meetings and while training staff members and volunteers.
- Develop and maintain relations with county and city housing authorities in order to expand the availability of safe and affordable housing for clients.
- Screen and assess applicants for the nine subsidized units for homeless AIDS patients; maintain the waiting list and make decisions on filling vacancies.

COMMUNITY SUPPORT SPECIALIST. Greater Lakes Mental Health Foundation. Assist case managers in a residential program for mentally ill adults by providing one-on-one preparation designed to aid in future independent living while regularly assessing and reporting on their progress.
- Provide liaison with community agencies in order to ensure each person receives all services available to help them reach their goals.

Prior experience:
ELIGIBILITY WORKER. County of San Bernardino, San Bernardino, CA (1995-00). Performed assessments of clients to determine eligibility for medical assistance in the form of Medi-Cal; became skilled in handling a heavy case load and became known for my accuracy in preparing large volumes of paperwork.
- Became acquainted with the vast interlocking network of social services organizations, and referred clients to those agencies and organizations as appropriate.
- Assisted clients in preparing personal budgets and managing their finances.
- Earned a reputation as a compassionate counselor and effective motivator while treating people from all walks of life with dignity.

OFFICE MANAGER'S ASSISTANT. M.T.S. Insurance Service, Brea, CA (1990-95). As the "right arm" of a busy office manager in a fast-paced insurance office, excelled in activities ranging from word processing, to invoicing, to customer service.

DATA ENTRY OPERATOR. The Broadway, Los Angeles, CA (1988-90). Used WordPerfect 5.1 while inputting data provided by sales associates; worked with customers in establishing delivery dates, and verified financial/accounting transactions.

PERSONAL   Am a patient, calm person who can handle a heavy work load and not get stressed out by tight deadlines. Have been told many times that I am a gifted counselor and communicator.

CAREER CHANGE

Date

HUMAN RELATIONS SPECIALIST

This individual seeks to return to a human services environment. He has been working in a profit-making business most recently, but he has structured his cover letter so that his previous experience is emphasized.

Dear Sir or Madam:

With the enclosed resume, I would like to express my interest in your organization and acquaint you with my skills and experience related to your needs.

As you will see from my resume, I hold a B.A. in Human Relations degree which I put to good use immediately after college when I served for 11 years as a District Executive with the Boy Scouts of America. In that capacity, I managed districts in Maine, Vermont, and Delaware and was responsible for recruiting, training, financial administration, program planning and management, and community liaison. Since Boy Scouts of America is an organization devoted to shaping youth in moral, ethical, and spiritual ways while teaching leadership ability as well as a variety of skills useful throughout life, I was continually involved in training and counseling young people. I acted as Director of Summer Camp operations during the summers, which involved planning and managing summer camp experiences for thousands of boys trying to earn Merit Badges and acquire skills in areas ranging from carpentry to first aid. I am a skilled counselor and program manager.

As a result of my involvement with the Boy Scouts, I gained numerous technical and mechanical skills which I subsequently put to use in production and manufacturing environments.

If you can use a dependable and experienced individual who offers a proven ability to adapt easily to new situations and rapidly master new tasks, I hope you will contact me. I enjoy being in a position in which I can help others, and I offer highly refined skills in dealing with the public. I can provide excellent personal and professional references at the appropriate time, and I hope I will have the pleasure of talking with you soon in person.

Yours sincerely,

Victor Amante

VICTOR AMANTE

1110½ Hay Street, Fayetteville, NC 28305 • preppub@aol.com • (910) 483-6611

OBJECTIVE I want to benefit an organization that can use a versatile professional who offers excellent counseling, training, administrative, and human resources skills along with extensive technical knowledge which I have applied in manufacturing and production environments.

EDUCATION Graduated with a **B.A. in Human Relations**, St. Joseph's College, Standish, ME.
• Previously completed courses at University of Maine before transferring to St. Joseph's. Completed extensive executive training sponsored by the Boy Scouts of America. Graduated from Davidson High School.
• Achieved the rank of **Eagle Scout.**

EXPERIENCE **STORE MANAGER.** Jenkins Enterprises, Standish, ME (2001-present). Worked at Joe's Convenience Store and Gas Station serving customers, stocking inventory, and operating a cash register.
• Was known for my honesty and attention to detail in handling and accounting for cash.

RESTAURANT MANAGER. Restaurants in Standish, ME (1998-01). Gained extensive experience in food service while working as Kitchen Manager and Manager at popular restaurants including The Chicken House and Miguel's Restaurant.

DISTRICT EXECUTIVE, BOY SCOUTS OF AMERICA. Boy Scout Units in Delaware, Maine, and Vermont (1982-98). After graduating from college, completed training to become an executive in this unique organization dedicated to helping youth grown morally as well as in numerous skills.

• In an essentially entrepreneurial role, was in charge of starting new units, recruiting and training volunteer leaders, and providing leadership to multiple units in the district.

• Was a frequent public speaker at scouting events.

• Handled extensive financial management responsibility; assisted in planning and administering a budget, and implemented aggressive fundraising campaigns to achieve ambitious budgetary goals.

• Was constantly involved in training and retraining adult leaders and youth leaders. Counseled adults and youth in personal, financial, and organizational areas; was known for my approachable manner and ability to relate to others easily.

• Acted as Director of Summer Camp operations which were week-long experiences in which boys earned Merit Badges; formulated the programs designed to help boys achieve those Merit Badges, hired and trained counselors, ordered supplies, and was responsible for a vast amount of property and equipment at each camp serving hundreds of boys each summer.

• Refined my counseling and communication skills while advising and nurturing troubled and impatient youth; helped young boys set and achieve high goals.

PERSONAL Can provide outstanding personal and professional references.

Date

Exact Name of Person
Exact Title
Exact Name of Company
Address
City, State, Zip

Dear Exact Name of Person (or Dear Sir or Madam if answering a blind ad):

With the enclosed resume, I would like to make you aware of my background in human services as well as my reputation as a resourceful and articulate professional who excels in helping others identify and resolve problems.

I grew up in Hampton and have recently relocated here to be near my aging parents. I am looking forward to continuing my career here and becoming reacquainted with this area as I make it my permanent home.

As you will see from my resume, I offer a reputation as an innovative and creative manager who excels in developing methods and procedures which allow human services programs to reach their target population and make a difference in their lives. My versatile background has included an emphasis on family preservation and providing home and community-based services for at-risk clients.

In my most recent job with the The Youth Center in Houston, TX, I was recruited to work with a population with mental health problems and provide assessment and treatment through individual, group, and family therapy. Prior to this job, I joined the Family Preservation Program and was responsible for its inception and effectiveness in handling a caseload of referrals from the Juvenile Courts. This program's emphasis was on reaching at-risk youth and helping prevent them from being placed in training schools by intervening with intensive counseling and support.

If you can use an experienced, compassionate, and effective professional who has long been recognized for uncompromising personal standards, I hope you will contact me soon to suggest a time when we might meet to discuss your needs. I can assure you in advance that I can provide outstanding references and could quickly become an asset to your organization.

Sincerely,

Adam Delph

ADAM DELPH

1110½ Hay Street, Fayetteville, NC 28305 • preppub@aol.com • (910) 483-6611

OBJECTIVE
To offer a distinguished background in human services counseling to an organization that can use a resourceful, articulate, and mature professional with strong management and communication skills along with a talent for identifying and resolving problems.

EDUCATION
M.Ed. in Counseling, Texas Southern University, Houston, TX, 1999.
B.S. in Psychology, Salt Lake City College, Salt Lake City, UT, 1988.
Graduated from Hampton High School, Hampton, VA.

TRAINING
Completed extensive professional seminars and training programs on family therapy,

EXPERIENCE
HUMAN SERVICES CLINICAL COUNSELOR. The Youth Center, Houston, TX (1996-present). Recruited for this job working with a population experiencing mental health problems, provide assessment and treatment services for families experiencing psychiatric, psychological, behavioral, developmental, and/or substance abuse difficulties.
- Work with clients in individual, family, and group therapy settings.
- Assess treatment needs.
- Open and maintain medical records.
- Prepare and submit requests for service authorizations.
- Provide intensive home/community-based family preservation services based on individual client and family strengths and need.

SUPERVISOR, FAMILY PRESERVATION PROGRAM. Eyes on Youth, Inc., Triton, UT (1992-96). Joined this agency when the Family Preservation Program was in the planning stages and was responsible for its inception and effectiveness in helping clients who consisted of troubled youth and families.
- Developed the model for delivering services by promoting collaboration with the Juvenile Court system in order to reduce the need for placing young offenders in training school programs.
- Trained and supervised two family preservation counselors and assisted in the development of treatment plans.
- Handled an active caseload of referrals from the Juvenile Courts and provided clients with intensive in-home, family-based placement prevention services.

DIRECTOR, INFORMATION AND REFERRAL/ASSESSMENT CENTER. Salt Lake Community College, Salt Lake City, UT (1983-92). Co-authored the grant which resulted in the $46,000 used to start up this new center which provided counseling services to evening college students.
- Coordinated planning and designed the procedures for the center which provided services which included assessment, career planning, and counseling as well as admissions testing and academic support.

PROFESSIONAL AFFILIATIONS
Past President, Utah Family-based Services Association, Triton, UT, region.
Past President, Guilford County Council on Youth.
Trainer, Assurance, Inc., family preservation services.

PERSONAL
Have relocated to Hampton where I grew up and am looking forward to making it my permanent home. Excellent references on request.

Date

Personnel Director
Parenting, Inc.

Dear Sir or Madam:

I am writing in response to your newspaper advertisement, soliciting applicants for the position of Family Support Group Coordinator. With the enclosed resume, I would like to make you aware of my background as a motivated and highly experienced human services professional with a strong background in juvenile corrections and the counseling of at-risk juveniles and their families.

In my most recent job at the Hanson Youth Institution, I have proven my dedication and ability, performing a dual role as Juvenile Corrections Officer and Case Manager. I have consistently excelled in these positions, supervising as many as 70 juvenile offenders while reviewing the cases of 6-8 clients to determine possible eligibility for reduction in sentencing or other rewards for good behavior. In previous positions as a Resource Teacher, Rehabilitation Specialist, and volunteer for the Guardian ad Litem program, I have shown my commitment to protecting and promoting the best interests of at-risk juveniles and insuring that they are provided with the counseling and services they need.

As you will see, I hold an Associate of Applied Science degree in Human Services from Northern State University, although I have supplemented with additional training courses. I believe that my strong combination of education and experience will be a great asset to any organization. Although I am highly regarded by my present employer and can provide excellent references at the appropriate time, I feel that my skills and talents would be better utilized in a direct-service, family-support environment.

If the Parenting, Inc. program could use a highly motivated, experienced human services professional with exceptional organizational and problem-solving skills and a background in providing support and services to juveniles, I hope you will contact me soon to discuss your needs. I can assure you in advance that I have an excellent reputation within the community and could quickly become a valuable addition to your organization.

Sincerely,

Abner Jerome Smith

ABNER JEROME SMITH

1110½ Hay Street, Fayetteville, NC 28305   •   preppub@aol.com   •   (910) 483-6611

OBJECTIVE

To benefit an organization that can use a highly motivated, experienced human services professional with a strong background in the counseling of at-risk juveniles and their families.

EDUCATION

Associate of Applied Sciences in Human Services, Northern State University, Aberdeen, SD, 1997.

Area Behavioral Health Services Training course, Slade Mental Health Center, Seven Lakes, SD, 2001.

Effective Teaching Training course, Northern State University, Aberdeen, SD, 2001.

EXPERIENCE

JUVENILE CORRECTIONS OFFICER/CASE MANAGER. South Dakota Department of Corrections, Hanson Youth Institution, Hoffman, SD (2000-present). At Hanson, currently perform two jobs with one salary, serving on the case management team in addition to my regular duties as a Juvenile Corrections Officer.
- Supervise as many as 70 juvenile offenders in addition to handling a caseload of six to eight clients whose cases have come up for review by the team.
- As a member of the Case Management Team, perform client assessments and make recommendations for changes in custody status.
- Counsel juvenile offenders and act as liaison between families and clients.
- Transport inmates to and from the facility in approved departmental vehicles.
- Give supervisory direction to juvenile offenders, and ensure compliance with local, state, and federal guidelines and policies.
- Perform computer data entry of client information and specifics of case files.

RESOURCE TEACHER. Mason County Board of Education, Redding, SD (1999-2000). Excelled in this position while working full-time and accepting increasing responsibilities at Hanson; was responsible for 17 students who were classified as "slow learners."
- Gathered materials to supplement regular classroom assignments and ensured that students stayed on-task with regular class work.
- Created and implemented lesson plans to maximize the interest and participation of the class and stimulate intellectual and emotional growth of each student.
- Developed different educational plans for each sub-group of 5-6 students, based on their differing levels of ability.

REHABILITATION TECHNICIAN. A.B.C. Services, Inc., Morris, SD (1996-1999). Educated and assisted mentally handicapped adults in a group home setting, helping them to recognize and achieve their potential and work toward living more independently.
- Implemented individual plans of care and documented client's progress accordingly.
- Administered medication according to doctor's orders.

VOLUNTEER, GUARDIAN AD LITEM PROGRAM. 20th Judicial District, Rose County Court House, Morris, SD (1995-1996). Protected and promoted the best interests of at-risk juveniles entering the court system due to allegations of abuse or neglect.
- Represented the juvenile in court and conducted follow-up investigations to determine the facts, assess the needs of the juvenile, and locate resources within the community to meet those needs.
- Discussed and explored options with the judge at the dispensation hearings to insure that the needs of the juvenile were being met.

PERSONAL

Outstanding personal and professional references are available upon request.

**INCOME
MAINTENANCE CASE
WORKER**

Dear Sir or Madam:

With the enclosed resume, I would like to make you aware of my interest in exploring employment opportunities with your organization upon my recent permanent relocation to New Jersey. I have just spent nearly two years in Oregon caring for my aging father, who had suffered a stroke. He has recovered, and I am returning permanently to New Jersey, which is my home.

As you will see from my resume, I am licensed and certified as a Social Worker by the State of New Jersey and offer seven years of experience with the Atlantic County Division of Economic Assistance in Atlantic City. You will note that I advanced rapidly with this agency. I was promoted to Income Maintenance Case Worker and was being groomed for promotion to Eligibility Specialist. I provided excellent support in several departments of this agency as I dealt with a wide range of clients as well as with attorneys and other professionals in the social services field.

I received advanced training in mediation and arbitration and earned my B.S. degree in Business Administration while excelling academically. With a reputation as a mature professional who thrives on challenges and pressure, I am skilled in taking on multiple simultaneous responsibilities and ensuring that each area is handled in a timely manner and with total accuracy.

In previous positions, I refined my communication and problem-solving skills working in human services, customer service, and bookkeeping/accounting jobs as well as in one position as a Police Dispatcher.

I hope you will contact me if you can use my experience and expertise in your agency. I would be delighted to make myself available for a personal interview at your convenience. Excellent professional and personal references will, of course, be available at the appropriate time.

Sincerely,

Heidi Stevens

HEIDI STEVENS

1110½ Hay Street, Fayetteville, NC 28305   •   preppub@aol.com   •   (910) 483-6611

OBJECTIVE

To offer superior motivational and communication skills to an organization that can benefit from my extensive experience in the social work and social services field as well as my adaptability shown in sales and office jobs and while utilizing automated systems.

EDUCATION

B.S. degree in Business Administration, with a concentration in Finance, Seaport State University, OR, 1990.

TRAINING AND CERTIFICATION

Received advanced training in mediation and arbitration.
Was licensed and certified as a Social Worker by the State of New Jersey, 2000.

EXPERIENCE

INCOME MAINTENANCE CASE WORKER. Atlantic County Division of Economic Assistance, Atlantic City, NJ (1994-present). Progressed rapidly to hold increasing levels of responsibility culminating in this job with a caseload of 100 clients.

- Promoted from Income Maintenance Technician, was being groomed for further promotion to Eligibility Specialist before voluntarily resigning to move to New Jersey to be near my aging parents and tend to my father who has recovered from a stroke.
- As an Income Maintenance Case Worker from 1998 to 2001: interviewed and processed food stamps and AFDC (Aid to Families with Dependent Children) applications for welfare recipients.
- Was selected to attend advanced training and seminars in crisis intervention along with technical training on applications using Dell computers.
- Maintained up-to-date awareness of agency policies and procedures in order to provide clients with all possible assistance in a timely manner.
- Gathered information through interviews, correspondence, and home visits and made initial determinations and redeterminations of eligibility.
- As an **Income Maintenance Technician from 1995 until my 1998 promotion,** interviewed clients and processed applications for aged and disabled clients in order to determine their eligibility for home care, nursing home, residential home, or hospice care.
- Worked closely with other professionals including attorneys and nursing home personnel in order to assure client services were provided according to guidelines.
- In my first job with this agency, was hired for the child care unit to assist clients in finding reliable caregivers and allow them to attend programs focusing on life skills, job readiness and searches, training, and employment offered by the county.
- Applied time management and organizational skills in a simultaneous 1999-01 job as a **Sales Representative** for group and individual life insurance products; refined computer skills while inputting data gathered from prospective customers by phone.

CUSTOMER SERVICE REPRESENTATIVE. Wildwood National Bank, Wildwood, NJ (1991-94). Handled a variety of daily activities including assisting customers opening accounts, entering data into computers, answering questions about bank services and products, and checking teller totals to ensure they balanced.

Highlights of earlier experience: Excelled in earlier jobs as a **Police Department Dispatcher, Bookkeeper, and Accounting Clerk.**

PERSONAL

Enjoy facing challenges and thrive under pressure. Am dedicated to finding a way to get things done and will not stop trying until I accomplish my goals. Excellent references.

Date

Personnel Committee
CC Partnership for Children
4200 Bradley Boulevard
Williamsburg, VA 78314

Dear Sir or Madam:

I would appreciate an opportunity to talk with you soon about how I could contribute to your organization through my proven leadership and management abilities along with my planning, organizational, and communication skills.

You will see from my enclosed resume that I am a hard worker who has excelled in working with numerous organizations providing services to children. Currently working at the Chatham County Department of Social Services, I have become knowledgeable of early childhood/family programs serving this culturally diverse community while determining client eligibility for income maintenance programs.

While earning my B.S. degree in Psychology and Human Development, I worked in two internships. In one internship, I assisted in setting up a new preschool facility within the Head Start program, and in the other internship, I worked as a teacher at a childcare facility. As a Hotline Counselor for a women's shelter while completing my degree, I helped women and children caught in situations of domestic violence and child abuse. I have also worked with Planned Parenthood, organizing portfolios about child sexuality and facilitating discussions with teenagers about sex. First Aid qualified, I am familiar with several popular software programs including Word and Excel.

You would find me in person to be an empathetic and caring person who is known for my positive, optimistic, and enthusiastic approach to life. I offer a reputation for being "mature beyond my years," and I have a strong desire to work in an area in which I am setting up new partnerships and ventures that enrich people's lives.

I hope you will write or call me soon to suggest a time when we might meet to discuss your needs and goals and how I might contribute to them. Thank you in advance for your time.

Sincerely yours,

Harriet E. Cleaver

HARRIET E. CLEAVER

1110½ Hay Street, Fayetteville, NC 28305   •   preppub@aol.com   •   (910) 483-6611

OBJECTIVE

I want to contribute to an organization that can use a confident and empathetic young professional who offers exceptionally strong leadership and communication skills.

EDUCATION

Bachelor of Science degree, **Psychology** and **Human Development**, Raymond University, Raymond, VA, 1998.
- Was elected **President** of Psi Chi Psychology Honor Society; used my leadership and motivational skills to increase morale and boost pride.
- Nominated "Outstanding Student" by Psi Chi Advisor.
- Served as a coordinator of Appalachian Conference on Behavioral Neurodynamics.

COMPUTERS

Familiar with Word, Excel, and a variety of software packages used by the Department of Social Services.

EXPERIENCE

INCOME MAINTENANCE CASEWORKER. Chatham County Department of Social Services, Chatham, AL (2000-present). Gained knowledge of and experience in administering early childhood/family programs serving this culturally diverse community while determining client eligibility for income maintenance programs; interviewed clients, verified information through third parties, explained program requirements and options, and referred clients to alternate services.
- Processed automated information.
- Have gained an excellent understanding of what resources are available to people seeking federal or state assistance.

HEAD COUNSELOR (SUMMER). Jewish Community Center, Chatham, AL (1999). Excelled in this seasonal job planning and supervising summer activities for children.

HOTLINE COUNSELOR. Women's Resource Center, Hot Springs, AL (1997-98). While earning my college degree, volunteered at a women's shelter helping women and children caught in situations of domestic violence and child abuse; processed new residents, referred callers to other appropriate agencies, and counseled hotline callers.
- With a reputation for being "mature beyond my years," was commended for my compassionate style as well as for my resourcefulness in "thinking on my feet" in emergencies.

INTERNSHIP: EDUCATION COORDINATOR. Head Start, Dolby, AL (1997). Assisted in setting up a new preschool facility/program as part of an internship related to earning my B.S. degree; learned how children with developmental delays can affect a classroom.

INTERNSHIP: TEACHER. Little Angels Playschool, Wheeling, AL (1996). In an internship from January-April, worked with teachers and parents while supervising children and ensuring their needs were met.

Prior jobs in which I have excelled include **EDUCATION COORDINATOR**, Wheeling, AL (1995) and three positions as **ASSISTANT TEACHER** Vamoose, AL (June-August 1995 and July-August 1996), and Macon, AL (January-April 1994).

PERSONAL

Am First Aid trained and qualified. Have a way of relating to people so that they see me as a friend and role model. Consider myself a good listener who is open-minded and flexible.

Date

**JUVENILE
COUNSELOR**

Dear Sir or Madam:

Can you use a poised communicator and effective problem solver with proven skills in the area of counseling?

As you will see by my enclosed resume, I offer extensive counseling experience through a combination of training, volunteer work, and positions in intake counseling, dispute resolution, and as a Social Worker with the Case County Department of Social Services.

In addition, you would find me to be a friendly professional with solid decision-making skills and the ability to be firm and remain fair and unbiased. I relate very well to people of all backgrounds. I would like to contribute my dedication and strong work ethic to become a valuable and productive member of your team.

I hope you will contact me soon to suggest a time convenient for us to meet and discuss your current and future needs and how I might serve them. Thank you in advance for your time.

Sincerely,

Randy Castillo

RANDY CASTILLO

1110½ Hay Street, Fayetteville, NC 28305   •   preppub@aol.com   •   (910) 483-6611

OBJECTIVE

To benefit an organization needing a versatile young professional with "top-notch" abilities in communication, leadership, and problem-solving.

EDUCATION

Bachelor of Science in **Criminal Justice** with a concentration in **Social Work**, Newport State University, Newport, RI, 1996; selected to **Who's Who Among College Students**.
- Completed internship with the Case County Adult Probation Division.

EXPERIENCE

HUMAN RESOURCES PLACEMENT SPECIALIST and **SOCIAL WORKER.** Case County Department of Social Services, Newport, RI (2001-present). Provide placement counseling and assistance to a heavy caseload of client families under the Work First program (TNF, FS, MIC).
- Create employment plans, working with clients and community resource representatives.
- Cultivate and maintain excellent working relationships with a number of community organizations in order to provide the necessary services for clients.
- Develop effective problem-solving skills, instilling clients with a desire to increase their independence.

CASE WORKER I. Case County Department of Social Services, RI (1998-2001). Interviewed clients to determine if they were eligible for food stamps and processed cases in a timely manner; suggesting alternate programs they might be eligible for.
- Received Computer-Based Training (CBT) in Aid for Families with Dependent Children (AFDC) and Adult Medicaid — extensive classroom training in adult Medicaid.
- Served as Chairman of I MAAC, an in-house group of caseworkers selected by our peers to represent all caseworkers concerning training and testing needs.

DISPUTE RESOLUTION MEDIATOR. Case County, RI (1995-1998). Licensed by the State of Rhode Island to mediate the resolution of conflicts in court-referred cases involving juveniles and adults.

JUVENILE INTAKE COUNSELOR. Victim/Offender Reconciliation Program, Case County, RI (1994-95). Use problem-solving techniques to help juvenile offenders and their victims understand causes and effects of crime while providing counseling and mediation.

JUVENILE COUNSELOR. Case Juvenile Detention Center, Newport, RI (1992-94). Maintained security and safety for 20-30 young men and women between the ages of eight and 17. Conducted group and one-on-one counseling sessions at any given time; counseled the families along with their child at the request of the family.

PURCHASING CLERK. Folsom Valley Medical Center, Newport, RI (1990-92). Handled the purchasing, shipping, and receiving of hospital supplies at a major medical center, which involved interpreting inventory data to make appropriate ordering decisions.

SPECIAL TRAINING

SECTION LEADER. Navy Reserves, West End, RI (1988-90). Supervised 15 people while excelling in special training courses, dispute resolution, mediation, and victim's rights.

ACTIVITIES

Counseled an 11-year-old youth in the Governor's **One-on-One Find-a-Friend Program** and won the **Community Service Award** through my participation in the Criminal Justice Club at Newport State University.

CAREER CHANGE

Date

Exact Name of Person
Exact Title
Exact Name of Company
Address
City, State, Zip

JUVENILE COUNSELOR

Dear Exact Name of Person (or Dear Sir or Madam if answering a blind ad):

With the enclosed resume, I would like to make you aware of my background as an educated young professional with exceptional communication and organizational skills who offers a track record of success in paralegal, community probation, juvenile counseling, and library environments.

In my most recent position as a Library Technician for the U.S. Army Library at Larson Barracks in Germany, I provided a wide range of administrative, clerical, and customer service support.

In an earlier job as a Paralegal Assistant, I read and analyzed blotter reports to prepare fact sheets for new cases. I also typed and prepared Letters of Reprimand, Articles 15s, and other documents, including notifications sent to personnel informing them of their assignment to court martial duty. While serving in this position, I simultaneously worked as a Community Probation Officer, providing administrative support, including composing and typing correspondence sent to the client to inform them of the action being brought against them and the date and time of their community appointment.

Prior to moving to Germany, I served as a Juvenile Counselor for the Wood County Juvenile Detention Center, providing counseling services and in-processing for new female residents being admitted to the Center. I instructed new residents in the rules of the center, informed them of what would be expected of them, and conducted individual and group counseling sessions.

As you will see, I have completed a Bachelor of Science degree in Criminal Justice, graduating **magna cum laude** from Dalton College. I was awarded an Honor Scholarship for academic excellence in Criminal Justice and was named to the National Dean's List for two consecutive years. I feel that my strong combination of educational excellence and practical work experience would make me a valuable addition to your organization.

If you can use an enthusiastic, hard-working professional whose skills related to human services, social work, and counseling have been tested in challenging environments worldwide, then I look forward to hearing from you soon.

Sincerely,

Rolanda Perkins

ROLANDA PERKINS

1110½ Hay Street, Fayetteville, NC 28305   •   preppub@aol.com   •   (910) 483-6611

OBJECTIVE   To benefit an organization that can use an educated young professional with exceptional communication and organizational skills who offers a track record of excellence in paralegal, community probation, juvenile counseling, and library environments.

EDUCATION   Earned a **Bachelor of Science** degree in **Criminal Justice**, Dalton College, Albany, GA, 2001. Course work included a class on diversity in the workplace.
- Graduated **magna cum laude**, maintaining a cumulative GPA of 3.5.
- Awarded an Honor Scholarship in Criminal Justice for academic excellence.
- Named to the National Dean's List for two consecutive years.
- Nominated for the National Collegiate Minority Leadership Award.
- Nominated for the Honor Society at Dalton College.

Completed 43 credit hours towards a liberal arts degree, Floyd College, Rome, GA, 1997-1998.

EXPERIENCE   **LIBRARY TECHNICIAN.** U.S. Army Library, Larson Barracks, Germany (2002). Provided customer service, clerical, and administrative support while assisting patrons and performing general upkeep, shelving, bookkeeping, and documentation for this busy branch library. Supervised seasonal employees, training them in library procedures, including proper shelving using the Dewey Decimal system and in-processing of new materials.
- Assisted library patrons in locating information, using sources such as the card catalog, Books in Print, and other reference materials.
- Instructed library patrons in the use of computers and the operation of computer-based library resources and databases, such as Sirs and Newsbank.
- Perform in-processing of materials coming into the library, completing paperwork necessary to log new resources into the system and allow us to track their usage.
- Process check-out and return of materials selected by patrons; process card renewals and interlibrary loans.

PARALEGAL ASSISTANT. Office of the Judge Advocate, Criminal Law Division, Germany (2001). Performed paralegal duties and provided clerical, administrative and general office support to this busy government agency.
- Read and analyzed information contained in blotter reports in order to prepare fact sheets for new cases.
- Prepared and typed Letters of Reprimand, Article 15s, and other legal documents.

COMMUNITY PROBATION OFFICER. Kitzingen, Germany (2001). While simultaneously serving in the above position, I provided administrative support to the probation office, gaining valuable experience related to the types and length of punishment imposed for certain offenses.
- Composed and typed correspondence sent to the client to inform them of their community appointment as well as the action being brought against them.

JUVENILE COUNSELOR. Wood County Juvenile Detention Center, Macon, GA (2001). Contributed to the operation of the detention center through my excellent communication and organizational skills, providing counseling services and in-processing to new residents; notified parents that their child was being held at the center.
- Conducted individual and group counseling for up to nine female students.

PERSONAL   Excellent personal and professional references are available upon request.

Date

Exact Name of Person
Exact Title
Exact Name of Company
Address
City, State, Zip

MENTAL HEALTH COUNSELOR

Dear Exact Name of Person (or Dear Sir or Madam if answering a blind ad):

With the enclosed resume, I would like to make you aware of my background as an articulate young professional with exceptional analytical and managerial skills, as well as of the strong educational background and interest in health care administration that I could put to work for your company.

As you will see from my resume, I am currently completing a dual-degree master's program, and will receive Master of Business Administration and Master of Health Administration from Phillips University in Austin, TX. This program included an emphasis on the legal issues surrounding health care administration as well as financial management and strategic management techniques. I have attended numerous seminars, in-service training courses, and workshops since earning a bachelor's degree in Criminal Justice and entering the social work field.

Since 1999 I have served as a social worker and counselor for the Laramie County Mental Health Center in Austin, TX. I provide clinical supervision to as many as three human services professionals providing one-on-one treatment according to existing plans. In addition, I have served on several important committees where my keen insights and the information that I provided have resulted in increased productivity and efficiency both within those committees and throughout the organization as a whole.

If you can use an articulate, bright, and well-educated young professional, I hope you will welcome my call soon when I try to arrange a brief meeting to discuss your goals and how my background might serve your needs. I can provide outstanding references at the appropriate time.

Sincerely,

Alexander Griffith

Alternate Last Paragraph:
I hope you will write or call me soon to suggest a time when we might meet to discuss your needs and goals and how my background might serve them. I can provide outstanding references at the appropriate time.

ALEXANDER GRIFFITH

1110½ Hay Street, Fayetteville, NC 28305 • preppub@aol.com • (910) 483-6611

OBJECTIVE   To contribute to an organization that could benefit from my education and interest in health care administration as well as my exceptional communication, motivational, analytical, and decision-making skills and my background of excellence in human services environments.

EDUCATION & TRAINING   Completing a rigorous dual-degree **Master of Business Administration/Master of Health Administration** program, Phillips University, Austin, TX; degree to be awarded 2003.
- Completed specialized course work which included organizational behavior and design, legal environment in health care, health care finance, managerial economics, strategic management, and MIS theory.

B.A., Criminal Justice, Allentown College of St. Francis DeSales, Center Valley, TX, 1996.
Completed extensive training by attending workshops, in-service training, and seminars.

EXPERIENCE   **SOCIAL WORKER** and **MENTAL HEALTH COUNSELOR.** Laramie County Mental Health Center, Austin, TX (2000-present). Provide clinical supervision to as many as three counselors performing one-on-one treatment according to existing service plans for clients while also personally providing individual, family, and group therapy.
- Contribute as a key member of the Human Relations Council and the Clinical Review Committee which makes treatment recommendations after analyzing case histories.
- Developed extensive knowledge of the complexities and procedures which must be complied with as a member of the agency's Accreditation Committee.
- Apply excellent communication and organizational skills while performing liaison with educators and school counselors, Department of Social Services personnel, juvenile court counselors, and representatives of other state and county programs.
- Provide input during the decision-making process as a member of the interdisciplinary team that makes treatment decisions for current and new clients.

CASE MANAGER, ADOLESCENT & ADULT INTENSIVE PROGRAM. Smitt Foundation for Mental Health, Sellersville, TX (1994-00). Was known for my ability to handle details in a program which operated at a hectic pace while servicing a large and varied caseload with an emphasis on arranging for educational, vocational, and living situations for mentally ill adolescents and young adults. Worked closely with hospitals, police, and probation departments to ensure young patients received proper diagnoses and treatment.
- Became thoroughly familiar with mental health emergency commitment laws and procedures as an Intensive Case Manager.
- Played a vital role in the transition of Children's Services to a managed care type of program and served on the Children's Services Committee.

SUPERVISORY MENTAL HEALTH WORKER. Lark House, Allentown, TX (1992-94). Supervised two groups of 13 children each in an afternoon treatment program while scheduling and conducting therapeutic activities.
- Was selected as one of only three members of the staff qualified to conduct psychosocial assessments of potential clients and their parents or guardians.
- Performed administrative duties including writing reports and evaluations, planning work assignments, and scheduling training activities.

PERSONAL   Studied the Spanish language and culture during a summer exchange program in Mexico. Am experienced in crisis intervention and in dealing with high levels of pressure and stress.

Date

Exact Name of Person
Exact Title
Exact Name of Company
Address
City, State, Zip

MENTAL HEALTH TECHNICIAN

Dear Exact Name of Person (or Dear Sir or Madam if answering a blind ad):

With the enclosed resume, I would like to make you aware of my background related to social work and mental health. I am interested in exploring employment opportunities with your organization.

As you will see from my resume, I have recently graduated with a degree in Sociology and Social Services. In my spare time during college I worked as a Residence Hall Counselor and Tutor. While helping students improve their decision-making and personal management skills, I gained experience in providing intervention for students who were suicidal on numerous occasions.

In a prior paid position as a Habilitation Technician, I provided direct care to profoundly mentally challenged clients, and I became knowledgeable of their legal rights. Subsequently as a Mental Health Technician, I provided care to mentally impaired adults, and I applied effective behavior modification techniques.

You would find me in person to be a vibrant, dedicated young social worker who is highly effective in establishing strong working relationships with everyone with whom I come into contact. I can provide outstanding references at the appropriate time.

Sincerely,

Charlotte J. Oliphant

Alternate Last Paragraph:
I hope you will write or call me soon to suggest a time when we might meet to discuss your needs and goals and how my background might serve them. I can provide outstanding references at the appropriate time.

CHARLOTTE J. OLIPHANT

1110½ Hay Street, Fayetteville, NC 28305 • preppub@aol.com • (910) 483-6611

OBJECTIVE To offer my ability to manage time and human resources as well as my organizational and planning skills and attention to detail to an organization that can use a fast learner who excels in relating to people from diverse backgrounds, ages, and socioeconomic levels.

EDUCATION Earned a **Bachelor's degree in Sociology and Social Services** from Morgan State University, Baltimore, MD, 2002.
- Graduated *cum laude.*
- Was honored with a Chancellor's Award of Merit in recognition of my accomplishments in sports, academics, and family activities, April 1996.
- Nominated by my peers, was elected president of the Economics and Finance Club, September 1996.
- Earned numerous awards and honors for my athletic abilities as a member of the university's basketball and volleyball teams.
- Was named to the All-Conference Teams, honored as Most Valuable Player, and an NCAA Division II All-American in both sports.

Previously attended The University of Maryland at College Park.

EXPERIENCE *Gained experience in positions where "people skills" and the ability to manage time and deal with problems professionally and calmly were of major importance while attending school full-time:*

SOCIOLOGY AND SOCIAL SERVICES STUDENT. Morgan State University, MD (1999-02). Refined my counseling and communication skills while completing this degree program as a full-time student.
- In my spare time, worked as a Residence Hall Counselor and Tutor. Helped many students gain self-confidence and improve their ability to make decisions.

YOUTH PROGRAM ASSISTANT. Kent Temporary Agency, Baltimore, MD (1998). Worked as part of a team of professionals providing care for three mentally handicapped children while ensuring that daily care was provided according to policies and procedures.

MENTAL HEALTH TECHNICIAN. X.Y. Contract Management Services, Baltimore, MD (1996-97). Provided direct care to five mentally handicapped adults with an emphasis on implementing and carrying out behavior plans and behavior modification techniques.
- Taught self-help and independent living skills as well as maintaining documentation on each client's progress or lack of visible progress.
- Protected the well-being and legal rights of my clients.
- Planned and put together a recreation book and scheduled outings which met the needs of the clients for socialization and integration into the outside world.

HABILITATION TECHNICIAN. WZT of Maryland, Baltimore, MD (1994-95). Provided direct care to profoundly mentally retarded clients.
- Applied my knowledge of the legal rights of this class of clients and provided support for them so that their well being and legal rights were protected.
- Transported clients for and from activities such as recreational and social outings as well as medical and counseling appointments.

Highlights of earlier experience: From 1992 to 1994, was a Bus Driver for the Devon County Schools, Baltimore, MD, and was entrusted with safely transporting children to and from the public schools.

Date

Exact Name of Person
Title or Position
Name of Company
Address (number and street)
Address (city, state, and zip)

**PERSONAL CARE
ASSISTANT**

Dear Exact Name of Person (or Sir or Madam if answering a blind ad):

I would appreciate an opportunity to talk with you soon about how I could contribute to your organization through my education and experience as well as through my personal strengths as an articulate, compassionate, and dedicated young professional.

With a degree in Psychology from The University of North Carolina at Greensboro, I have applied my time management and organizational skills to maintain a high GPA while also gaining work experience in health care settings ranging from a medical office to a facility for mentally and developmentally disabled adults. In addition to course work in my major area of concentration, I also excelled in courses in the science field including microbiology, biology, chemistry, and physiology.

I am a well-rounded and adaptable individual with good listening skills, the ability to quickly learn and apply new ideas and methods, and outstanding organizational skills.

I hope you will welcome my call soon to arrange a brief meeting to discuss your current and future needs and how I might serve them. Thank you in advance for your time.

Sincerely,

Anabel P. Lee

Alternate last paragraph:
I hope you will call or write me soon to suggest a time convenient for us to meet and discuss your current and future needs and how I might serve them. Thank you in advance for your time.

ANABEL P. LEE

1110½ Hay Street, Fayetteville, NC 28305   •   preppub@aol.com   •   (910) 483-6611

OBJECTIVE
To offer a combination of a newly earned degree in psychology, a reputation as a self-motivated fast learner, and experience in the health care field to an organization that can use an outgoing and enthusiastic young professional with superior communication skills.

EDUCATION
Graduated from The University of North Carolina at Greensboro with a **B.A. in Psychology**, 2002.
- Placed on the Dean's List for the College of Arts and Sciences.
- Excelled in specialized course work including:

  abnormal psychology   child psychology   basic chemistry   anatomy
  human development   microbiology   biology   physiology

- A member of Pi Beta Phi Sorority, held elected offices including serving on the planning and organizational committee for the Pi Phi 5-mile race which raised money for a women's shelter and was elected to the Standards Board which met each week to discuss financial and membership concerns.
- Attended a summer Study Abroad program in Italy, 2000.

EXPERIENCE
While attending college full-time, gained experience in volunteer and part-time jobs in a broad spectrum of health care settings as well as in sales and service industries where I earned a reputation as an articulate, dependable, and talented young professional:
PERSONAL CARE ASSISTANT. Home Health Services, Inc., Greensboro, NC (2002-present). Assisted in daily living activities, behavior management, and recreational activities in a group home for mentally and developmentally disabled adults.
- Volunteered with this organization previously in 1997 and gained experience in a children's group home.
- Provided support and assistance for daily activities such as hygiene, meal preparation, safety, and fire safety as well as in helping clients develop independence.
- Provided companionship and counseling.
- Learned how to plan and implement behavioral modification and management programs and write case notes.

NANNY. Babysitting Network, Inc., Greensboro, NC (2001). Gained personal awareness of my capacity for compassion, kindness, and patience while dealing with children from four-week-old infants to 12-year-olds for various area families.

RECEPTIONIST and **FILE CLERK.** Clark Drive OB-GYN, Wilmington, NC (1998 and 2000). During college holiday breaks, gained experience in a professional medical office environment and became familiar with office procedures while filing, answering phones, and assisting with other support activities.

PERSONAL CARE GIVER. Care Center, Raleigh, NC (1997). Became aware of the special problems of profoundly mentally and developmentally disabled children while providing companionship as well as assisting the center's nurse.

VOLUNTEER CARE GIVER. Shady Oaks, Chapel Hill, NC (1996). Became acquainted with the needs of the elderly while providing companionship and assistance in daily living.

PERSONAL
Am self-motivated to excel in everything I attempt. Offer the ability to adapt to changing circumstances and handle pressure and crisis situations.

Date

Exact Name of Person
Title or Position
Name of Company
Address (no., street)
Address (city, state, zip)

PRISON COUNSELOR

Dear Exact Name of Person (or Dear Sir or Madam if answering a blind ad.):

Can you use a mature young professional with experience in law enforcement and security along with a degree in Sociology/Social Work? I am particularly interested in pursuing employment opportunities as a Prison Counselor.

While serving in the U.S. Army with the Military Police, I received law enforcement training and excelled in providing security for multimillion-dollar equipment as well as facilities and personnel. I was entrusted by the U.S. government with a Secret security clearance and, as you will see by my resume, became a skilled marksman with the M16 rifle as well as .45 and .38 caliber pistols.

Since leaving military service I have returned to college full time and in May 2002, I received my Bachelor of Arts degree in **Sociology and Social Work**. I completed a rigorous internship as a youth counselor in a group home where I participated in individual and group counseling. Through my concern and nonjudgmental attitude I was able to win the confidence and respect of the young people in the home.

I feel confident that through my skill as a counselor, law enforcement/security background with the military, and knowledge of supply and inventory control I could be a valuable asset to your organization.

I hope you will welcome my call soon to arrange a brief meeting at your convenience to discuss your current and future needs and how I might serve them. Thank you in advance for your time.

Sincerely yours,

Irene R. Donne

Alternate last paragraph:
I hope you will call or write soon to suggest a time convenient for us to meet and discuss your current and future needs and how I might serve them. Thank you in advance for your time.

IRENE R. DONNE

1110½ Hay Street, Fayetteville, NC 28305   •   preppub@aol.com   •   (910) 483-6611

OBJECTIVE

To apply my "newly minted" degree and experience to an organization that can use my abilities related to security, law enforcement, and counseling as well as my personal qualities of maturity, dedication, and concern for others.

EDUCATION

Bachelor of Arts (B.A.) degree in Sociology/Social Work, University of California, Santa Barbara, CA, May 2002.
- Placed on the Chancellor's List, 2001-02, and the National Dean's List, 2000-2001, with a 3.7 GPA.
- Excelled in specialized course work including:

sociology of deviant behavior	crime and delinquency
contemporary social theory	race and ethnic relations
sociology of gender	sociology of religion
social stratification/change	culture and personality
marriage and the family	sociology of sex roles

EXPERIENCE

YOUTH COUNSELING INTERN. Progressive Youth Services, Los Angeles, CA (2002-presemt). Refined my counseling skills while learning to remain objective and nonjudgmental as an observer and participant in individual and group counseling sessions.
- Gained experience in applying techniques of behavioral management and alternative ways of handling inappropriate behavior.
- Earned the confidence of troubled young people through my listening skills, judgment, and willingness to spend time with them "one-on-one."

INVENTORY CONTROL SPECIALIST. U.S. Army Reserves, Ft. Bragg, NC (1998-2002). Handled the issue, receipt, and storage of equipment while also conducting regular stock inventories.
- Learned to manage time effectively while attending college on a full-time basis and furthering my inventory control skills in this part-time job.
- Became familiar with the efforts needed by every member of a team to ensure group goals were met.

SECURITY AND LAW ENFORCEMENT SPECIALIST. U.S. Army, Germany (1994-97). Earned a reputation for my maturity and dependability while refining my knowledge of industrial and personnel security and community law enforcement.
- Guaranteed the safety and security of multimillion-dollar assets and personnel while securing entrance gates on maintenance sites and to the main military compound.
- Guarded facilities while standing watch in secure lookout towers.
- Assisted the unit armorer by issuing and receiving weapons and ammunition.
- Conducted ammunition and weapons inventories.

SPECIAL SKILLS
- Through training and experience am skilled in providing security for industrial facilities, supplies, weapons, and personnel
- Am qualified as a driver/mechanic for wheeled vehicles.

CLEARANCE

Was entrusted with a **Secret** security clearance.

PERSONAL

Enjoy seeing open communication and have concern for helping people cope with their problems. Will relocate.

DAISY G. BUCHANAN

Psychiatric Nurse and Social Worker

1110½ Hay Street, Fayetteville, NC 28305   •   preppub@aol.com   •
(910) 483-6611

CURRICULUM VITAE

PROFESSIONAL CREDENTIALS

**PSYCHIATRIC
SOCIAL WORKER**

Licensed as a **Registered Nurse**, South Carolina and Illinois
Certified by the American Nurses' Association as a **Mental Health/Psychiatric Nurse**
Received **Nursing Administration certification** from the American Nurses' Association

PROFESSIONAL ORGANIZATIONS
AND COMMUNITY ACTIVITIES

Hold membership in Sigma Iota Epsilon, a Central Michigan University Honor Society for graduate-level business majors.
Am a member of the following professional organizations:

 National Association of Social Workers (NASW)
 American Nurses' Association
 South Carolina Nurses' Association
 South Carolina Nurse Executives' Association
 USC School of Social Work Alumni Association

EDUCATION

Completed **Master of Social Work (M.S.W.) degree** from The University of South Carolina, degree awarded May 1997.

Completed **M.S.A. degree program in Health Administration,** Central Illinois University, Chicago, IL; degree awarded May 1995.

B.A., Human Services, University of North Carolina at Chapel Hill, NC, 1990.

A.D.N., Nursing, Belleville Area College of Nursing, Belleville, IL, 1985.

EXPERIENCE

Family Therapist (1994-present), under contract with the Metropolitan Health Clinic of Atlanta, GA. Provide individual and family therapy for children and adolescent family members.

Interim Director of Nursing (1990-93) and **Consultant and Adult Services Manager** (1984-91), Bellview Psychiatric Hospital, Bellview, GA. As Interim Director of Nursing, was selected to manage the 24-hour nursing care department of a 175-bed private psychiatric hospital with 225 nursing department employees. As the Adult Services Manager and a Consultant, handled a range of administrative and marketing activities while supervising approximately 50 medical and mental health employees. Managed employees in three units: a 42-bed "open" acute care section, an 11-bed "locked" unit, and a 20-bed adolescent/adult chemical dependency unit.

Psychiatric Head Nurse (1980-90), Trelawny Memorial Hospital, Trelawny, GA. Supervised 52 health care professionals in a 45-bed comprehensive medical care unit. Provided care which included chemical detox and medical and psychiatric needs for patients ranging in age from five years old to geriatric patients in a 45-bed comprehensive medical care unit. Advanced to this position on the basis of my proven knowledge and skills in earlier jobs as a Staff Nurse and later as the Shift Supervisor for 15 employees.

ACCOMPLISHMENTS

While attending USC in the M.S.W. degree program:
- Learned about the economic and social changes that have taken place in central Europe following the fall of Communism through lectures, discussion groups, and personal observation while participating in a summer study tour of Hungary and Czechoslovakia sponsored by the School of Social Work.
- Acted as the School of Social Work's representative on the university's student government "honor court."
- Completed a nine-month internship in the Affective Disorders Unit at the Mayo Clinic.
- Participated in an Internship as the Social Work Intern for the Mayo Clinic.
- Received several awards including recognition by Nurses' Association as one of the "Great 100" nurses in the state
- Developed and implemented programs including a Quality Assurance Program for nursing services.
- Facilitated Cumberland Hospital as a clinical placement site for four RN nursing programs.
- Ensured the facility complied with all regulatory standards and specifications including the JCAH (Joint Commission on Accreditation of Hospitals) and the Standards of Psychiatric Mental Health Nursing.
- Was selected on two separate occasions to serve as a consultant for other medical facilities preparing for JCAH surveys: instructed classes and provided advice and guidance to clinical directors which enabled them to successfully complete their evaluations.

CAREER CHANGE

Date

Exact Name of Person
Exact Title
Exact Name of Company
Address
City, State, Zip

Dear Exact Name of Person (or Dear Sir or Madam if answering a blind ad):

With the enclosed resume, I would like to make you aware of my background as an educated, articulate young professional who offers exceptional communication and organizational skills as well as experience in dealing with diverse populations in customer service and public speaking environments.

I am in the process of relocating to the Savannah area due to my husband's transfer from GTE. I will be permanently established in the area by June 1, and I would appreciate the chance to speak with you concerning career opportunities within your organization.

As you will see from my resume, I have recently completed a Bachelor of Arts in Psychology with a concentration in Counseling from Helton State University, where I graduated **magna cum laude** with a **3.7 cumulative GPA**. Throughout my collegiate career, I have excelled academically while managing a family and a home. Earlier, I graduated **cum laude** with an Associate of Arts with a concentration in Education at Spokane Community College, maintaining a **3.5 GPA**. I also completed a number of travel industry management and training courses through my employers, and am highly computer literate.

Although my previous experience has been as a Branch Manager and Travel Agent for various companies in the travel industry, I feel that the exceptional communication skills, strong "people" focus, and public speaking ability which I have honed in this field will serve me well in counseling environments.

I hope you will welcome my call soon when I try to arrange a brief meeting to discuss your goals and how my background might serve your needs. I can provide outstanding references at the appropriate time.

Sincerely,

Yolanda Maria Bell

YOLANDA MARIA BELL

1110½ Hay Street, Fayetteville, NC 28305   •   preppub@aol.com   •   (910) 483-6611

OBJECTIVE To benefit an organization that can use a human services professional with exceptional communication, organizational, and customer service skills who offers an education in psychology and counseling as well as experience in dealing with diverse populations.

EDUCATION **Bachelor of Arts** in **Psychology** with a concentration in Counseling, Helton State University, Helton, IN, 2002.
- Graduated **magna cum laude**, maintaining a **3.7 cumulative GPA**.
- Completed research projects examining the long-term effect of uniform school dress codes on achievement scores and the effects of culture on teenage pregnancy; received "A's" on both projects.

Courses related to counseling and psychology included:

Abnormal Psychology	Principles of Sociology I & II	General Psychology
Cognitive Psychology	Theories of Personality	Theories of Learning
Physiological Psychology	Social Psychology	Psychology of Aging
Child Psychopathology	Psychological Statistics	

Psychological Testing & Measurement
Psychology of Personal Adjustment
Introduction to Clinical Psychology & Counseling

Associate of Arts with a concentration in Education, Spokane Community College, Spokane, Washington, 1999.
- Graduated **cum laude**, with a **3.5 cumulative GPA**.

COMPUTERS Familiar with many of the most popular computer operating systems and software, including: Windows 95 and Microsoft Word, PowerPoint, Works, and Publisher.

EXPERIENCE **COLLEGE STUDENT.** Helton State University, Helton, IN (2000-present). Honed my time management skills, attending college full-time while managing a home and family.

BRANCH MANAGER. Palm Travel, Muncie, IN (1995-1999). Oversaw all operational aspects of this local travel agency; interviewed, hired, and trained a travel agent while assisting customers with the planning and scheduling of hotel, airline, rental car, and cruise ship reservations and travel itineraries.
- Completed a company-sponsored management training program; coordinated and negotiated with vendors, and set up new customer accounts.
- Created and implemented innovative and effective marketing strategies and promotions which resulted in quadrupling the office's sales within a one-year period.
- Conducted public speaking engagements at meetings, presenting Sato's products and services to local consumers.
- Streamlined bookkeeping procedures and implemented an improved filing system to increase office efficiency.

COLLEGE INSTRUCTOR. Helton Technical Community College, Helton, IN (1994-1995). Conducted a 12-week program of classes for prospective travel agents, preparing the students in all areas of the travel industry.
- Instructed students in the operation of the SABRE reservation system, as well as the use of the Official Airline Guide (OAG) and other travel industry guides and directories.

PERSONAL Excellent personal and professional references are available upon request.

Date

Exact Name of Person
Exact Title
Exact Name of Company
Address
City, State, Zip

PSYCHOLOGY STUDENT

Dear Exact Name of Person (or Dear Sir or Madam if answering a blind ad):

With the enclosed resume, I would like to make you aware of my background related to social work. I am interested in exploring employment opportunities with your organization.

As you will see from my resume, I have recently graduated with a degree in Psychology which I earned after making the decision to change careers from the business world into the social services environment. In my senior year, I was handpicked for a prestigious assignment as assistant to a prominent psychologist, and in that capacity I refined my research and writing skills while playing a major behind-the-scenes role in a research project. I was also elected Vice President of the Psychology Club even though I worked nearly full-time in a restaurant in order to finance my education.

I am a mature individual who desires to make significant contributions to the social work field and to the lives of those in need, and I am confident that I could become a valuable member of your department of social services. I can provide outstanding references at the appropriate time.

Sincerely,

Emeline Y. Osborne

Alternate Last Paragraph:
I hope you will write or call me soon to suggest a time when we might meet to discuss your needs and goals and how my background might serve them. I can provide outstanding references at the appropriate time.

EMELINE Y. OSBORNE

1110½ Hay Street, Fayetteville, NC 28305 • preppub@aol.com • (910) 483-6611

OBJECTIVE I want to contribute to an organization that can use a hard-working young professional who offers a proven "track record" of hard work and dependability along with strong planning, organizational, and management skills.

EDUCATION Earned **B.A. degree in Psychology**, The University of Iowa, Iowa City, IA, 2002.
- Worked every weekend for four years (1998-2002) as a manager at Happy Burger in order to finance my college education, which required me to travel from Iowa City to Cedar Rapids every weekend.
- Was handpicked for a prestigious six-month assignment my senior year as **Assistant to Psychologist**; refined my research and writing skills while compiling and organizing statistics and operating a computer.

Completed course work to receive certification in Food Service Management, Westerville Technical Community College, Westerville, GA, 1991.

Graduated from Johnson High School as an **Honor Roll Student**, 1987.
- Was elected Vice President of the Psychology Club.
- Member, Beta Club.

EXPERIENCE **MANAGER**. Happy Burger Restaurant, Cedar Rapids, IA (2002-present). Used my psychology education to help create and implement motivational programs that boosted employee productivity and improved morale.
- Trained and supervised up to 10 employees.
- Controlled cash flow of up to $16,000 daily; made bank deposits.
- Ordered and controlled an inventory of perishable and nonperishable goods which experienced a rapid turnover.
- Developed a highly motivated team known for providing excellent customer service.

MATH LAB ASSISTANT. University of Iowa Math Department, Iowa City, IA (1998-2002). Was successful in helping many students eliminate their "math fear" while monitoring students with math deficiencies, administering and grading tests, and tutoring students on levels ranging from basic to advanced mathematics.
- Began as a tutor in the Math Lab and quickly advanced to help plan and manage all tutoring services provided.
- Assisted athletes in "time management": aided in planning their course schedules and establishing specific study sessions to help them acquire good study habits.
- In my spare time, also worked as an **Aerobics Tutor**.

OFFICE ASSISTANT/PAYROLL CLERK. U.S. Department of Commerce, Cedar Rapids, IA (Mar-Aug 1997). Assisted with the U.S. census by interviewing personnel and handling payroll.

CASHIER. Happy Burger Restaurant, Cedar Rapids, IA (1995-96). Was commended for my poise in handling the public in my first job; learned to work in a fast-paced environment which required accurate handling of money while rapidly assembling orders.

BUS DRIVER. Cole Elementary School, Cedar Rapids, IA (1995-96). Became known as a disciplined hard worker and was named "Bus Driver of the Year" because of my perfect safety record and courteous behavior.

PERSONAL Offer a proven ability to motivate others. Am highly motivated to excel.

Date

Exact Name of Person
Title or Position
Name of Company
Address (no., street)
Address (city, state, zip)

Dear Exact Name of Person (or Dear Sir or Madam if answering a blind ad):

I would appreciate an opportunity to talk with you about how I could contribute to your organization as your Rape Crisis Center Supervisor. I am responding to your recent advertisement in the Chicago Times. I offer a proven ability to nurture people who are in pain, and I have excelled in positions as a Psychotherapist, Medical Care Coordinator, and Social Worker.

As you will see from my resume, I have a broad base of experience ranging from coordinating community alternative care projects, to rape crisis counseling, to social worker for adults and for children in hospital settings. I feel that I am most effective in settings where outpatient and client services are provided and I can draw on other team members to ensure the highest quality of care possible. Very effective with clients of all ages, cultures, and races, I am able to deal with crisis including responding to the terminally ill as well as providing grief counseling for the bereaved.

My educational background includes a Master of Social Work (M.S.W.) degree from East Lansing University and a B.S. in Social Work from Wayne State University. During two years as a graduate intern, I worked extensively with two terminally ill women. One of them was a social worker with AIDS who taught me a lot about how this disease destroys lives and made a major impact on my life and career choices. I am a social worker with a reputation as a sensitive and empathetic professional who is very effective in crisis situations.

Always eager to learn and grow, I am proud of my accomplishments in changing careers and earning a master's degree while in my thirties. I have always been described as a "people person" and feel that the field of social work gives me valuable opportunities to contribute to others.

I hope you will welcome my call soon to arrange a brief meeting at your convenience to discuss your current and future needs and how I might serve them. Thank you in advance for your time.

Sincerely yours,

Dana J. Pirate

DANA J. PIRATE

1110½ Hay Street, Fayetteville, NC 28305   •   preppub@aol.com   •   (910) 483-6611

OBJECTIVE

To offer my skills in social work for the benefit of an organization that can use a professional skilled in individual and family counseling, dealing with crisis situations, and public speaking.

EDUCATION

Master of Social Work (M.S.W.), East Lansing University, Lansing, MI, 2000.
B.S. in Social Work, Wayne State University, Detroit, MI, 1987.
* Graduated *magna cum laude* with a 3.93 GPA.
* Was accepted for the Chancellor's Scholarship Program on the basis of grades and "life experience" and the 1985 edition of *Who's Who in American Colleges and Universities*.

A.A.S., Mechanical Engineering Technology, Northwood University, Midland, MI.

TRAINING

Completed programs in rape crisis training, hospital discharge, and long-term care regulations and two years in psychological assessment, counseling and other social services work.

EXPERIENCE

SOCIAL WORKER. Cornelius Medical Center, East Lansing, MI (2000-present). Provide services including crisis counseling, discharge planning, and assistance with disability applications to patients in a number of different areas of the hospital.
* Became familiar with disability eligibility requirements and claims processing.
* Was able to pass my knowledge on to medical personnel who may not have been fully aware of the scope of social programs available to their patients.

MEDICAL CARE COORDINATOR. Ford County Hospital, Dearborn, MI (1998-00). As the hospital's first "in-house" social worker in a role which had previously been held by a nurse, managed four social workers assigned to an "alternative care" program.
* Was instrumental in reviving a county-wide, hospital-based health care program which allowed many people to remain at home instead of having to enter nursing homes.
* Was named to the advisory board for the county-wide comprehensive health care plan and a special council on aging.

COLLEGE INSTRUCTOR. Kellogg Community College, Battle Creek, MI (1996-97). Based on my experience, accomplishments as a student, and speaking skills, was invited to become a part-time instructor for two courses: Policies II and Human Behavior II.

PSYCHOTHERAPIST. Ford County Hospital, Dearborn, MI (1995). Refined techniques for guiding the course of group therapy while conducting individual, family, and group therapy sessions in a children's unit. Learned the importance of teamwork in treatment and discharge planning while dealing with professionals from the Department of Social Services and mental health workers.

VOLUNTEER COORDINATOR. Rape Crisis Volunteers of Ford County, Dearborn, MI (1993-94). Handled the details of scheduling and training volunteers available 24 hours a day, producing a newsletter, educating the public, and counseling sexual assault victims.

MENTAL HEALTH WORKER. Gladstone Hospital, Flint, MI (1987-1992). Became aware of the importance of teamwork in an acute care situation while counseling and supervising acutely ill patients.

Highlights of other experience: Learned about two very different cultures as a Summer Missionary: provided social services to Hispanic and Haitian migrant workers.

Date

JOB
P.O. Box 5555
Fayetteville, NC

Dear Sir or Madam:

     I would appreciate an opportunity to talk with you soon about how my organizational, interpersonal, and communication talents could make me the person you are looking for to fill the position of Coordinator for the Newport News Habitat for Humanity program.

     As you will see from my resume I offer outstanding time management and organizational abilities along with a talent for getting along well with others. The jobs I held while attending college required strong abilities in those areas and allowed me the opportunity to earn a reputation as a mature young professional who could be counted on to "get things done." After graduating with a B.A. in Social Services Administration, I obtained my first job in my field -- Rape Crisis Counselor. I have excelled in providing counseling to women and children (and some men) who are in distress, and I have recently initiated a special counseling and educational program with the local prison in Newport News.

     In prior experience, I displayed the ability to work with clients and understand their needs as a tax preparation specialist and while working in a law office and financial investment firm. I feel certain that you would find me to be a poised and caring individual who is able to interact gracefully with committees, volunteers, victims, and families.

     I hope you will welcome my call soon to arrange a brief meeting at your convenience to discuss your current and future needs and how I might serve them. Thank you in advance for your time.

Sincerely yours,

Mary L. Sunshine

MARY L. SUNSHINE

1110½ Hay Street, Fayetteville, NC 28305 • preppub@aol.com • (910) 483-6611

OBJECTIVE   To contribute through my reputation as a hard-working young professional who offers outstanding organizational abilities, verbal and written communication skills, and a talent for motivating and working with others.

EDUCATION   **B.A., Social Services Administration,** Hollins College, Roanoke, VA, 1998.
- Was recognized as an honor student for academic excellence.

TRAINING   Completed a 25-hour IRS course and qualified as a "Volunteer Income Tax Assistant," 1997.

COMPUTER SKILLS   Excelled in computer classes and built a broad base of operating knowledge on mainframes as well as Macintosh and IBM PC's.
- Discovered a "knack" for using computers and learning new systems and software easily and quickly.

EXPERIENCE   **RAPE CRISIS COUNSELOR.** Rape Crisis Volunteers of Loudon County, Newport News, VA (2000-present). Provide counseling by telephone or in person for victims of violent assault, informing them about courses of legal action as well as victim's compensation and assistance and mental health services available.
- Served on an "on-call" basis a few times a month.
- Maintained contact with victims, providing additional counseling after discharge from medical institutions.
- Participated in fund-raising activities for the center.

TAX PREPARATION ASSISTANT ADMINISTRATOR. U.S. Government, Ft. Bragg, NC (1997-99). Contributed to the organization, set up, and operation of a tax assistance center for 60,000 military personnel and their families at the nation's largest military base.
- Polished my interpersonal skills by encouraging clients to attend tax preparation classes.
- Became familiar with government regulations applicable to tax return preparation.

TEACHER'S AIDE. Head Start, Roanoke, VA (1996). Created and developed educational programs and arts and crafts projects while working with children individually and in groups.
- Became skilled in communicating with disadvantaged children and their families.

ADMINISTRATIVE ASSISTANT and **RECEPTIONIST.** Investment Holdings, Inc., Richmond, PA (1993-95). Handled a variety of functional areas in the busy and hectic atmosphere of a financial investment firm: greeted and assisted clients, answered phones, typed, and filed. Gained knowledge of planning investments and financial matters.
- Placed purchase and sell orders for clients, posting transactions to the proper accounts.

LEGAL SECRETARY. Barrington and Associates, Philadelphia, PA (1991-92). Became familiar with legal proceedings working in a law office by assisting clients and working with staff members as an administrative assistant.

Other experience: Contributed creative ideas for improving services and procedures in a health clinic while screening patients and organizing health and nutrition programs.

PERSONAL   Work well with and can communicate with people of all ages and backgrounds. Have a talent for public speaking and reputation as a dedicated hard worker.

Date

Exact Name of Person
Exact Title
Exact Name of Company
Address
City, State, Zip

Dear Exact Name of Person (or Dear Sir or Madam if answering a blind ad):

With the enclosed resume, I would like to make you aware of my interest in exploring employment opportunities with your organization. I am in the process of relocating to the Godfrey area, which will permit me to live closer to my extended family.

As you will see from my resume, I have been working since I was 15 years old and partially financed my college education through a variety of jobs. In one job at a community college, I worked as an Adjunct Faculty Member and was responsible for promoting educational programs while occasionally substituting for teachers in the classroom. I also worked in sales and retail jobs. As a teenager, I worked for three years for a small drug store chain in Florida, handling a variety of receiving and merchandising duties in addition to sales. As a college student, I worked for the fashion retailer Steven's Clothing for three years. While in college at Parkland College, I also excelled in part-time jobs as an Account Executive with a small publishing company and as a Telefundraiser for Parkland College Foundation.

After earning my B.A. in English, I accepted a position in the mental health field and have been working as a member of a small team concerned with the care of mentally ill residents. I was attracted to this job because I felt it would give me an opportunity to help others.

Although I am highly regarded in my current position and have enjoyed contributing to the well being of the mentally ill, I have decided that I would prefer utilizing my strong communication skills and management abilities in a profit-making company. While working in previous sales jobs, I became accustomed to having my results measured on the bottom line, and I would like to be a part of dynamic organization with ambitious goals. I am confident that my outgoing personality and ambitious nature would be well suited to an organization which values initiative, discipline, and resourcefulness.

If you can use a hard-working young professional with strong written and oral communication skills, I hope you will contact me soon to suggest a time when we might meet to discuss your needs. I can provide outstanding references at the appropriate time.

Sincerely,

Eden Caulfield

EDEN CAULFIELD

1110½ Hay Street, Fayetteville, NC 28305   •   preppub@aol.com   •   (910) 483-6611

OBJECTIVE   To benefit an organization that can use an articulate young professional with strong communication, marketing, and public relations skills who excels in handling multiple responsibilities and deadlines in a resourceful, dedicated manner.

EDUCATION   **B.A., Sociology and Social Work**, Parkland College, Champaign, IL, 2000.
A.A., English, Lewis and Clark Community College, Godfrey, IL, 1997.

EXPERIENCE   **Have established a reputation as a reliable, personable, and resourceful young problem solver in full-time, part-time, and volunteer positions in both high school and college as well as after college graduation:**
UNIT TREATMENT REHABILITATION SPECIALIST. Illinois Evaluation and Treatment Center, Champaign, FL (2000-present). After college graduation, accepted a full-time position in the mental health field which has given me extensive insight into the judicial system; have been commended for my meticulous attention to detail in a therapeutic environment which requires careful recordkeeping on behalf of mentally ill residents.
- Was attracted to this job because I felt it would give me an opportunity to apply my talents while improving the lives of others.
- As a respected member of a small professional team, implement specialized treatments as directed by the therapeutic team.
- Have earned respect for my ability to articulately and persuasively communicate with team members, medical professionals, residents' family members, and others.

CUSTOMER SERVICE & SALES REPRESENTATIVE. Steven's Clothing, Champaign, IL (1997-99). Partially financed my college education in this job which strengthened my sales, customer service, merchandising, and inventory control skills.
- Became skilled at merchandising with planograms; contributed numerous ideas which improved customer relations and boosted repeat business.
- Learned the art of fashion merchandising while gaining excellent sales skills.
- Was commended for my strong motivational abilities, and I was strongly encouraged to enter company's management trainee program after college graduation.

ADJUNCT FACULTY MEMBER. Lewis and Clark Community College Adult High School, Godfrey, IL (1996-97). While completing my A.A. degree, worked as an Adjunct Faculty Member; promoted educational programs and registered students for classes; maintained attendance statistics and substituted for teachers in various classes.

SALES REPRESENTATIVE & CUSTOMER SERVICE REPRESENTATIVE. Thomas Drugs, Godfrey, IL (1993-96). Began working when I was 15 years old, and became a dedicated and reliable employee of this small drug store.

Other experience: While earning my college degree, worked part-time in these jobs which refined my sales, communication, and customer service skills.
ACCOUNT EXECUTIVE. Brian Publications, Champaign, FL; **SALES   ASSOCIATE/ CASHIER.** Maynard's, Champaign, IL; and **TELEFUNDRAISER.** Parkland College Foundation, Champaign, IL.

PERSONAL   Enjoy reading, playing the piano, exercising, listening to music, spending time with family and friends, and writing. Am considered to be "a good listener." Excellent references.

Date

Exact Name of Person
Exact Title
Exact Name of Company
Address
City, State, Zip

SCHOOL COUNSELOR   Dear Exact Name of Person (or Dear Sir or Madam if answering a blind ad):

With the enclosed resume, I would like to make you aware of my background as an articulate, enthusiastic human services professional whose exceptional skills in classroom instruction and counseling have been proven while working with diverse populations in a variety of challenging environments.

As you will see from my resume, I have excelled throughout my academic career, maintaining a **3.88 cumulative GPA** en route to completing my Masters of Education degree at the University of California. I graduated **magna cum laude** while earning a Bachelor of Science in Psychology from the University of Florida, where I was named to the Dean's List each semester for three consecutive years and was voted Most Distinguished Student by the faculty in recognition of my academic excellence and community involvement.

In my most recent position, I taught Psychology at Miami-Dade Community College, providing classroom instruction to 35 students as well as preparing lesson plans, assignments, and other written materials.

Previously I honed my counseling and teaching skills while completing challenging internships in various environments, where I built a reputation as a motivated team player while working with diverse consumer populations. As a School Counselor Intern for a junior high school and an elementary school in Georgia, I provided individual and group counseling to troubled students while acting as liaison in difficult and sensitive situations between the student, parent, teachers, and administration.

While completing a 21-month M.S.W. Internship at the Davis Veteran's Center, I worked with traumatized, substance abusing, and grieving adolescent and adult consumers, coordinating and facilitating group counseling sessions as well as providing individual counseling.

If you can use an articulate communicator, skilled teacher, and compassionate counselor, I hope you will welcome my call soon when I try to arrange a brief meeting to discuss your goals and how my background might serve your needs. I can provide outstanding references and letters of recommendation at the appropriate time.

Sincerely,

Maggie Holcomb

MAGGIE HOLCOMB

1110½ Hay Street, Fayetteville, NC 28305   •   preppub@aol.com   •   (910) 483-6611

OBJECTIVE   To benefit an organization that can use a motivated, articulate human services professional who offers a strong background in classroom instruction as well as in individual and group counseling of diverse populations in public schools and long-term care environments.

EDUCATION   **Masters of Education** in **Counseling**, University of California, Santa Cruz, CA, 2000; graduated with a **3.88 cumulative GPA.**
Bachelor of Arts in **Psychology**, University of Florida, Gainesville, FL, 2000; graduated **magna cum laude** with a **cumulative GPA** of **3.68 overall, 4.0 in my major.**
- Named to the **Dean's List** each semester from 1997-1999.
- Honored by the faculty members with the **Most Distinguished Student** award for my academic excellence and commitment to community involvement.

AFFILIATIONS   Member, American Counseling Association
Student Member, American Psychological Association
Member, Psychology Association

EXPERIENCE   **PSYCHOLOGY INSTRUCTOR.** Miami-Dade Community College, Miami, FL (2002-present). Taught psychology to 35 students at this local community college; presented course materials through oral presentations, role playing, and other methods; prepared lesson plans, projects, reports, and assignments.
- Evaluated individual performance through formal examination and personal observation; counseled and assisted students who were having difficulty with the course materials.

SCHOOL COUNSELOR INTERN. Augusta Junior High School, Augusta, GA (2002). Provided individual and group counseling to seventh and eighth grade students while completing a five-month internship at this local junior high school; interacted with students, parents, teachers, and administrators to facilitate the counseling process.
- Counseled troubled students on an individual basis as well as coordinating and facilitating counseling groups; assisted with the Peer Leadership Training program.
- Provided materials for, and frequently made presentations at Special Education meetings and Alternative Education meetings; tutored special needs students on an individual and group basis.

SCHOOL COUNSELOR INTERN. Athens Elementary School, Athens, GA (2001). Counseled troubled students in kindergarten through sixth grade while completing a five-month internship at this local elementary school; wrote a successful grant to provide funding for a substance abuse prevention program.

M.S.W. INTERN. Davis Veteran's Center, Davis, CA (1998-00). While completing my Master of Education, provided individual and group counseling during a 21-month internship; conducted research into Vicarious Traumatization. Counseled adolescents and adults who were facing issues related to physical, emotional, or psychological trauma, substance abuse, and grief management. Coordinated and facilitated group counseling for Post-Traumatic Stress Disorder, Substance Abuse, and Self Esteem.

Highlights of earlier experience: Excelled in earlier human services positions as a **HABILITATION SPECIALIST**, obtaining MANDT training while working with dual-diagnosis patients and as a **RECREATION ASSISTANT** in a long-term care facility.

CAREER CHANGE

Date

Arthur A. Smith
District Manager
Whoville District Office
302 Main Street
Whoville, NC

SCHOOL PSYCHOLOGIST

Dear Mr. Smith:

With this letter and resume, I would like to enthusiastically follow up on our enjoyable and informative meeting in person on January 26. Thank you very much for your hospitality. I am interested in a second career with the Social Security Administration, and I feel I have much to offer.

As you will see from my resume, I have worked hard to earn a Master's degree, Bachelor's degree, and Associate's degree. I offer a versatile background and history of advancement based on expertise in analyzing situations, solving problems, and dealing with people in culturally diverse work environments. While performing with distinction in demanding jobs requiring frequent travel and long hours, I received extensive technical and managerial training emphasizing resource management, budgeting, quality assurance, and automated systems applications. In every job I held, I resourcefully discovered ways to cut costs while improving quality.

Known for my ability to develop, implement, and manage support programs, I offer a wide range of expertise in analyzing situations, developing and implementing workable solutions, training personnel and building teams known for their emphasis on providing timely support under tight deadlines and pressure. Accustomed to achieving exceptional results with limited resources, I am an expert in maximizing the potential of individuals while encouraging each person to work toward achieving team goals and standards.

Respected for my analytical skills and sound judgment, I am known for my ability to deal with people in a productive style. If you can use a versatile and mature management professional, I hope you will contact me soon to suggest a time we might meet to discuss how I could contribute to your organization. I can provide excellent professional and personal references at the appropriate time. Thank you for your time and consideration.

Sincerely,

Connie H. Waters

CONNIE H. WATERS

1110½ Hay Street, Fayetteville, NC 28305   •   preppub@aol.com   •   (910) 483-6611

OBJECTIVE

To apply my background as a school psychologist with skills in handling difficult situations calmly and with control and a strong combination of practical and theoretical experience.

EDUCATION & TRAINING

M.S. in School Psychology in a 60-hour program, Lewis University, Romeoville, IL, 1997.
B.S. in Psychology and Anthropology, Illinois State University, Normal, IL, 1995.
Participated in more than 200 hours of workshops/seminars in areas ranging from substance abuse, to "mainstreaming" the LD child, to rape crisis intervention, to multiculturalism, to traumatic brain injury assessment/intervention.

CERTIFICATION & AFFILIATIONS

Am certified as a Level II School Psychologist, North Carolina and Michigan, 1996.
Hold Preliminary Certification as a School Psychologist in Michigan, 1995.
Hold membership in professional organizations including:
     Council for Exceptional Children (CEC)
     Children with Attention Deficit Disorders Support Group (CHADD)
     National Association of School Psychologists (NASP)

EXPERIENCE

SCHOOL PSYCHOLOGIST. Wake County Schools, Raleigh, NC (2000-present). Am further refining my counseling, time management, research, and communication skills working in a county with a highly diverse and unique ethnically and socioeconomically mixed population of students including a large transient military population.

- Applied tact and sensitivity while responding to traumatic situations affecting students and their families including crisis situations such as the Gulf War, sexual assault, violence, suicide, and death — in both group and individual counseling sessions.
- Received a certificate of appreciation from the staff at one high school for my support to students during a period when many of their parents were in the Middle East.
- Polished my assessment and interpretation skills while evaluating children from age five up for educational diagnoses and eligibility determinations for special programs; planned interventions and evaluated progress and change.
- Acted as liaison between the school system and various agencies in order to ensure students and their families received appropriate services.
- Served on the School-Based Committee which made determinations of eligibility for Special Education programs, a team which met with teachers to develop appropriate strategies for "at-risk" students, the Crisis Team, and the ADHD screening committee.

Gained practical experience in internships/practicums which built on an educational base:
SCHOOL PSYCHOLOGIST. Detroit Public School System, MI (1990-2000). Learned techniques for assessing and working with autistic children while also providing assistance to the director of a Child Find Developmental Screening Program.

EVALUATOR. Madison County Community School Corp., Wichita, KS (1987-89). Gained experience in several assessment techniques and polished my interpersonal communication skills while evaluating candidates for "exceptional children's" programs.

Highlights of other experience: Helped a family with a handicapped child by implementing educational plans, and taking him to occupational and speech therapy, and introducing him to age-appropriate activities.

PERSONAL

Provided research, editorial assistance, and support for the author of a well-received book on the impact of geographical relocation — "Kids on the Move" — published by NASP.

Date

Exact Name of Person
Exact Title
Exact Name of Company
Address
City, State, Zip

SCHOOL SOCIAL WORKER

Dear Exact Name of Person (or Dear Sir or Madam if answering a blind ad):

With the enclosed resume, I would like to make you aware of my interest in employment as a School Social Worker with your school.

As you will see from my resume, I have completed my School Social Work Certification from Marquette College, and I previously completed a B.S. in Psychology as well as extensive course work related to Special Education.

After leaving the military, I became a high school teacher in the Milwaukee City school system for a year, and I taught students with special learning disabilities who were in grades 9-12. It was during that time that I decided I wanted to become a School Social Worker.

I am confident that I could make significant contributions to the lives of others through my resourcefulness as well as my genuine desire to help others. I have demonstrated my ability to influence and inspire others during my experience as a high school teacher as well as during my recent internship as a School Social Worker.

I would certainly enjoy an opportunity to meet with you to discuss my background and your needs, and I hope you will contact me to suggest a time when your schedule might permit a brief meeting. I can provide outstanding references. Thank you in advance for your time.

Yours sincerely,

Barbara Ava Dean

BARBARA AVA DEAN

1110½ Hay Street, Fayetteville, NC 28305   •   preppub@aol.com   •   (910) 483-6611

OBJECTIVE

To contribute to an organization that can use an accomplished young professional who offers strong leadership, management, and communication skills along with a proven ability to motivate, counsel, influence, and inspire others.

EDUCATION

School Social Work Certification, Marquette College, Milwaukee, WI, May 2001.
Extensive formal training and hands-on experience related to these and other areas:

Effective teacher training	Family support	Mental health
Domestic violence	Juvenile offenders	Home visits
Communication Skills	Counseling	Leadership

Bachelor of Science in Psychology, University of Wisconsin, Green Bay, WI, 1990-1994.
Phi Alpha (National Honor Society in Social Work), Sigma Omega Chi (National Honor Society Sociology, Social Work, Criminal Justice).

EXPERIENCE

SOCIAL WORKER INTERN. Milwaukee City Schools, Milwaukee, WI (2002-present). Have gained respect for my communication and interpersonal skills at Lincoln High School. Work under the direction and mentorship of School Social Worker Jane Smith.

- Assist the school Social Worker in promoting the maximum development of all students by emphasizing prevention of problems that interfere with learning and mastery.
- Have become well acquainted with issues related to adolescent pregnancy, domestic violence, substance abuse, and other problems which interfere with the ability of teenagers to learn.
- Perform assessment of student needs while playing a role in program planning and evaluation.
- Have established congenial relationships with outside agencies in the process of referring students to outside organizations for specialized and intensive help.

FULL-TIME GRADUATE STUDENT & SUBSTITUTE SCHOOL TEACHER. Hayes County School, Madison, WI (1998-01). Substituted in grades 1-12 in Hayes County while pursuing completion of my School Social Worker Certification.

SCHOOL TEACHER. Madison City Schools, Madison, WI (1996-97). Made the decision that I wanted to earn my School Social Worker Certification as I taught students with special learning disabilities who were in grades 9-12.

- Was told on numerous occasions that my natural love for children "shined through" as I worked diligently to help students succeed in setting and achieving high personal and career goals.
- Provided a goal plan specifying the approval performance of each student as I supervised 48 students daily.

Military experience: Served with distinction in the U.S. Army and was promoted to Captain in this track record of advancement:
SPECIAL PROJECTS MANAGER. Ft. Dix, NJ (1992-94). Was specially selected to take responsibility for a project which involved creating "from scratch" the only Prisoner of War Information Center in existence in the U.S.

OPERATIONS OFFICER. Ft. Bragg, NC (1989-92). As a Lieutenant (P), was handpicked to assume responsibilities normally held by a Major; worked at the Police Station of this large military base and was continuously involved in counseling others involved in problems including domestic violence.

Date

Exact Name of Person
Exact Title
Exact Name of Company
Address
City, State, Zip

Dear Exact Name of Person (or Dear Sir or Madam if answering a blind ad):

**SENIOR SOCIAL
WORKER**

With the enclosed resume, I would like to make you aware of my interest in employment as a Social Worker.

In my current position as a Senior Social Worker, I work diligently and resourcefully to remove potential barriers for employment for the most disadvantaged and challenged in our society. I maintain a caseload of extremely challenged clients while continuously solving problems and assisting my colleagues with their most difficult caseload issues.

In a previous position as a Case Manager, I managed programs including Income Maintenance and Food Stamps. A strong believer in getting involved in the community, I always donate some of my spare time to worthy causes, and I have been a dedicated rape crisis counselor.

I would certainly enjoy an opportunity to meet with you to discuss my background and your needs, and I hope you will contact me to suggest a time when your schedule might permit a brief meeting. I can provide outstanding references. Thank you in advance for your time.

Yours sincerely,

Aletha F. Blake

ALETHA F. BLAKE

1110½ Hay Street, Fayetteville, NC 28305   •   preppub@aol.com   •   (910) 483-6611

OBJECTIVE   To benefit an organization through my skills in counseling, communication, and administration.

EXPERIENCE   *Berry County Department of Social Services, Erie, PA (2000-present). Have served in these positions of increasing responsibility:*
SENIOR SOCIAL WORKER. (2001-present). Interview, counsel, assess, and assist clients in removing potential barriers for gaining employment; access computer information.
- Arrange and provide supportive services including day care and transportation; teach job hunting skills.
- Monitor progress, solve problems, and maintain a caseload of 50 people.

CASE MANAGER. (1995-2000). Interviewed clients, determining and verifying information for eligibility in social service programs including Income Maintenance, AFDC, MAF, and Food Stamps.
- Contacted and coordinated with other agencies and individuals to obtain assistance for clients.
- Explained all eligibility programs and requirements as well as the rights and responsibilities of clients.
- During this period, also served as a **rape crisis volunteer**, providing help and support to rape victims and their families.

COMMUNICATIONS OPERATOR. Merritt Telephone & Telegraph Services, Easton, PA (1994). Received calls, took orders, and accessed data on IBM TRC computers.

COURT REPRESENTATIVE. Thomas & Victor Bonding, Fairfield, CT (1991-93). Refined my knowledge of the legal system while notifying and assisting clients for court appearances.
- Handled legal follow up on judgement and negotiations.
- Established rapport and effective working relationships with judges, attorneys, and the entire court staff.
- Conducted criminal investigations; picked up bond jumpers.
- Developed office, administrative, and accounting skills including typing, filing, answering telephones, public relations, accounts payable and receivable, ledgers, and making deposits.

UNDERCOVER DETECTIVE. Gray's Department Store, Fairfield, CT (1990). Detected, apprehended, and detained shoplifters; prepared and filed reports.

JUVENILE COUNSELOR. Norris Detention Center, Newark, DE (1989). Supervised, counseled, motivated, and planned activities for clients, ensuring their security, health, morale, and welfare.
- Implemented activities tailored to individual client needs.
- Assigned detention and restriction for clients displaying aggressive deviant behavior.

EDUCATION   **Bachelor of Science (B.S.) degree**, **Criminology** and **Bachelor of Arts (B.A.) degree**, **Psychology,** 1988.

PERSONAL   Am a mature, reliable, hard-working young professional who approaches each task with total dedication. Have an ability to communicate effectively and establish rapport with people.

CAREER CHANGE

Date

Arthur A. Smith
District Manager
Whoville District Office
302 Main Street
Whoville, NC

Dear Mr. Smith:

With this letter and resume, I would like to enthusiastically follow up on our enjoyable and informative meeting in person on January 26. Thank you very much for your hospitality. As we discussed, I will be retiring from the Army and available for employment immediately. I am interested in a second career with Social Services, and I feel I have much to offer.

As you will see from my resume, I have worked hard to earn a Master's degree, Bachelor's degree, and Associate's degree while continuing to excel in full-time management positions while in military service. I offer a versatile background and history of advancement based on expertise in analyzing situations, solving problems, and dealing with people in culturally diverse work environments. While performing with distinction in demanding jobs requiring frequent travel and long hours, I received extensive technical and managerial training emphasizing resource management, budgeting, quality assurance, and automated systems applications. In every job I held in the military, I resourcefully discovered ways to cut costs while improving quality.

As a U.S. Army professional, I was recognized as a subject matter expert in emergency and disaster preparedness, hazardous material handling, and Nuclear/Biological/ Chemical (NBC) defense and program development, I have been handpicked for vital roles as a consultant, advisor, and program manager.

Known for my ability to develop, implement, and manage support programs, I offer a wide range of expertise in analyzing situations, developing and implementing workable solutions, training personnel and building teams known for their emphasis on providing timely support under tight deadlines and pressure. Accustomed to achieving exceptional results with limited resources, I am an expert in maximizing the potential of individuals while encouraging each person to work toward achieving team goals and standards.

Respected for my analytical skills and sound judgment, I am known for my ability to deal with people in a productive style. If you can use a versatile and mature management professional, I hope you will contact me soon to suggest a time we might meet to discuss how I could contribute to your organization. I can provide excellent professional and personal references at the appropriate time. Thank you for your time and consideration.

Sincerely,

Lonnie M. Hewey

LONNIE M. HEWEY

1110½ Hay Street, Fayetteville, NC 28305 • preppub@aol.com • (910) 483-6611

OBJECTIVE To contribute through a versatile blend of experience and knowledge gained in management and supervisory roles where the ability to maximize all available resources and diverse work forces while planning and coordinating projects/programs under pressure was vital.

EDUCATION **Master's degree in Management** (2000), **B.S. in Management** (1999), and **A.S. in**
& TRAINING **Management** (1999), Summit University of Louisiana, New Orleans, LA.
Received extensive training emphasizing resource management, budgeting, and automated systems applications as well as specialized technical training related to emergency/disaster preparedness, hazardous material handling, and environmental protection.

EXPERIENCE *Advanced to the rank of Sergeant First Class in managerial roles, U.S. Army:*
RESIDENTIAL HOUSING INSPECTOR. Ft. Bragg, NC (2000-present). Oversee property management for a housing development with hundreds of residential units; inspect exteriors and outside yards for compliance with government standards for upkeep.
- Mediate disputes over housing issues; assure security of the neighborhood for residents.

ADVISOR. Saudi Arabia (2000). Recognized as a subject matter expert and handpicked for this job, worked throughout the Middle East as the Nuclear/Biological/Chemical (NBC) Specialist on a team providing antiterrorism and personnel protection assessments.
- Conducted inspections; prepared analytical reports and suggestions for improvements.
- Provided sound security support and controlled access to commercial buildings and vehicles despite the drawbacks of coping with a rapid turnover of qualified personnel.

PROGRAM MANAGER. Ft. Bragg, NC (1998-99). Cited for my ability to take charge and meet challenges head on, managed NBC training and defense for a diverse multifunctional 603-person organization; consistently achieved equipment readiness rates above 95%.
- Emphasized training and encouraged personnel to take advantage of every opportunity; trained two supervisors to manage educational program scheduling and attendance.

GENERAL MANAGER. Ft. Bragg, NC (1997-98). Was selected for a supervisory role ahead of my peers to oversee NBC support for a 147-person transportation organization.
- Trained and supervised 36 people and controlled a $100,000 equipment inventory.
- Established a personnel retention program rated as the best in the parent organization.

CONTROLLER & CHEMICAL DEFENSE SUPERVISOR. Korea (1996). Cited as a major factor in the unit's recognition as "the best chemical company in the U.S. Army," provided expertise as supervisor of five people and controller of a $350,000 inventory of specialized equipment.

SUPERVISOR OF PLANS, TRAINING, AND OPERATIONS. Ft. Bragg, NC (1990-96). Supervised six people while serving as the senior evaluator and training specialist for six separate organizations; conducted quarterly assistance visits and evaluated subordinate programs after constructing the NBC defense plans for a finance support center.

Highlights of earlier U.S. Army experience: Advanced rapidly into leadership roles while building knowledge of chemical/environmental and telecommunications operations.

PERSONAL Entrusted with Secret security clearance. Earned recognition with three U.S. Army Commendation and four Achievement Medals. Knowledgeable of Microsoft Office.

Date

Exact Name of Person
Title or Position
Name of Company
Address (no., street)
Address (city, state, zip)

SOCIAL SERVICES DIRECTOR

Dear Exact Name of Person (or Dear Sir or Madam if answering a blind ad):

I would appreciate an opportunity to talk with you soon about how I could contribute to your organization through my background of distinguished performance due to my strong leadership, planning, and public speaking abilities. I am interested in exploring opportunities for a senior social services professional.

Having built a reputation as a talented manager of human resources, I have been very effective in developing and carrying out successful new programs which have been described as models for other similar departments to follow. During my career in state government I rose to the position of Director of the Ohio Division of Social Services and was the only person to have held this political appointment under two different governors representing different political parties!

As you will see from my resume, this position and my earlier track record of accomplishments, allowed me to polish skills ranging from planning and directing multimillion-dollar projects, to developing written documentation and presenting briefings to large groups including various government officials. In addition, I developed close working relations with agencies and personnel throughout the nation, as well as at the state, county, and local government levels.

Through my versatile educational background which includes degrees and course work in social work, secondary education, and law, I offer a unique background which will allow me to step into consulting, administrative, instructional or managerial roles.

I hope you will welcome my call soon to arrange a brief meeting at your convenience to discuss your current and future needs and how I might serve them. Thank you in advance for your time.

Sincerely yours,

Kitty A. Rembrant

KITTY A. REMBRANT

1110½ Hay Street, Fayetteville, NC 28305 • preppub@aol.com • (910) 483-6611

OBJECTIVE

To offer a track record of distinguished performance as a dedicated, innovative professional with proven analytical, motivational, and planning skills along with a reputation for excellence in program development, research, technical writing, and public speaking.

EDUCATION

Master of Social Work (MSW) degree, Ohio State, Columbus, OH, 1987.
Certificate of completion, Public Management Program (PMP), The State of OH Office of State Personnel.
B.S., Secondary Education, Ohio Central University, Toledo, OH, 1982.

HONORS

- Chosen to serve on numerous national task forces, was honored by the American Public Welfare Association (APWA) as an outstanding contributor to efforts to simplify welfare programs.
- Was appointed to the National Welfare Simplification and Advisory Committee by the U.S. Department of Agriculture.
- Was appointed to The Presidential Commission on Childhood and Youth Deaths.
- Received a U.S. Department of Agriculture Unit Award for Distinguished Service for superb efforts in implementing a unique cooperative federal, state, and local initiative to reduce erroneous benefit payments.

EXPERIENCE

PROFESSIONAL DIRECTOR, OHIO DIVISION OF SOCIAL SERVICES, Columbus, OH (2000-present). Supervised the administration of 50 county social services departments through a staff of 2,000 employees and a billion-dollar-plus budget.
which totaled $6.3 million in the program's first year.

- Applied my diplomatic skills working with the governments of each of the counties to ensure their programs met federal and state regulations while also dealing regularly with administrators of other state agencies (health, commerce, and the court system).
- Acted as the legislative liaison for the Division by lobbying for funding and bills which were advantageous for the Division of Social Services.
- Was the only person to hold this appointed position under two governors (from different political parties) and the only person to "come up through the ranks" to this level.

ASSISTANT CHIEF, SOCIAL SERVICES DIVISION. OH Department of Human Resources, Toledo, OH (1996-00). Streamlined and simplified procedures and developed policies while supervising 25 employees.

- Created and implemented a model program to prevent repeat adolescent pregnancies.
- Oversaw the monitoring, evaluation, and certification of 400 contracts.

CONSULTANT. OH Department of Human Resources, Toledo and Columbus, OH (1987-95). Developed a model training plan and peer supervision program as a technical advisor/ consultant for a ten-county region's Aid to Dependent Children programs.

- As Regional Services Supervisor, designed and administered successful marketing strategies that increased multi-disciplinary approaches to Child Welfare Service delivery in the 17 regional counties.

COMPUTER KNOWLEDGE

Knowledgeable of numerous computer applications.
Attended IBM-sponsored information systems training for human services specialists.

PERSONAL

Outstanding personal and professional references.

CAREER CHANGE

Date

Exact Name of Person
Title or Position
Name of Company
Address (no., street)
Address (city, state, zip)

Dear Exact Name of Person (or Dear Sir or Madam if answering a blind ad):

I would appreciate an opportunity to talk with you soon about how I could contribute to your organization through my managerial and supervisory abilities, communication and public speaking skills, and reputation as an adaptable and versatile professional.

You will see from my resume why I have earned a name as an adaptable leader with a reputation as a powerful team builder. Because of my creativity and versatility, the Air Force tested me in a variety of jobs. As a personnel recruiter I exceeded all sales quotas in "selling" the advantages of a military career to talented youth. Most recently I have been involved in developing training videos for personnel in the aerospace industry, and I have traveled around the country to introduce those interactive computer software programs. I have also excelled in management and supervisory positions in a career field in which there is "no room for error" — munitions management. In one job I supervised 38 employees while managing a fleet of transportation assets.

Throughout my military career, I have been promoted ahead of my peers and placed in roles where my communication and leadership skills have been essential assets. I strongly believe in the concept of "leadership by example," and I am known for my willingness to take the time to help my associates develop their skills and job knowledge to the maximum potential. I believe that effective team building is based on helping each individual team member develop.

I hope you will welcome my call soon to arrange a brief meeting at your convenience to discuss your current and future needs and how I might serve them. Thank you in advance for your time.

Sincerely yours,

Blake A. Markley

Alternate last paragraph:
I hope you will call or write me soon to suggest a time convenient for us to meet and discuss your current and future needs and how I might serve them. Thank you in advance for your time.

BLAKE ALLEN MARKLEY

1110½ Hay Street, Fayetteville, NC 28305   •   preppub@aol.com   •   (910) 483-6611

OBJECTIVE

To contribute to an organization that can use a hard-working young professional with an education in psychology and sociology and outstanding communication skills.

EDUCATION

Earned a **Bachelor of Science (B.S.)** degree with a major in **Psychology** and a minor in **Sociology**, Florida State University, Tallahassee, FL, 2000.

abnormal psychology	statistics
study of gerontology	physiological psychology
psychological tests and measurements	experimental psychology

TRAINING

Completed two training programs sponsored by Dade County: how to evaluate and process distress calls as a "Contact" program volunteer (64 hours), 1999 , and dispute resolution for mediation service volunteers (20 hours), 1997

COMMUNITY INVOLVEMENT

After completing the county training programs, volunteered my time in two separate community service programs:

- Contributed two five-hour shifts a month as a Contact volunteer involved in answering calls from people with personal emergencies and in need of someone to listen to them and provide assistance in locating sources to help them out of their crisis.
- Participated in a program which saved the court system time and money by using volunteer mediators to act as go-between and help settle disputes.

EXPERIENCE

SALES ASSOCIATE. Martin's Autos, Tallahassee, FL (2001-present). Further applied my sales skills working in the parts department of this major new and used car dealer.

COLLEGE STUDENT. Florida State University, FL (1995-00). Attended college full time and completed requirements for a bachelor's degree.

Built a strong base of experience in sales and customer service, Tallahassee, FL:
SALES REPRESENTATIVE and **STOCK PERSON.** Royal Carpet and Interiors (1994). Further refined my communication skills dealing with commercial and retail customers while working part time and attending college.

- Learned how to calculate and measure floor coverings as well as how to design and set up displays using carpet and tile.

SERVICE ADVISOR and **SALES ASSOCIATE.** Martin's Autos (1992-93). Learned to manage my time wisely while working in two separate operational areas for this dealership: greeted customers and made sure that requested maintenance and repairs were documented so they could be taken care of properly, while also learning the techniques for selling new and used vehicles.

- Became adept at "defusing" difficult situations, handling irate and difficult customers, and settling their problems to their satisfaction.
- Received a Letter of Commendation on the recommendation of a satisfied customer.

DEPARTMENT MANAGER and **SALES ASSOCIATE.** Murry's (1990-91). Oversaw daily operations in the Garden Center as well as Automotive and Photo departments, while also ensuring that the stock room was kept organized and merchandise properly shelved.

PERSONAL

Offer basic knowledge of computer operations including word processing and retail point-of-sale applications. Enjoy helping people and have a reputation for being tactful.

CAREER CHANGE

Date

Exact Name of Person
Title or Position
Name of Company
Address (number and street)
Address (city, state, zip)

Dear Exact Name of Person (or Dear Sir or Madam if answering a blind ad):

I would appreciate an opportunity to talk with you soon about how I could contribute to your organization through my education and high level of interest in the human services field by applying my knowledge related to social work and counseling.

As you will see from my enclosed resume I graduated *magna cum laude* from the University of Idaho in Moscow, ID, with a Bachelor of Social Work degree. My areas of concentration included 15 credit hours in Family and Children's Services and an additional 21 hours of Psychology which included Adolescent, Child, and Developmental Psychology.

During an internship at Allen Memorial Hospital in Boise, ID, I feel that I was able to make myself known and earn the respect of medical professionals in a hospital setting where the social work aspect of patient care was of secondary importance. During this period I gained experience in areas such as interviewing patients and their family members, assessing their needs, and networking through the community in order to make referrals to outside agencies and resources.

I have developed a reputation through practical work experience and volunteer activities as an empathetic and caring professional with excellent listening and analytical skills. I am very patient and nonjudgmental and respect the need for confidentiality in client care. An excellent manager of time, I am familiar with proper and accepted procedures for collecting data, identifying and assessing needs, and keeping complete and accurate records.

I hope you will welcome my call soon to arrange a brief meeting at your convenience to discuss your current and future needs and how I might serve them. Thank you in advance for your time.

Sincerely yours,

Laura B. Tree

Alternate last paragraph:
I hope you will call or write me soon to suggest a time convenient for us to meet and discuss your current and future needs and how I might serve them. Thank you in advance for your time.

LAURA B. TREE

1110½ Hay Street, Fayetteville, NC 28305   •   preppub@aol.com   •   (910) 483-6611

OBJECTIVE

To contribute through my education and interest in the field of social work and counseling to an organization that can benefit from my personal qualities and reputation as an empathetic and caring professional who is good at listening, interviewing, and counseling.

EDUCATION

Bachelor of Social Work (B.S.W.) degree, University of Idaho, Moscow, ID, 2002.
- Graduated *magna cum laude* with a 3.68 GPA from one of only three accredited schools of social work in the state.
- Was elected to membership in Phi Kappa Phi honor society in recognition of my placement in the top 5% of my class.
- Earned recognition from the Golden Key National Honor Society for my academic accomplishments.
- Completed 15 semester hours of work with a concentration in Family and Children's Services.
- Excelled in 21 hours of studies in Psychology which included courses in Adolescent Psychology, Child Psychology, and Developmental Psychology.

EXPERIENCE

SOCIAL WORK INTERN. Allen Memorial Hospital, Boise, ID (2002). Gained practical experience in a hospital setting by conducting interviews with patients and their families, arranging for home health care, coordinating plans for hospice care, and arranging for patients to be placed in nursing homes or rest homes.
- Became familiar with local assets and referred clients and their families to support agencies and services within the community.
- Completed paperwork and proper documentation of all interviews and actions.
- Learned the importance of following procedures for identifying and assessing needs, collecting data, interviewing, and keeping complete and accurate records.

ADMINISTRATIVE ASSISTANT. Wharton, Stone, & Roe, Attorneys at Law, Boise, ID (1999-present). As an assistant in the Real Estate Department, have polished my communication skills while dealing on a regular basis with professionals ranging from attorneys, to real estate agents, to mortgage and insurance company personnel, to people at title companies.
- Gained knowledge of real estate law and the mortgage closing process while working up to 35 hours per week while carrying a full course load.

SALES ASSOCIATE. Water's Department Store, Lewiston, ID (1999). Learned valuable time management skills while assisting with customer purchases, returns, or layaway.

PHYSICAL THERAPY CLINIC VOLUNTEER. Pocatello Regional Rehabilitation Center, Pocatello, ID (1998). Contributed more than 100 hours of time to work with pediatric physical therapy patients by assisting the physical therapy staff members in moving the children, playing with them and giving them individual attention, and observing their physical and emotional condition.

CUSTOMER SERVICE SPECIALIST. Meadows Department Store, Lewiston, ID (1996-97). Learned to be adaptable and quickly master new tasks: took care of such day-to-day activities as accounting for petty cash/register money, wrapping gifts, typing, taking credit applications, processing gift certificates, and handling returned checks/layaways/complaints.

PERSONAL

Skilled at interviewing — concisely paraphrase, clarify, and summarize what others have said. Am patient and non-judgmental with respect for the importance of confidentiality.

Exact Name of Person
Exact Title
Exact Name of Company
Address
City, State, Zip

SOCIAL WORK SUPERVISOR

Dear Exact Name of Person (or Dear Sir or Madam if answering a blind ad):

With the enclosed resume, I would like to make you aware of my background as an articulate, experienced human services professional whose exceptional skills in social services supervision and training, classroom instruction, and counseling have been proven while working with diverse populations.

As you will see from my resume, I have excelled throughout my academic career, maintaining a **3.8 cumulative GPA** en route to completing my Master of Arts in Psychology degree at University of Maine. Earlier I earned a Bachelor of Arts in Sociology from St. Josephs College, and I supplemented my formal education with numerous additional training courses in social services management and supervision.

I am currently excelling in dual roles, teaching Psychology as an Adjunct Instructor at Bergen Community College while simultaneously working full-time as a Social Work Supervisor III with the Miles County Department of Social Services. At HTCC, I provide classroom instruction to as many as three classes per week with up to 35 students in each class. I prepare lesson plans, assignments, and other written materials, such as the course syllabus and testing materials, and I counsel and assist students who are having difficulty with the course materials.

During my years of service to the Miles County Department of Social Services, my exemplary performance has been rewarded with consistent promotion to positions of increasing responsibility. Adept at program development and management, I have initiated, organized and implemented a number of important In-Home Services programs within the county, including the Community Alternatives Program (for which I wrote the grant), the Personal Care Program, and the Adult Care Home Case Management Program. In addition to authoring the county guidelines and procedures for many of these new programs, I also supervised and trained the staff that facilitated them.

If you can use an articulate communicator, skilled teacher, and counselor, I hope you will write or call me soon to suggest a time when we might meet to discuss your needs and goals and how my background might serve them. I can provide outstanding references at the appropriate time.

Sincerely,

Lauren Moore

LAUREN MOORE

1110½ Hay Street, Fayetteville, NC 28305   •   preppub@aol.com   •   (910) 483-6611

OBJECTIVE

To benefit an organization that can use an experienced, articulate human services professional who offers a strong background in the development and training of social services staff and client/family education as well as in classroom instruction and program management.

EDUCATION

Master of Arts in **Psychology**, University of Maine, Orono, ME, 1995; graduated with a **3.8 cumulative GPA**.

Bachelor of Arts in **Sociology**, St. Josephs College, Standish, MA.

Completed additional training in social services which included four 14-hour modules of the Adult Services Supervisor's Curriculum and the Interactive Management Training Course sponsored by the Georgia Division of Social Services.

EXPERIENCE

PSYCHOLOGY INSTRUCTOR (Adjunct Instructor, Part-Time). Bergen Community College, Paramus, NJ (2002-present). Teach psychology to up to 35 students in one to three classes at this local community college; present course materials through oral presentations, written material, role playing and other methods, preparing lesson plans, projects, and reports.

With the Miles County Department of Social Services, Standish, MA, have advanced in the following "track record" of increasing responsibilities:
2000-present: **SOCIAL WORK SUPERVISOR III.** Adult Services Section. Promoted to this position from Social Work Supervisor II; coordinate, implement, and manage a wide range of In-Home Services programs, to include the Adult Care Home Case Management Program, Community Alternative Program, In-Home Aides program, and Personal Care Program.

- Provide managerial oversight and training for five supervisors and one clerical worker; responsible for all 73 professional and paraprofessional employees of the unit.
- Developed, organized, and implemented the Adult Care Home Case Management Program in Miles Country from inception to integration with other county services.
- Managed a number of In-Home Services Programs that generate more than $750,000 in revenues from various state and local reimbursement services.

1995-1999: **SOCIAL WORK SUPERVISOR II.** Family & Children Section. Provided a wide variety of management, consultation, budgeting, and staff development skills while directing the work of six social services personnel and a clerical worker.

Highlights of earlier experience:
SOCIAL WORK SUPERVISOR I & II. Adult Services Section. In my first supervisory role with the Department of Social Services, conducted orientation, instruction, and training for new staff members under my supervision; supervised up to 11 Social Workers and support staff members. Was instrumental in creating, organizing, implementing, and managing the Community Alternatives Program and the Personal Care Program in Miles County; authored the guidelines and procedures for both; wrote the grant for the Community Alternatives Program.

SOCIAL WORKER. Adult Services Section. Provided social work services to consumers in a long-term care environment; monitored rest homes throughout Miles County to ensure compliance with local, state, and federal laws, regulations, and guidelines.

Date

Exact Name of Person
Exact Title
Exact Name of Company
Address
City, State, Zip

SOCIAL WORKER   Dear Exact Name of Person (or Dear Sir or Madam, if answering a blind ad):

With the enclosed resume, I would like to introduce you to my background as a Social Worker and Investigator with specialized experience in assisting children who are victims of sexual abuse, physical abuse, and neglect. On October 15, I resigned my position as a Social Worker in Worcester, Massachusetts because my husband and I have relocated to Georgia due to his new job assignment. We are thrilled to be back in the area because I am from Georgia and my extended family lives here.

While earning my Bachelor of Science in Social Work (B.S.W.) from Clark University, I volunteered for two years at a women's shelter and I helped to make a difference in the lives of many women who were victims of violence. After excelling in an internship with the Clark County Department of Social Services, I was offered a full-time position as a Social Worker. Subsequently I advanced to the position of Investigator for Child Protective Services, and I directed services to the child and family in an attempt to protect the child from further neglect and abuse.

In my most recent position as a Social Worker III Child Placement Unit, I have handled a caseload of 27 cases while specializing in sexual abuse cases where the children has already been removed from the home or were in foster care. I am skilled at numerous legal processes, including terminating parental rights, and I have become very knowledgeable about the variety of programs and services which are available to provide intervention and problem solving for abusive parents and their children.

I believe that through my enthusiasm, motivational abilities, empathy, and compassion for others, I can make valuable contributions to an organization such as yours. I hope you will welcome my call soon when I try to arrange a brief meeting to discuss your goals and how my background might serve your needs. I can provide outstanding references at the appropriate time.

Sincerely,

Sandy M. Jenkins

SANDY MAE JENKINS

1110½ Hay Street, Fayetteville, NC 28305   •   preppub@aol.com   •   (910) 483-6611

OBJECTIVE

To offer my reputation as a compassionate, dedicated, and enthusiastic professional to an organization that can use my education and experience related to social work and human services as well as my willingness to go the extra mile for my clients.

EDUCATION

Bachelor of Science in **Social Work (B.S.W.)**, Clark University, Worcester, MA, 1996. Previously completed social work courses at Macon Community College, Macon, GA. Completed numerous training programs including the following:

MAPP Certification	Core I Training	Core II Training
Crossing Threshold	Risk Assessment Training	ChildAbuse Summit
Stress Management	Civil Rights Training	Deciding Together
The Carolinas Project	Child Sexual Abuse Training	

Child Development in Families at Risk
AFCARS Training, Child Placement
Life Books for Children Experiencing the Trauma of Separation and Loss
Legal Aspects of Child Protective Services
Medical Aspects of Child Protective Services

EXPERIENCE

SOCIAL WORKER III, CHILD PLACEMENT UNIT. Clark County Department of Social Services, Worcester, MA (2000-present). Handled a caseload of 27 cases while specializing in sexual abuse cases in which the children had already been removed from the home or were in foster care.

- Gained experience in writing petitions and summons, and am experienced in handling non-secure hearings. After trial dates are set, testify in criminal court. Am experienced in handling the judicial proceedings involved in terminating parental rights.
- Thrived on the challenge of bringing stability, good parenting, and a sense of permanence into the lives of children whose biological parents were incapable of fulfilling their parental obligations.
- Became skilled at assessing parenting capabilities of potential adoptive or foster parents.
- Taught Model Approach to Partnership in Parenting (MAPP) to foster and adoptive parents.
- Conducted individual and group interviews to make assessments of families and child.
- Handled resource development, community liaison, and all aspects of case management.
- Became experienced in dealing with people who don't want to be told what to do; believe strongly in the value of working with other social workers to share ideas.

INVESTIGATOR, SOCIAL WORKER III, CHILD PROTECTIVE SERVICES. Clark County Department of Social Services, Worcester, MA (1996-00). Investigated allegations of child abuse and neglect by interviewing, observing, and interpreting verbal and nonverbal behavior of the child, perpetrator, family, and other collateral witnesses.

- Assessed the risk level of the identified child, analyzing and documenting assembled facts pertinent to the child's situation to facilitate effective decision making.
- Developed and implemented effective treatment plans, and/or removed the child from the abusive environment to protect the child from further neglect or abuse.
- Completed and filed juvenile court petitions, summons, and court reports; provided courtroom testimony in child abuse cases.

PERSONAL

Excel in interviews and in confrontations about sensitive subjects. Am very persistent — will not give up until I am sure that I have obtained the very best assistance for my client.

Jeff Smith
Director of Marketing
Coordinated Health Services

SOCIAL WORKER Dear Mr. Smith:

I am writing to express my interest in a position as a Qualified Mental Health Professional with your company. With the enclosed resume, I would like to make you aware of the considerable knowledge and experience in providing mental health services to consumer populations which I could put to work for your organization.

As a Social Worker II in Dayton, OH, I provide in- and outpatient treatment services for children as a member of a professional treatment team. I am involved in promoting community living skills for Willie M case members who reside in residential treatment group homes, therapeutic homes, biological DSS foster homes, and independent and supervised apartment living program. Because of my work, I won the Social Worker of the Year award.

I hope you will welcome my call soon when I try to arrange a brief meeting to discuss your goals and how my background might serve your needs. I can provide outstanding references at the appropriate time.

Sincerely,

Mary Jane Miller

Alternate Last Paragraph:
I hope you will write or call me soon to suggest a time when we might meet to discuss your needs and goals and how my background might serve them. I can provide outstanding references at the appropriate time.

MARY JANE MILLER

1110½ Hay Street, Fayetteville, NC 28305   •   preppub@aol.com   •   (910) 483-6611

OBJECTIVE   To contribute to an organization that can use a skilled human services professional with strong clinical and administrative skills and experience in dealing with various consumer populations.

CERTIFICATIONS   Completed numerous certification and training programs, which included: Working with the Substance Abusing, Mentally Ill, Mentally Retarded (Thomas S.) Client, Helping the Helpless: Treatment and Case Management for the Chronic Substance Abuser, Supported Employment Service for Individuals with Severe Disabilities, Getting Services to Persons with AIDS, Outcome Measurement: The Basics, and Caregivers Training Course for Trainers. Qualified **Developmental Disabilities Professional** and **Mental Health Professional**

EXPERIENCE   **COORDINATOR** and **SOCIAL WORKER (Part-time).** Home Health Care Agency, Dayton, OH (2000-present). Provide my expertise in development of Policies and Procedures while assisting the Founder and Director in preparing for the opening of this local home health care business.

Earned rapid advancement from Intern, to Social Worker I, to my current position of Social Worker II, Other Family, Inc., as well as serving on a contractual basis for the Thomas S Program, Dayton, OH (1990-present):
SOCIAL WORKER II. Other Family, Inc., Dayton, OH (1995-present). Provide in- and outpatient treatment services for children as a member of a professional treatment team promoting community living skills for Willie M case members who reside in residential treatment group homes, therapeutic homes, biological DSS foster homes, and independent and supervised apartment living program.
- Supervise interns from University of Dayton.
- Earned formal recognition by the Dayton Programmatic Unit of the National Association of Social Workers as *"Social Worker of the Year."*

CONTRACT CASE MANAGER/SOCIAL WORKER II. Thomas S Services, Dayton, OH (1991-95). Served as case manager for Thomas S case members; was responsible for arranging, coordinating, and integrating multiple services for Thomas S clients.

RELIEF STAFF THERAPIST (part-time). Warren HSA Substance Abuse Hospital, Dayton, OH (1990). Led Alcoholics Anonymous meetings; participated in community activities involving AA participants; maintained medical records.

EDUCATION   **Bachelor of Science,** with a major in **Social Work,** Malone College, Canton, OH, 1990.
Social Work Internship: Home Health Care Agency, Dayton, OH.
- Supervised up to 20 employees and contract providers, including CNAs, LPNs, and other medical professionals; interviewed, hired, and trained employees, including direct care contractors.
- Planned and assigned daily duties for each employee, as well as preparing weekly work schedules; performed periodic performance appraisals for all employees.
- Maintained record of required updates to training and certifications, informing employees when it was necessary for them to complete additional training or continuing education.

PROFESSIONAL ORGANIZATIONS   Hold active membership in the following organizations: Malone College Social Work Advisory Board and Dayton Regional Mental Health Risk Management Team.

Date

Mrs. Dorothy G. Smith, Ph.D.
Director of Special Programs (TRIO Programs)

Dear Dr. Smith:

With the enclosed resume, I would like to make you aware of my interest in being considered for the position as Academic Advisor. I trust that you will have some positive memories of me from my days as a freshman student in your Introduction to Sociology class. It was that class that cemented my desire to make Sociology/Social Work my major, and I am grateful to you for the numerous times and ways in which you challenged me to excel.

Since graduation I have been aggressively recruited to enter the management trainee programs of several large corporations, but I am yearning to find a situation in which I can use my education while also applying some of my field experience in social work. You will see from my resume that I completed a Social Work Internship at Stillwater High School where I earned a reputation as a highly motivated individual who was most effective in working with at-risk juveniles. Indeed, as an upperclassman during my junior and senior years at East Central University, I served as a Peer Mentor helping incoming freshmen transition into college life. Through my experience as a Peer Mentor and as a Social Work Intern, I gained insights into the particular problems faced by first-generation college students and by low-income students.

In a part-time job while earning my degree, I refined my counseling and interviewing skills as a M.A.S. Administrator at the V.A. Medical Center, where I interviewed Persian Gulf and Vietnam veterans.

While in college I had several field experiences relevant to social work and sociology. In one situation I functioned as a Home Assistant, working with Thomas S (mentally challenged adults) and assisted those consumers in acquiring more independence and mastery of their everyday activities. In another situation as an Autism Therapist, I worked with an autistic child in a private home.

I hope you will give me an opportunity to talk with you in person about the Assistant School Counselor position because I believe that I am the dedicated and knowledgeable young professional you are seeking. I am a loyal and industrious worker who would be committed to the success of every student with whom I came into contact, and I believe I have much to offer that could be valuable to Rose State's students. Thank you in advance for your consideration.

Sincerely,

Scott Norwood

SCOTT NORWOOD

1110½ Hay Street, Fayetteville, NC 28305 • preppub@aol.com • (910) 483-6611

OBJECTIVE

I wish to contribute to Rose State College as an Academic Advisor, and I offer an in depth understanding of the university, experience in working with at-risk and low-income students, as well as numerous field experiences related to social work and sociology.

EDUCATION

Bachelor of Arts (B.A.), Sociology/Social Work, East Central University, Ada, OK, 2002.
- As an upperclassman, served as a **Peer Mentor** helping incoming freshmen transition into college life; visited classes in order to provide information about programs, university resources, and campus life. Gained insights into the special needs of low-income and potential first-generation college students.
- Was a member of the **Sociology Club**; also was a member of the **Modeling Club** and participated in several fashion shows sponsored by major area retailers.

TRAINING

P.I.C. Certified (self-defense tactics and techniques used by group home workers)
CPR Certified

COMPUTERS

Experienced with Microsoft Word, Lotus 1-2-3, WordPerfect, Excel; skilled in using Internet

EXPERIENCE

SOCIAL WORK INTERN & SCHOOL COUNSELOR. Stillwater High School, Stillwater, OH (2002). In an internship at this area high school, gained a reputation as a highly motivated individual with excellent counseling skills as well as a strong desire to help others.
- Made home visits to at-risk students and counseled at-risk juveniles.
- Maintained and filed attendance records.
- Served as a "big brother" role model to students just a year or more younger than I was.
- Chaperoned field trips with at-risk students.
- Took pride in the fact that many students told me that my intervention in their lives was the main reason they stayed in school or returned to school.

HOME ASSISTANT. Innovative Programming Associates, Stillwater, OK (2000-01). In a part-time job while in college in which I functioned in the role of a Home Assistant, worked with Thomas "S" clients (mentally challenged adults) and maintained records of their progress.
- Chaperoned consumers on field trips, including to parks and malls.
- Assisted consumers in becoming more independent in activities which included bathing, hygiene, dressing, and similar daily tasks.

M.A.S. ADMINISTRATOR. V.A. Medical Center, Stillwater, OK (1998-99). In a part-time job while earning my college degree, refined my interviewing skills conducting patient interviews, including interviews with Persian Gulf and Vietnam veterans.
- Assisted consumers in becoming more independent in activities which included bathing, hygiene, dressing, and similar daily tasks.
- Utilized a computer to input data and maintain a database of information.

AUTISM THERAPIST. Private family, Stillwater, OK (1995-98). Worked with an autistic child in a private home; helped sharpen the child's oral, written, and analytical skills.
- It was during this period in my life when I decided that I wanted to become a social worker. I began taking college courses in my spare time toward my degree.

PERSONAL

Can provide outstanding personal and professional references. Am known as a very hard worker with excellent counseling and communication skills.

Date

Exact Name of Person
Exact Title
Exact Name of Company
Address
City, State, Zip

**SUBSTANCE ABUSE
COUNSELOR**

Dear Exact Name of Person (or Dear Sir or Madam, if answering a blind ad):

With the enclosed resume, I would like to introduce you to my background as a Social Worker.

In my current position as a Substance Abuse Counselor, I have performed intake and assessment in order to gather information from school, family, and social agencies. I have handled responsibility for case management and client advocacy as well as for resource development and outreach. A key responsibility is preparing treatment planning based on client needs as presented by client and client family and support system. I also maintain treatment records to meet Medicare, private insurance, and managed health care criteria.

Known for my strong communication and counseling skills, I have facilitated group sessions for clients and conducted individual counseling on a weekly or bi-weekly basis for client case loads. I have also developed and conducted classes to educate community, school, and court support systems concerning drug awareness.

I am confident that I could contribute significantly to your private practice through my in-depth background in substance abuse counseling, and I would like to talk with you about your needs in that area. I hope you will welcome my call soon when I try to arrange a brief meeting to discuss your goals and how my background might serve your needs. I can provide outstanding references at the appropriate time.

Sincerely,

Ursula D. Homer

URSULA D. HOMER

1110½ Hay Street, Fayetteville, NC 28305   •   preppub@aol.com   •   (910) 483-6611

OBJECTIVE

I want to contribute to an organization that can use an experienced social worker with excellent supervisory and program management skills along with a reputation as a creative, caring, and compassionate individual.

EDUCATION

B.S.S.W. degree in Social Work, University of Arizona, 2000.
* Made the Dean's List 1995, 1996, 1997, 1998, 1999, and 2000.

Completed 38 hours of graduate study in Social Work, University of Arizona, Tucson, AZ, 2000-01.

Have completed numerous seminars and courses which included the North Carolina School for Alcohol and Drug Studies, UNC, Wilmington, 2000:

     Reality Therapy (30 hours)   Healing the Whole Person (two hours)

     Rational Behavior Therapy (six hours)   Ethical Dilemmas (three hours)

     Adolescent Counseling/Crisis Intervention (three hours)

     Case Coordination Techniques (three hours)

* In 2000, completed the Alcohol and Drug Prevention Program (120 hours)
* In 1999, completed Family Counseling/Working with Families in Crisis (30 hours)
* In 1998, completed Working with Families and Couples (30 hours)

AFFILIATIONS

National Association of Social Work and American Association of Counseling Development

EXPERIENCE

SUBSTANCE ABUSE COUNSELOR II. Tucson Mental Health Center, Tucson, AZ (2001-present). Performed intake and assessment to include gathering collateral information from school, family, and social agencies; was responsible for case management and client advocacy as well as for resource development and outreach.
* Prepared treatment planning based on client needs as presented by client and client family and support system.
* Maintained treatment records to meet Medicare, private insurance, and managed health care criteria.
* Facilitated group sessions for clients and conducted individual counseling on a weekly or bi-weekly basis for client case loads.
* Developed and conducted classes to educate community, school, and court support systems concerning drug awareness and community services.
* Acted as community school and court liaison to advocate clients' progress and needs.

DRUG & ALCOHOL ABUSE SPECIALIST. Department of Psychiatry, Alcohol & Drug Resident Treatment Facility, Nuernberg USAH MEDDAC, Germany (1989-94). Received an Army Commendation Award for my exceptional performance in this job in a 40-bed facility; assessed patients upon admission to determine appropriate course of treatment while supervising three people.
* Presented case histories in multi-disciplinary staffing environment.
* Served as a primary counselor to over 100 patients and family members; facilitated primary patient and couples groups which consisted of 10-12 people and 5-6 couples; facilitated AA training groups in order to familiarize patients with this self-help program.
* Trained and supervised counselors Europe-wide through the Alcoholism Training Program to familiarize them with the disease concept of alcoholism and family dynamics.

PERSONAL

Received a Certificate of Appreciation for my efforts in Alcoholism Education from the Girl Scouts of America and from the LIFE Group. Can provide excellent references upon request.

Date

Exact Name of Person
Exact Title
Exact Name of Company
Address
City, State, Zip

VICTIM ADVOCATE   Dear Exact Name of Person (or Dear Sir or Madam if answering a blind ad):

With the enclosed resume, I would like to introduce you to my background as an articulate communicator and experienced social worker whose outstanding organizational and case management skills have been proven in challenging environments where I have worked with various consumer populations.

As you will see from my resume, I have earned a Bachelor of Science in Sociology with a minor in Social Work from Towson University, which I have supplemented with additional courses in Case Management, Staff Development training, and Law Enforcement Response to Sexual Assault.

My case management experience has been both extensive and versatile, and I have worked with social services consumers ranging from victims of domestic violence and sexual assault, to the homeless and the chronically/severely mentally ill, to substance abusers and inmates in maximum security correctional facilities. Throughout my career in counseling and social work, I have managed heavy caseloads while developing effective cooperative relationships with community officials and other service providers.

Most recently, I single-handedly developed and ran a satellite office for an organization which provides counseling, victim advocacy, and referral services to victims of domestic violence and sexual assault. While overseeing all counseling, operational, and administrative functions of the office, I liaised with officials from the local law enforcement and judicial communities as well as local service providers and other outside agencies to provide assistance to victims who were involved in prosecution.

In earlier positions, I assisted homeless and substance abuse consumers with vocational counseling and housing issues and worked with individuals suffering from chronic and severe mental illness to provide them with increased independence and encourage them to take advantage of community resources.

If you can use a versatile and highly skilled human services professional, I hope you will write or call me soon to suggest a time when we might meet to discuss your needs and goals and how my background might serve them. I can provide outstanding references at the appropriate time.

Sincerely,

Jane L. Goodfellow

JANE L. GOODFELLOW

1110½ Hay Street, Fayetteville, NC 28305 • preppub@aol.com • (910) 483-6611

OBJECTIVE

To benefit an organization that can use a dedicated human services professional with exceptional communication and organizational skills who offers a strong background in case management of a wide range of mental health consumers.

EDUCATION

Bachelor of Science degree in **Sociology**, with a minor in **Social Work**, Towson University, Towson, MD, 1992.
Completed additional course work in social services which included the Bowie State University Case Management training, University Center for Psychiatric Rehabilitation; a 40-hour Staff Development Training course, and Arkansas Coalition Against Domestic Violence

EXPERIENCE

VICTIM ADVOCATE. Crisis Center, Baltimore, MD (2000-present). Provided individual supportive counseling, assessment, case management, and advocacy to victims of domestic violence and sexual assault while managing an office of this organization.
- Oversaw all operational, administrative, and counseling functions of a satellite office serving a two-county area.
- Performed assessments and referred consumers to other appropriate agency- or community-sponsored programs, when needed.
- Managed as many as 20 open cases at any time, providing court advocacy, information, and support to victims who were participating in the judicial process.
- Served as a key member of the Multi-Disciplinary Team Community Action Committee; networked with local law enforcement community and judicial system, service providers, and community leaders to raise awareness and increase convictions in domestic violence cases.
- Developed and distributed a variety of informational handouts and materials to domestic violence and sexual assault victims; distributed materials to other service providers.

INTENSIVE CASE MANAGER. Mental Health Agency, Detroit, MI (1995-1999). Serviced a heavy case load of chronically/severely mentally ill consumers as well as substance abusers and the homeless, providing continual assessment of consumer needs and crisis intervention.
- Trained new case managers/team members and medical students completing practicums.
- Provided case management to as many as 30 consumers, working to increase their level of independent functioning and use of community resources while reducing hospitalization.
- Assisted homeless and mentally ill consumers to obtain a stable living environment.

CASE MANAGER and **GRANT MANAGEMENT TEAM MEMBER.** Ford Connection, Highland, KS (1994). Provided assessment, counseling, vocational education, job placement assistance, and child care to 20 families at the James S. Ford housing development facility.
- Assisted consumers with development of problem-solving skills; provided crisis intervention and referrals to other service providers within the community.

Started with Roadways as a Crisis Line Counselor, and quickly advanced to positions of increasing responsibility: Worked as a **MENTAL HEALTH CASE MANAGER.** Highland, KS (1993-1994) and as an **ADJUNCT INSTRUCTOR.** Eastern Kansas Correctional Complex, St. Louis, MO (1992), teaching college-level courses to maximum-security inmates.

CRISIS COUNSELOR. St. Louis, MO (1990-1991). Served as a team member on an eight-bed crisis unit for homicidal/suicidal consumers while also operating a 24-hour crisis line.

CAREER CHANGE

Date

Exact Name of Person
Title or Position
Name of Company
Address (no., street)
Address (city, state, zip)

Dear Exact Name of Person (or Dear Sir or Madam if answering a blind ad):

I would appreciate an opportunity to talk with you soon about how I could contribute to your organization through my distinguished career as a military officer who is known as a talented communicator, administrator, and planning and operations manager.

As you will see from my resume, I offer an M.S. degree in Personnel Counseling and Human Services. Throughout my military career, I have been placed in positions where I have been called on to guide, counsel, and lead military and civilian employees in a wide range of training and daily operations activities as well as under combat conditions during the war in the Middle East.

I have consistently been singled out as an exceptionally skilled writer and briefer who can present complex concepts in an easily understood manner. Known for my keen intellect, common sense, and ability to think on my feet, I have been effective in dealing with people ranging from high school and college students, to military personnel of all ranks and years of service, to foreign dignitaries.

I am an aggressive, energetic, and enthusiastic individual who has earned a reputation as a good listener. I have always been proud of my reputation as a caring and empathetic leader who shows concern for his employees.

Through my success in demanding jobs as a pilot as well as through my talents as a leader, communicator, mentor, and manager, I am confident that I have earned my reputation as an adaptable and innovative decision maker and problem solver.

My experience in training planning and management includes exposure to multi-service and multi-level operations. I am experienced in supervising vocational counselors and personnel recruiters as well as in providing counseling for troubled adolescents and handicapped people through various volunteer programs and community activities.

I hope you will welcome my call soon to arrange a brief meeting at your convenience to discuss your current and future needs and how I might serve them. Thank you in advance for your time.

Sincerely yours,

Maurice P. Vieling

MAURICE P. VIELING

1110½ Hay Street, Fayetteville, NC 28305 • preppub@aol.com • (910) 483-6611

OBJECTIVE

To offer my exceptional abilities in counseling, instructing, and training personnel as well as in managing material and fiscal assets to an organization that can use an innovative and versatile professional with a track record of distinguished service as a military officer.

EDUCATION & TRAINING

M.S., Personnel Counseling/Human Services, Mercer University, Macon, GA, 1992
- Graduated *summa cum laude* with a perfect 4.0 GPA.

B.S., Health and Physical Education, Valdosta State University, Valdosta, GA.
- Was honored as a Distinguished Military Graduate for placing **first** in my class.
- Was **Honor Graduate**, Command and Staff College.

EXPERIENCE

Have earned a reputation as a "gifted" communicator and creative problem-solver while becoming recognized as one who sets the standard, U.S. Army:

TRAINING CONSULTANT. Ft. Bragg, NC (2000-present). As the senior advisor to a general officer, oversee a program which handles investigations, inspections, and assistance for 144 university Reserve Officer Training Corps (ROTC) programs throughout the eastern United States from Maine to Florida and 418 high school JROTC programs.
- Applied analytical, research, and communication skills to conduct a study on the merits of JROTC summer camps — my plan was adopted for nationwide implementation.

DIRECTOR OF MAINTENANCE, LOGISTICS, AND OPERATIONS. Ft. Bragg, NC (1999-00). Administered a multimillion-dollar budget for a unique 378-person, 48-helicopter, 57-vehicle organization: ensured the most productive use of assets so that each department and the whole organization became known for exceptional performance.
- Earned a respected Meritorious Service Medal for leading the maintenance, inventory, and logistics sections to recognition as the best in the parent organization.

OPERATIONS AND TRAINING MANAGER. Ft. Bragg, NC (1997-98). Polished my ability to develop multi-level training and operations as the senior planner for a 400-person organization which participated in worldwide national-level operations.
- Recognized as "cool, clearheaded, and a keen thinker," represented this unique Kiowa helicopter unit as the liaison with personnel operating in Bahrain and Kuwait.

DIRECTOR FOR PLANNING AND OPERATIONS. Germany and Saudi Arabia (1995-96). Received the Bronze Star Medal for my expertise in single-handedly writing and preparing the briefing plans used to move 1,500 people, 103 helicopters, and 350 vehicles to the inhospitable desert environment and managed successful combat actions.

GENERAL MANAGER. Ft. Hood, TX, and Germany (1992-94). Guided two 200-person helicopter units through functional reorganizations including relocating all personnel, their families, and equipment to Germany; was accountable for $64 million in equipment.

SALES AND PUBLIC RELATIONS DIRECTOR. Monroe, LA (1990-91). Handpicked to direct an experimental program, successfully in communicated with university and high school faculty, administration, and students while "selling" the idea of a military career to qualified young people throughout Louisiana.

PERSONAL

Enjoy meeting people and learning about different cultures: have lived in five countries. Was entrusted by the U.S. Government with a **Top Secret** clearance.

Date

Exact Name of Person
Exact Title
Exact Name of Company
Address
City, State, Zip

**VOCATIONAL
GUIDANCE
COUNSELOR**

Dear Exact Name of Person (or Dear Sir or Madam, if answering a blind ad):

With the enclosed resume, I would like to introduce you to my background as a Vocational Guidance Counselor.

In my current position as a Vocational Guidance Counselor at the Veterans Administration, I have worked closely with veterans of military service to help them formulate career goals and realistic plans to achieve those goals. I am knowledgeable of a wide range of testing instruments including Myers-Briggs as well as the Differential Aptitude Test and the Kuder Preference Record. Through my own 25 years of military experience, I possess the knowledge of military occupational specialties needed to help the veteran "translate" his or her background into civilian equivalents.

I thoroughly enjoy working in the career counseling field, because I believe strongly that unless a man or woman is gainfully employed to his or her optimal level, that individual cannot achieve the kind of self respect which promotes independence and self-reliance. I am proud of the hundreds of individuals whom I have helped in the vocational counseling area.

I am confident that I could contribute significantly to your school through my in-depth background in vocational counseling, and I would like to talk with you about your needs in that area. I hope you will welcome my call soon when I try to arrange a brief meeting to discuss your goals and how my background might serve your needs. I can provide outstanding references at the appropriate time.

Sincerely,

Tom B. Workman

TOM B. WORKMAN

1110½ Hay Street, Fayetteville, NC 28305   •   preppub@aol.com   •   (910) 483-6611

OBJECTIVE   To act as a contractor with the Veterans Administration to provide educational and vocational guidance counseling.

EDUCATION   **Master of Arts** degree in Counseling/Human Services, Kettering University, Flint, MI, 1987.
Bachelor of Arts degree in Social Science, Calvin College, Grand Rapids, MI, 1985.
Associate of Arts degree in General Education, Spring Arbor College, Spring Arbor, MI, 1983.

EXPERIENCE   **CONTRACT EDUCATIONAL/VOCATIONAL COUNSELOR.** Veterans Administration, Fort Benning, GA (2000-present). Perform activities, under contract for Veterans Administration at Fort Benning, which include administering testing and providing initial educational counseling interviews.

- From 7 July 2000 to 19 January 2002, completed more than 650 cases.
- Counseled and interviewed veterans to formulate plans for continued education and job hunting.
- Administered tests that assessed interests, aptitudes, and abilities to assist the individual in making informed career decisions; became skilled in analyzing the results of tests including the Differential Aptitude Test (DAT) and the Kuder Preference Record (KPR).
- Applied my extensive knowledge of military occupational specialties gained through 25 years of military experience in helping veterans determine what civilian occupations their military experience is most related to.

DEPUTY GARRISON COMMANDER. U.S. Army, Ft. Bragg, NC (1996-99). As the principal assistant to the Ft. Bragg Garrison Commander, played a key role in managing a major Army installation which supports a work force of 43,000 soldiers and 7,000 civilian employees with an annual budget of $435 million.

- Was directly responsible for coordinating these and other areas:

logistics engineering and housing	contracting
resource management	provost marshal
reserve component	civilian personnel
information management personnel and community activities	

- Assisted in the planning, coordination, and execution of emergency action plans for the world's largest U.S. military base.
- Became skilled in all aspects of strategic planning and contingency planning.
- Was a popular public speaker known for my ability to communicate effectively with people of all ages and educational levels.
- Reorganized and streamlined administrative procedures while also reducing overtime costs by 15%.

CHIEF OF FORCE STRUCTURE. U.S. Army, Ft. Bragg, NC (1994-95). Was primary assistant to the commanding general that took action to establish, modify, and change the personnel and equipment structure of the Army units under his command.

CLEARANCE   Held a Top Secret security clearance while in military service.

PERSONAL   Offer a proven ability to work well with others and help them determine career goals.

Date

Exact Name of Person
Exact Title
Exact Name of Company
Address
City, State, Zip

Dear Exact Name of Person (or Dear Sir or Madam if answering a blind ad):

With the enclosed resume, I would like to introduce you to a highly motivated and well-rounded professional with a reputation for effectiveness in counseling, human relations, and educational activities. One of my greatest strengths is my people-oriented skills. Consistently recognized as a person whom others are comfortable approaching for advice and guidance, I excel in educating, redirecting and reeducating people and helping them set and achieve their goals.

As you will see from my enclosed resume, I received my M.A. in Counseling and earned a B.S. in Social Work. One element of my graduate degree program was a 300-hour practicum in counseling with the Brainerd County Department of Social Services. As a Facilitator and Counselor with DSS, I continued to work with victims of domestic violence and with their abusers and family members in group and individual settings. This work has allowed me to see the first-hand results of how listening and helping others in a fair and non-judgmental setting can bring about positive changes to the lives of these individuals.

I am currently excelling in my first job in the social work field. I accepted a position as a Probation Officer, and I have made significant contributions to the lives of numerous individuals. Although I can provide excellent references at the appropriate time, I am selectively exploring opportunities outside the probation system.

As a military spouse and native of the West Indies, I can offer life experiences gained while living and working in Europe and in the Caribbean. I believe that this multi-cultural background has given me perspective in dealing with people of varied backgrounds and also helped me become an adaptable individual who can provide initiative, a sense of adventure, and a high degree of flexibility and who can relate life experiences to the situations of others in a helpful manner.

If you can use an experienced counselor and educator with a special interest in helping others through excellent communication and motivational skills, please call or write me soon to suggest a time when we might have a brief discussion of how I could contribute to your organization.

Sincerely,

Barbara Simmons

BARBARA SIMMONS

1110½ Hay Street, Fayetteville, NC 28305 · preppub@aol.com · (910) 483-6611

OBJECTIVE
To benefit an organization that can use a skilled professional with exceptional communication and organizational skills who offers a background of excellence in a variety of challenging customer service, education, and social work environments.

EDUCATION
Bachelor of Social Work (BSW) degree from the University of Minnesota, Duluth, MN, 2001; graduated with a **3.35 cumulative GPA**.
Internship #1: Vocational Specialist. Bemidji Vocational Center, Bemidji, MN (2001). Planned and organized client evaluation workshops as well as assisting with the supervision of a large number of clients with various disabilities during situational assessments.

Internship #2: Facilitator. Atlantic Bridge for the Blind, Waukegan, MI (2002). Supervised production workers, guided visitors and potential employees in addition to acting as liaison between blind employees and public transportation officials.
* Named to the Honor's List for the Fall semester of 1999.
* Attended Northwest Technical College before transferring to the University of Minnesota.
* Named to the President's List for academic excellence, winter and spring quarters, 1999.

CERTIFICATIONS
Certified Reading Tutor for Illiterate Adults.

AFFILIATIONS
Member, National Association of Social Workers, 2001-present.
Served as a member of the Northwest Campus Association of Social Workers.

EXPERIENCE
PROBATION OFFICER. Department of Corrections, Adult Probation and Parole, Brainerd, MN (2001-present). In my first job in my field, provide counseling, clerical, and intake services to adult clients in the probation and parole system.
* Conduct initial intake interviews on new clients entering the system.
* Conduct detailed examinations of all criminal and financial records for each client.

Simultaneous part-time jobs in college while earning my B.S.S.W. degree:
SUBSTITUTE TEACHER and **MOTOR COACH OPERATOR.** St. Paul, MN (1997-01). Demonstrated my time management and customer service skills, working simultaneously as a Driver for Coach Lines and a Substitute Teacher with the St. Paul Schools.
* As a Motor Coach Operator, provided exceptional customer service; frequently handle disputes, misunderstandings, and complaints between passengers, using exceptional communication skills to tactfully resolve conflicts in a fair and equitable manner.
* As a Substitute Teacher, effectively maintained discipline and order.

READING TUTOR. St. Paul Reading Center, St. Paul, MN (1994-96). Volunteer as a tutor, instructing illiterate adults in reading and writing as well as some basic mathematics skills; read books aloud for translation onto audiotape to assist clients in learning to read.

SUBSTITUTE TEACHER & DRIVER. Garden of Learning, St. Paul, MN (1990-93). Provided transportation for and served as a Substitute Teacher at this busy daycare center; assisted with meals, performed clerical and administrative tasks in the front office, and helped children with computer literacy and art projects.

PERSONAL
Excellent personal and professional references are available upon request.

Date

Exact Name of Person
Title or Position
Name of Company
Address (no., street)
Address (city, state, zip)

VOLUNTEER TRAINING SUPERVISOR

Dear Exact Name of Person (or Dear Sir or Madam if answering a blind ad):

I would appreciate an opportunity to talk with you soon about how I could contribute to your organization through my education and experience as well as my project planning, coordinating, and communication skills.

I was recently awarded **two** master's degrees: one in **Public Administration** and the second in **International Relations**, both from Clarkson University in Potsdam, NY. As you will see by my resume, I applied my research and analytical skills to complete industry program evaluations in connection with each degree. In one case my research partner and I made recommendations regarding the City of Potsdam's commercial refuse plan which resulted in the city council's changing a previously adopted policy.

While working for the American Red Cross, I have contributed by reorganizing operational plans, coordinating for disaster preparedness, training and supervising volunteers, and conducting classes on health and safety-related subjects. I received the Red Cross's highest honor, the "Clara Barton Award," and the governor of the state of Georgia singled me out for a prestigious award recognizing my achievements.

During several years of working for the U.S. Civil Service system, I became known as a highly skilled administrative assistant and executive secretary. In addition to organizational skills, those positions required a professional who could plan, coordinate, and handle details. I am a person who fits into many situations with ease.

I hope you will welcome my call soon to arrange a brief meeting at your convenience to discuss your current and future needs and how I might serve them. Thank you in advance for your time.

Sincerely yours,

Beatrice Alligheri

BEATRICE ALLIGHERI

1110½ Hay Street, Fayetteville, NC 28305 • preppub@aol.com • (910) 483-6611

OBJECTIVE
To apply my analytical, coordination, and organizational abilities to an organization that can use an intelligent and energetic self-starter.

EDUCATION
M.A., Public Administration, Clarkson University, Potsdam, NY, 2000.
- Made recommendations which led to changes in policy by the city council after evaluating the City of Potsdam's commercial refuse system.

M.A., International Relations, Clarkson University, Potsdam, NY, 2000.
- Received positive feedback from Davidson Agricultural Co. after evaluating their Potsdam, NY, and Sao Paulo, Brazil, operations and developing public relations plans for both locations.

B.S., Social Science, Ithaca College, Ithaca, NY, 1990.

EXPERIENCE
Contributed through counseling and management skills to the American Red Cross::
COUNSELOR/ASSISTANT MANAGER. Charlotte, NC. (2000-present). Applied a variety of skills by training personnel, rewriting the site disaster plan, interviewing applicants and determining needs, and making referrals.
- Reorganized the health and safety plan to make it profitable.
- Coordinated emergency preparedness planning with Army, Air Force, and area civilian personnel.

EDUCATION AND VOLUNTEER TRAINING SUPERVISOR. Ft. Benning, GA (1997-99). Recruited, trained, and supervised 80 adult and 50 youth volunteers.
- Used my communication skills to prepare and conduct first aid, CPR, health, and safety classes throughout the community.
- Received the "Clara Barton Award," the Red Cross's highest honor, and the "Georgia Governor's Award for Volunteerism."

ADVANCED WITH THE U.S. CIVIL SERVICE:
ADMINISTRATIVE ASSISTANT. Peterson AFB, Ft. Carson, CO (1994-97). Earned frequent promotions and supervised as many as seven clerk/typists while working in communications, medical administration, and civil engineering.
- Gained experience in purchase order and contract preparation.
- Received congressional inquiries and saw that they received responses.

EXECUTIVE SECRETARY. Ft. Benning, GA (1990-93). Polished my administrative and office management skills providing secretarial support for a transportation office, a psychiatry and psychology clinic, and an engineering department.
- Coordinated air/ground travel arrangements and researched suppliers for the "best buys."
- Handled numerous functional areas: maintained managers' schedules, prepared correspondence from dictation and rough draft, maintained files and publications, and managed personnel files.

TECHNICAL KNOWLEDGE
Am experienced in using computer software including: Excel, PowerPoint, Access, Word, and numerous other software applications.

PERSONAL
Was entrusted with a **Top Secret** security clearance. Am a member, American Society of Public Administrators. Thrive on hard work and challenges.

Date

Exact Name of Person
Exact Title
Exact Name of Company
Address
City, State, Zip

WILLIE M
GROUP HOME
MANAGER

Dear Exact Name of Person (or Dear Sir or Madam, if answering a blind ad):

With the enclosed resume, I would like to introduce you to my background as a Social Worker.

In my current position as Supervisor at a Willie M. Group Home, I assist in the supervision of nine emotionally disturbed children living in a group home. In addition to controlling medication and ensuring the general health and welfare of children, I compile and write weekly and monthly behavior summary reports.

Known for my strong communication and counseling skills, I have conducted individual counseling and I have also sought opportunities to educate community, school, and court support systems concerning group homes.

I am confident that I could contribute significantly to your organization through my in-depth experience with the Willie M. population, and I would like to talk with you about your needs in that area. I hope you will welcome my call soon when I try to arrange a brief meeting to discuss your goals and how my background might serve your needs. I can provide outstanding references at the appropriate time.

Sincerely,

Pierre Soire

PIERRE A. SOIRE

1110½ Hay Street, Fayetteville, NC 28305 • preppub@aol.com • (910) 483-6611

OBJECTIVE   To benefit an organization seeking a hard-working individual experienced in personnel supervision, leadership, and inventory management, who possesses excellent planning, organizational, and time-management abilities.

EDUCATION   Earning my Bachelor of Science in Social Work, University of Knoxville, TN; degree to be awarded in 2004.
Graduated from American Samoa High School, Pago Pago, 1989.
Completed a wide range of continuing education courses, including classes in leadership, chemistry, and personnel management.

EXPERIENCE   **SUPERVISOR.** Willie M. Group Home, Knoxville, TN (2001-present). Assist in the supervision of nine emotionally disturbed children living in a group home.
- Control medication and ensure general health and welfare of children.
- Compile and write weekly and monthly behavior summary reports.
- Transport children to school and medical appointments.
- In a simultaneous position as **SECURITY SUPERVISOR.** Protection Security Service, Knoxville, TN, head a security staff at the Tasty Soup Company in Knoxville while performing my supervisory functions at the Willie M. group home.

Refined my managerial, inventory, and communication skills while serving in these positions in the U.S. Army, 1991-01.
PERSONNEL TRAINER. (1997-01). Refined management and communication skills instructing and training a 56-employee organization in basic and advanced technical skills.
- Conducted both classroom and practical classes and tests.
- Ensured all personnel gained proficiency in each required skills area.

INVENTORY MANAGER/PERSONNEL TRAINER. (1995-97). Trained and supervised a crew of 15 personnel while controlling a multimillion-dollar inventory of nuclear weapons.
- Coordinated and directed cannon and Howitzer operations training exercises.
- Conducted counseling sessions.
- Signed for all disbursements of nuclear weapons.

INVENTORY/PERSONNEL MANAGER. (1993-95). Trained, supervised, and evaluated a 15-person staff while managing a multimillion-dollar inventory of weapons.
- Evaluated personnel and recommended for promotion or disciplinary actions.

INVENTORY MANAGER/PERSONNEL TRAINER. (1991-93). Oversaw a large inventory of armaments while training, evaluating, and supervising special weapons crews in emergency and safety situations.
- Designed and wrote all lesson plans, exercises, training tasks, schedules, performance ratings, and counseling manuals.

PERSONAL   Am a versatile professional who enjoys problem-solving, decision-making, and challenges. Work well as either a team member or a team leader. Am computer literate. Earned numerous awards, including the Army Achievement Medal and Army Commendation Medal.

Date

Exact Name of Person
Title or Position
Name of Company
Address (no., street)
Address (city, state, zip)

**YOUTH OUTREACH
DIRECTOR**

Dear Exact Name of Person (or Dear Sir or Madam if answering a blind ad):

I would appreciate an opportunity to talk with you soon about how I could benefit your organization with my knowledge and experience in social work, counseling, case management, and creating and implementing developmental programs.

As you will see from my resume, I offer a Bachelor of Social Work degree and have gained excellent counseling experience during my position as a social worker at Council of Community Services. I developed programs to aid human services agencies with children with educational and emotional needs, as well as resourcing community and allied health agencies for supplemental services.

Highlights of other social work experience include providing counseling functions and program development as liaison between the Ashland Shelter and various human services agencies in Ashland, OR. While serving as a Behavioral Specialist in the U.S. Army, I polished my drug, alcohol, family therapy, and sexual abuse therapy skills.

You would find me to be an honest, versatile professional dedicated to improving the quality of life of needy and troubled children and families.

I hope you will call or write me soon to suggest a time convenient for us to meet and discuss your current and future needs and how I might serve them. Thank you in advance for your time.

Sincerely,

Alice I. Wonder

Alternate last paragraph:
I hope you will welcome my call soon to arrange a brief meeting at your convenience to discuss your current and future needs and how I might serve them. Thank you in advance for your time.

ALICE I. WONDER

1110½ Hay Street, Fayetteville, NC 28305   •   preppub@aol.com   •   (910) 483-6611

OBJECTIVE

To benefit an organization seeking a hard-working professional experienced in social work, counseling, case management, and creating and implementing developmental programs.

EDUCATION

Bachelor of Social Work degree, University of Oregon, Eugene, OR, 1999.
Associate of Arts degree in History, Oregon State University, Corvallis, OR, 1992.
Completed a wide range of continuing education courses, including classes in the treatment and prevention of substance abuse, FACMT operation, and juvenile drug and alcohol addiction.

EXPERIENCE

SOCIAL WORKER. Portland County Schools, Portland, OR (2000-present). Refined assessment, organization, and evaluating skills while volunteering, currently developing community outreach programs to help children with educational and emotional needs.
- Utilize excellent communication skills while conferring with children and their families.

SOCIAL WORKER. Council of Community Services, Ashland, OR (1999). Helped transform a small, nonprofit agency into a self-supporting community services agency.
- Formed task forces to study, find solutions, and implement those solutions, for issues and problems concerning the community.
- Developed community programs, including the "Wish List" program for human services agencies.
- Refined public speaking and organizational skills.
- Access community and allied health agencies for supplemental counseling and information.

SOCIAL WORKER. Ashland Shelter, Ashland, OR (1998). Volunteered part-time to provide direct client care to homeless individuals and families.
- Performed *pro bono* family therapy sessions for shelter residents.
- As liaison between the shelter and various human services agencies, coordinated and implemented work/study programs, allowing homeless families to become independent.

SOCIAL WORK INTERN. Project Concern, Eugene, OR (1997). Gained excellent hands-on experience assisting social workers in the case management and counseling of clients with various mental health disabilities.
- Redesigned existing medical record forms, decreasing processing time by over 40%.

PRESCHOOL TEACHER. Funtime Daycare, Warwick, WA (1995-96). Taught children aged 3-4 years basic educational material.
- Learned to utilize a tactful but firm approach with parents when discussing the learning, social, and emotional needs of their children.

BEHAVIORAL SCIENCE SPECIALIST. U.S. Army, Various Locations (1990-94). Provided counseling for military personnel and dependents while serving as a counselor and social worker for both the Drug and Alcohol and Mental Health Services. Developed a comprehensive drug/alcohol/sexual abuse safety class for children. Taught Parent DARE classes.

MEMBERSHIPS

Member of National Association of Social Workers, Children's Task Force, and Council of Community Services

PERSONAL

Am a versatile professional who enjoys challenges, problem-solving, and maximizing resources. Sincerely aspiring to improve both an individual's and a family's quality of life.

Date

Exact Name of Person
Exact Title
Exact Name of Company
Address
City, State, Zip

**YOUTH PROGRAM
ADMINISTRATOR**

Dear Exact Name of Person (or Dear Sir or Madam if answering a blind ad):

With the enclosed resume, I would like to express my interest in exploring employment opportunities with your organization. I am seeking an employer who can use a highly intelligent and totally reliable young professional with an outstanding work history.

In my most recent position, I programmed and managed a variety of youth services at a military base in Hawaii, and I handled the responsibility of creating written flyers and newsletters while also training and managing youth counselors. I was promoted to handle senior management responsibilities because of my strong communication and problem-solving skills.

In prior positions with the Honolulu Police Department as well as with the Logistic Support Division in Hawaii, I excelled as a Communicators Operator and Dispatcher. I have become skilled at handling emergency situations with common sense and insight. At the Honolulu Police Department, I monitored the activities of more than 30 officers per shift as I performed liaison with 911 and various elements of the Honolulu Police Department.

If you can use a dedicated young professional who offers the proven ability to produce quality results in any type of work environment, I hope you will contact me soon to suggest a time we might meet to discuss how I could contribute to your organization. I can provide excellent professional and personal references at the appropriate time. Thank you for your time and consideration.

Sincerely,

Priscilla B. Verdra

PRISCILLA B. VERDRA

1110½ Hay Street, Fayetteville, NC 28305   •   preppub@aol.com   •   (910) 483-6611

OBJECTIVE

I want to contribute to an organization that can use an experienced young professional who offers strong problem-solving and communication skills along with an enthusiastic customer service attitude.

EDUCATION & TRAINING

Completed two years toward Bachelor's degree with a concentration of course work in human resources and sociology, Hawaii Pacific University; am finishing my degree in my spare time.

Extensive training in emergency communications sponsored by the Honolulu Police Department. Completed the Air Force Child Care Modules, Child Abuse Training, training certifying me to become an Administrator of Medications, Food Handlers training, Moving Ahead (4-H) Military Child Care Training, and training pertaining to ADHD and ODD Children and anger diffusion.

EXPERIENCE

LEAD COUNSELOR and PROGRAM ADMINISTRATOR. 15TH Services, Honolulu, Hawaii (1998-present). For the Youth Programs at a large military base in Hawaii, was the lead counselor for up to 233 school-age children K-12; supervised up to 12 other caregivers.

- Programmed daily activities in a variety of areas including academics, art, science, and physical education; managed several new programs. Was Coordinator of Project Learn, and Programmer for the Boys and Girls Clubs.
- Coordinated activities that enhanced learning and growth; played a key role in organizing and implementing community activities such as carnivals, Halloween and Santa Claus events, military appreciation activities, talent shows, Easter egg hunts, and others.
- Conducted parents' meetings and handled accounts receivable. Have been praised for keen negotiating skills.
- Worked closely with children diagnosed with ADHD, ODD, autism, bi-polar disorders, and physical challenges.
- Created flyers, calendars, and newsletters while also writing reports.

DISPATCHER. 15TH Logistic Support Division, Honolulu, Hawaii (1996-98). Was recruited as a Dispatcher for the Logistic Support Division, and was rapidly promoted to Manager of the Protocol Division, which involved organizing and managing arrangements for visiting VIPs.

POLICE DEPARTMENT DISPATCHER & C0MMUNICATIONS OPERATOR. Honolulu Police Department, Honolulu, HI (1988-96). Established an excellent reputation within the Knoxville community and participated in many emergency situations.

- Processed emergency and non-emergency information to officers.
- Was promoted to train new dispatchers; monitored the activities of more than 30 officers per shift while also monitoring and operating seven police channels.

Other experience: Became a part of the work force in Hawaii by becoming a temporary worker with Luau Temporary Service in Honolulu.

- Performed data entry and utilized Microsoft Word to write letters and reports.
- Read blueprints; handled filing; answered phones.

COMPUTERS

Proficient in using computers with MS Word, Excel, PowerPoint, and other software.

PERSONAL

Thrive on solving problems. Held one of the nation's highest security clearances: Top Secret.

Date

Dear Sir or Madam:

I would appreciate an opportunity to talk with you soon about how I could contribute to your organization through my enthusiastic and energetic manner, adaptability, and outstanding ability to relate to and work with people of all ages and developmental levels.

As you will see from my resume, I am a versatile professional with a broad base of experience in mental health and social services. My experience includes involvement with substance abuse education and counseling, residential management, therapeutic recreation program supervision and planning, and administrative operations.

Currently pursuing a bachelor's degree in Sociology after completing three years of study in Psychology while in Germany, I have shown myself to be a compassionate and caring professional who can handle crisis and high-risk situations. I have worked with clients ranging from the elderly, to violent and emotionally disturbed youth, to rape and abuse victims of all ages, to substance abusers of all ages. I have consistently earned the respect, trust, and confidentiality of my clients and their family members as well as the mental health, medical, and legal professionals with whom I am in frequent contact.

I am confident that I possess a thorough knowledge of the concepts, practices, and techniques of the field of mental retardation and developmental disabilities of clients and the population served to include the areas of habilitation planning and program administration.

Although I am a productive and valued professional in my present situation, I have family and friends in your area and I am in the process of permanently relocating to your community.

If you are looking for a dedicated and reliable professional with a reputation for being well-rounded, approachable, and self-reliant, I hope you will call or write me soon to suggest a time convenient for us to meet and discuss your current and future needs and how I might serve them. Thank you in advance for your time.

Sincerely,

Charity S. Sweet

CHARITY S. SWEET

1110½ Hay Street, Fayetteville, NC 28305   •   preppub@aol.com   •   (910) 483-6611

OBJECTIVE

To combine my education and professional work experience in the field of mental health/ social service operations to benefit an organization in need of an enthusiastic professional who excels in dealing with people, defusing difficult situations, and solving problems.

EXPERIENCE

YOUTH PROGRAM ASSISTANT. Madison County Mental Health Center, Madison, WI (2001-present). Provide psycho-educational services to "Willie M," juvenile sex offenders, and emotionally disturbed adolescents in a high-risk adolescent facility: ensure that clients who require out-of-home care due to their psychiatric needs receive focused attention to assist them in the development of social skills, independent living skills, and behavioral management.

- Plan and implement group activities and monitor participation; provide and administer medication.
- Interact daily with in-house therapists, social workers, probation officers, and other mental health professionals.
- Prepare weekly summaries, treatment plans, record keeping for individual and group adolescent facility client funds, MAR (Medical Administration Record) notes, High-Risk Intervention notes, and incident and accident reports.
- Design, develop, and organize new and on-going activity programs and have become well-versed in the principles and techniques of therapeutic recreation methods.
- Teach behavior modification techniques and gained experience in crisis intervention, high-risk intervention, and crisis management in an environment working with adolescent males.

DAY PARENT. Family Outreach, Inc., Madison, WI (2001-present). In this part-time position simultaneous with the above, taught developmental skills and handled daily documentation, training, and formal/informal assessments for emotionally/physically handicapped and MR/DD clients of all ages; provide support in activities including counseling, case management, behavior management, and community skills training.

DAY PARENT and **CERTIFIED NURSING ASSISTANT.** Madison, WI (1999-01). In a self-employed position as a private contractor, provided outpatient services to mentally retarded/developmentally disabled clients.

- Provided a wide range of services including assistance with gross and fine motor skills, as well as social, self-help, and cognitive skills as well as physical and speech therapy; assisted with personal hygiene and medication control.

SUBSTANCE ABUSE COUNSELOR. Wade & Associates, Inc., Teaneck, NY (1997-99). Provided individual, group, and family counseling as well as education for substance abuse treatment services including referrals, screenings, and assessments.

- Liaised between the criminal justice system and other community resources.
- Moved within the company to SAC in 1991 after two years as a **YOUTH SUPPORT MANAGER** at a "Willie M" residential facility, supervised male and female adolescent youth with emotional and violent behavior problems.

CHILD ABUSE COUNSELOR AND PROGRAM COORDINATOR. Holt Psychiatric Clinic, Germany (1995-97). Conducted research, planned, and carried out a child abuse educational program which included workshops and seminars as well as counseling activities.

EDUCATION

Carroll College, Waukesha, WI, **B.S. in Sociology** in progress (1999-present).

Date

Joe Smith
Personnel Specialist
City of Salem Personnel Department
Room 222, City Hall
333 Market Street
Salem, NC

YOUTH PROGRAM DIRECTOR

Dear Mr. Smith:

I would appreciate an opportunity to talk with you soon about how I could benefit the City of Salem as a Recreation Center Supervisor. I am certain that I offer the experience, skills, and abilities required to be effective in this position.

With a degree in Psychology, and a minor concentration in Sociology, I am very interested in using my knowledge and skills to work with the youth of our community. As the Program Director for the Park Terrace Boys and Girls Club, I have been successful in establishing an effective program which provides young people living in a public housing project a safe and healthy place to gather close to their homes. I was recognized with the Linville County Pioneer Award for my vision in recognizing the need for this program and then seeing it through.

One of my major contributions to this program was the implementation of basketball and football teams — I coach the basketball team and selected and trained the coaches for the football team. In addition to overseeing the recreational aspect of operating this type of facility, my responsibilities include such activities as writing grant proposals, preparing monthly reports on activities and enrollment levels, and making the decisions on the scope and type of activities. I prepare the monthly activity calendars and represent the club within the community.

I am very effective in counseling and dealing with the problems of at-risk youth and attempt in everything I do to act as a positive role model. I am the kind of person who meets challenges head on and uses my creativity and high level of self motivation to reach others.

I hope you will call me soon to arrange a brief meeting to discuss how I can contribute to the Salem community as a Recreation Center Supervisor through my knowledge and abilities as well as through my enthusiasm and drive to excel.

Sincerely yours,

Rod C. Bass

ROD C. BASS

1110½ Hay Street, Fayetteville, NC 28305 • preppub@aol.com • (910) 483-6611

OBJECTIVE

To offer experience and a strong interest in working with young people to an organization that can use a dedicated young professional who possesses excellent communication, public relations, and counseling skills.

EDUCATION & TRAINING

B.S. degree in **Psychology** with a minor concentration in **Sociology,** University of Oregon, Eugene, OR, 2000.
* Maintained at least a 3.0 GPA throughout my college career.
Completed training programs on effective techniques for communicating with at-risk youth and a "Smart Moves" course emphasizing intervention.

EXPERIENCE

Developed innovative and highly successful recreational programs for young people in the community while gaining managerial skills with the Boys and Girls Club of Linville County, Salem, OR:
UNIT DIRECTOR. (2001-present). After a six-month learning period, took on the job of directing all aspects of operating a facility which provided a safe place for young people living in a public housing project, Park Terrace, to participate in recreational and social activities.
- Established basketball and football teams: coached the basketball team of 13-15 year olds which reached the county playoffs.
- Received the Pioneer Award from the county for my efforts in developing this facility and building it into a successful program.
- Oversaw activities for an average of 38 students a day and provided tutoring, cooking classes, and computer classes as well as recreation.
- Organized a female drill team which gave participants a chance to combine modern, African, and jazz moves in their routines.
- Refined my communication skills writing grant proposals.
- Selected and trained staff members; evaluated their performance.
- Prepared and filed monthly reports on club activities and enrollment.
- Made decisions on the number and type of activities to be held and prepared the monthly schedule of events.
- Became adept at representing a positive image of the club to members of the community and calming the fears of people who had doubts about the program's success in the environment of a public housing area.

TEMPORARY UNIT DIRECTOR. (1998-00). Learned and refined the skills necessary to operate and maintain a youth recreation center and to supervise staff members so that programs were carried out in such a way as to interest young people in participating in safe and healthy activities.
- Introduced the idea of a youth club in a public housing complex and then started the Park Terrace Boys and Girls Club.

PROGRAM DIRECTOR and **COUNSELOR.** (1995-97). Gained a broad range of experience in coordinating social, cultural, and recreational activities for the Park Road Boys and Girls Club.
- Created and implemented the "Adopt a Grandparent" program which allowed club members an opportunity to visit rest homes and learn from senior members of the community.

PERSONAL

Always meet challenges head on. Will persist until I reach my goal. Am proud to have been the first male in my family to earn a college degree.

Date

Exact Name of Person
Exact Title
Exact Name of Company
Address
City, State, Zip

YOUTH PROGRAM
DIRECTOR

Dear Exact Name of Person (or Dear Sir or Madam if answering a blind ad):

With the enclosed resume, I would like to make you aware of my education and extensive experience related to social work and human services. I offer a reputation as a compassionate, dedicated, and enthusiastic professional with a proven willingness to go the extra mile to help my clients.

For the last six years, I have served as a Juvenile Probation Officer for Chad County Youth Services in New Jersey. In this position, I managed a caseload of over 100 active probationary juveniles, counseling them and their families and acting as liaison between my clients and local law enforcement, school systems, and other supporting agencies. I reported directly to the Chief Probation Officer, and I was being groomed to take over that position when my father passed away, and I decided to return home to Jackson to be with my mother.

With a Master's degree in Counseling and Psychology and a Bachelor of Science in Social Work, I have a solid educational background in addition to my years of experience. In previous positions, I have utilized my proven ability to coordinate services between agencies as well as my strong skills in youth counseling, patient evaluation and assessment, and substance abuse counseling. Though my main experience has been in providing crisis intervention, rehabilitation, and guidance to at-risk youth, I feel that my exceptional counseling skills and highly developed organizational, supervisory, and communication skills would be a strong asset in any counseling environment.

If your organization can use the skills of a highly experienced, motivated counselor or program director, I look forward to hearing from you to arrange a convenient time when we could meet to discuss your present and future needs and how I might serve them.

Sincerely,

Ebony Haigler

EBONY HAIGLER

1110½ Hay Street, Fayetteville, NC 28305   •   preppub@aol.com   •   (910) 483-6611

OBJECTIVE

To offer my reputation as a dedicated, and enthusiastic professional to an organization that can use my education and experience related to social work and human services.

EDUCATION

Master's Degree in Counseling and Psychology, Troy State University, Gotham, NY, 1999.
Bachelor of Science in Social Work, Troy State University, Gotham, NY, 1991.

EXPERIENCE

JUVENILE PROBATION OFFICER. Chad County Youth Services, Paterson, NJ (2000-present). As the front-line officer for more than 100 active probationary juveniles and their families, was involved in a wide range of human resources management activities in addition to providing crisis counseling; on any given day, provided leadership and problem-solving related to multiple crises arising in clients' family/home environment, school situation, and community activities.
* Acted as liaison between local law enforcement, school systems, the judicial system, and other agencies charged with the care and supervision of these juvenile offenders.
* Prepared accurate paperwork for court procedures, state commitments, and case maintenance.
* Counseled clients and their families to assist them in dealing with problems arising within the family/home environment, school, and community.
* Dealt with day-to-day issues and crises confronting clients while providing oversight for the home, school, and community activities of more than 100 juveniles aged eight to 18.
* Scheduled and conducted probationary supervision meetings with clients and families.

YOUTH SERVICES SPECIALIST. Glory County Youth Services, Paterson, NJ (1999). Performed individual, group, and family counseling for clients in this busy regional office.
* Coordinated with directors of other agencies and assisted clients in obtaining referrals.
* Provided support counseling to local group homes as well as the diversion center.

APARTMENT MANAGER. Enterprise Management, Inc., Enterprise, NJ (1996-1998). Managed 68 rental units, ensuring the upkeep and appearance of the property, keeping the account books accurate and up-to-date, and collecting rent from the tenants.

ADDICTIONS COUNSELOR I. Addictions Recovery, Inc., Jackson, MS (1994-1995). Counseled and offered rehabilitative guidance to adolescents with identified chemical dependency problems.
* Performed preliminary intake and evaluation of assigned clients, and developed psychosocial assessments to determine a proper course of counseling and treatment.
* Acted as liaison between local agencies and youths in my care to assure that each client was provided with comprehensive, high-quality services.
* Participated in an addiction team formulated to educate and assist at-risk children in the local school system with drug and alcohol-related issues.

OUTPATIENT COUNSELOR. Eastern Missouri Drug Council, Inc., St. Louis, MO (1993). Provided outpatient treatment and counseling.
* Assessed each assigned referral client to determine services needed.
* Provided individual, group, and family counseling and worked with clients to establish treatment plans.

PERSONAL

Excellent personal and professional references are available upon request.

Date

Exact Name of Person
Title or Position
Name of Company
Address (number and street)
Address (city, state, and zip)

YOUTH PROGRAM MANAGER

There are a couple of things you can learn from this resume. Notice that the address line on the resume has two addresses—the address where he currently resides, and the address to which he will be moving shortly. In the first paragraph of the cover letter, he alerts his reader to the fact that he is relocating because of his wife's job. This will reassure the prospective employer that he is not leaving his current position because of work-related problems.

Dear Exact Name of Person: (or Dear Sir or Madam if answering a blind ad.)

With the enclosed resume, I would like to indicate my interest in your organization and my desire to explore employment opportunities. My wife and I have recently relocated to Atlanta because my wife has been promoted and relocated by her employer, Farmington Industries. We have bought a house and are hoping to make Atlanta our permanent home.

As you will see from my enclosed resume, I have excelled in a track record of outstanding results within the social services and human services field. I am a dedicated social worker who "found my field" after a distinguished "first career" serving in the Air Force in the recreational and transportation fields. As a manager in the Air Force, I thoroughly enjoyed the challenges involved in training and counseling young soldiers, and I was successful in helping many troubled young people turn their lives around and become positive, contributing, and well-adjusted members of society. After military service I earned my Bachelor of Science in Social Work (magna cum laude). As a Social Worker, I have discovered that I have a "gift" for comforting both the young and elderly, and I have been enriched by work experience in hospice, hospital, and mental health environments.

I hope you will welcome my call soon to arrange a brief meeting at your convenience to discuss your current and future needs and how I might serve them. I can provide excellent references. Thank you in advance for your time.

Sincerely yours.

Frederick Hallgarth

Alternate last paragraph:
I hope you will call or write me soon to suggest a time convenient for us to meet and discuss your current and future needs and how I might serve them. Thank you in advance for your time.

FREDERICK HALLGARTH

Until 12/15/02: 1110½ Hay Street, Decatur, GA 28305   (910) 483-6611
After 12/16/02: 538 Pittsfield Avenue, Atlanta, GA 58401   (805) 483-6611

OBJECTIVE   I want to contribute to an organization that can use a dedicated social worker who is known for my caring manner and for my belief that the elderly as well as children deserve to be honored and given a helping hand by sincere, empathetic professionals.

EDUCATION   Earned a Bachelor of Science in Social Work (B.S.W.) **magna cum laude** with a 3.83 GPA, Georgia College, Decatur, GA, 1996.

CERTIFICATIONS Certified in CPR and First Aid by the American Red Cross
Received Certification of Completion from a Personal Intervention Course (PIC)

EXPERIENCE   **YOUTH PROGRAM MANAGER.** Decatur County Mental Health, Decatur, GA (2000-present). In a group home for nine male juvenile sex offenders aged 14-18, monitored and assisted children on a 24-hour-a-day basis.
- Administered prescription medicine for charts; was responsible for safety of my clients.
- Transported clients to appointments and to outings as deemed appropriate by Decatur County Mental Health.
- Became very knowledgeable of the special needs of this particular client population, and excelled in handling and diffusing hostile situations with clients.
- Learned how important it is to assure proper administration of prescription medicines to clients.

HOSPICE INTERN. Home Health Care of Decatur, Decatur, GA (Sept-Dec 1999). Derived enormous satisfaction from this four-month internship in a hospice environment.
- It gave me a great feeling of accomplishment to help someone through his last journey in life in a peaceful way; I also learned that the dying still have much to contribute to those around them, and I greatly enjoyed listening and providing a comforting presence to the little children and the elderly whom I saw die.
- Learned how gratifying it is for people to die in their own natural surroundings.

SOCIAL WORKER TRAINEE/VOLUNTEER. Veterans Administration Hospital, Decatur, GA (1992-98). While earning my B.S.W. degree, worked more than 3,000 hours with older people in the Intermediate Ward; became skilled in working with older people with AIDS, Hepatitis C, cancer, and with amputees.
- Functioned as the personal assistant to many elderly people, and took them to doctors' appointments, on outings, and to activities.
- Became a favorite assistant of the nursing staff; often assisted them in various activities.

TRANSPORTATION SPECIALIST. U.S. Air Force, various locations (1982-92). Worked in the purchasing, logistics, and transportation field training and managing up to six individuals; became skilled in purchasing items ranging from paper clips to heavy industrial equipment.
- Developed excellent supervisory and personnel administration skills.

RECREATIONAL SPECIALIST. U.S. Air Force, various locations (1982). Developed a recreational program which was voted "best" in the parent organization while advancing to top management positions in the recreational management field.
- Supervised up to eight recreational assistants while supervising athletic events, overseeing the maintenance of athletic fields, and overseeing a wide range of athletic events, competitions, tournaments, and activities.

PERSONAL   Can provide outstanding personal and professional references. Have a true love of geriatric patients and children and feel that they are often the "throwaway citizens" in society.

ABOUT THE EDITOR

Anne McKinney holds an MBA from the Harvard Business School and a BA in English from the University of North Carolina at Chapel Hill. A noted public speaker, writer, and teacher, she is the senior editor for PREP's business and career imprint, which bears her name. Early titles in the Anne McKinney Career Series (now called the Real-Resumes Series) published by PREP include: *Resumes and Cover Letters That Have Worked, Resumes and Cover Letters That Have Worked for Military Professionals, Government Job Applications and Federal Resumes, Cover Letters That Blow Doors Open,* and *Letters for Special Situations.* Her career titles and how-to resume-and-cover-letter books are based on the expertise she has acquired in 20 years of working with job hunters. Her valuable career insights have appeared in publications of the "Wall Street Journal" and other prominent newspapers and magazines.

PREP Publishing Order Form

You may purchase any of our titles from your favorite bookseller! Or send a check or money order or your credit card number for the total amount*, plus $4.00 postage and handling, to PREP, Box 66, Fayetteville, NC 28302. You may also order our titles on our website at www.prep-pub.com and feel free to e-mail us at preppub@aol.com or call 910-483-6611 with your questions or concerns.

Name: _____

Phone #:_____

Address: _____

E-mail address:

Payment Type: ☐ Check/Money Order   ☐ Visa   ☐ MasterCard

Credit Card Number: _____ Expiration Date: _____

Check items you are ordering:

☐ $16.95—REAL-RESUMES FOR MANUFACTURING JOBS. Anne McKinney, Editor

☐ $16.95—REAL-RESUMES FOR AVIATION & TRAVEL JOBS. Anne McKinney, Editor

☐ $16.95—REAL-RESUMES FOR POLICE, LAW ENFORCEMENT & SECURITY JOBS. Anne McKinney, Editor

☐ $16.95—REAL-RESUMES FOR SOCIAL WORK & COUNSELING JOBS. Anne McKinney, Editor

☐ $16.95—REAL-RESUMES FOR CONSTRUCTION JOBS. Anne McKinney, Editor

☐ $16.95—REAL-RESUMES FOR FINANCIAL JOBS. Anne McKinney, Editor

☐ $16.95—REAL-RESUMES FOR COMPUTER JOBS. Anne McKinney, Editor

☐ $16.95—REAL-RESUMES FOR MEDICAL JOBS. Anne McKinney, Editor

☐ $16.95—REAL-RESUMES FOR TEACHERS. Anne McKinney, Editor

☐ $16.95—REAL-RESUMES FOR CAREER CHANGERS. Anne McKinney, Editor

☐ $16.95—REAL-RESUMES FOR STUDENTS. Anne McKinney, Editor

☐ $16.95—REAL-RESUMES FOR SALES. Anne McKinney, Editor

☐ $16.95—REAL ESSAYS FOR COLLEGE AND GRAD SCHOOL. Anne McKinney, Editor

☐ $25.00—RESUMES AND COVER LETTERS THAT HAVE WORKED.

☐ $25.00—RESUMES AND COVER LETTERS THAT HAVE WORKED FOR MILITARY PROFESSIONALS.

☐ $25.00—RESUMES AND COVER LETTERS FOR MANAGERS.

☐ $25.00—GOVERNMENT JOB APPLICATIONS AND FEDERAL RESUMES: Federal Resumes, KSAs, Forms 171 and 612, and Postal Applications.

☐ $25.00—COVER LETTERS THAT BLOW DOORS OPEN.

☐ $25.00—LETTERS FOR SPECIAL SITUATIONS.

☐ $16.00—BACK IN TIME. Patty Sleem

☐ $17.00—(trade paperback) SECOND TIME AROUND. Patty Sleem

☐ $25.00—(hardcover) SECOND TIME AROUND. Patty Sleem

☐ $18.00—A GENTLE BREEZE FROM GOSSAMER WINGS. Gordon Beld

☐ $18.00—BIBLE STORIES FROM THE OLD TESTAMENT. Katherine Whaley

☐ $14.95—WHAT THE BIBLE SAYS ABOUT... *Words that can lead to success and happiness* (large print edition) Patty Sleem

☐ $10.95—KIJABE An African Historical Saga. Pally Dhillon

_____ **TOTAL ORDERED (add $4.00 for postage and handling)**

PREP offers volume discounts on large orders. Call us at (910) 483-6611 for more information.

THE MISSION OF PREP PUBLISHING IS TO PUBLISH
BOOKS AND OTHER PRODUCTS WHICH ENRICH
PEOPLE'S LIVES AND HELP THEM OPTIMIZE THE
HUMAN EXPERIENCE. OUR STRONGEST LINES ARE
OUR JUDEO-CHRISTIAN ETHICS SERIES AND OUR
BUSINESS & CAREER SERIES.

Would you like to explore the possibility of having PREP's writing
team create a resume for you similar to the ones in this book?

For a brief free consultation, call 910-483-6611
or send $4.00 to receive our Job Change Packet to
PREP, Department SPR2002, Fayetteville, NC 28302.

QUESTIONS OR COMMENTS? E-MAIL US AT PREPPUB@AOL.COM

Made in the USA
Lexington, KY
24 March 2013